HOUSE OF LORDS   SES

SELECT COMMITTEE ON
THE EUROPEAN COMMUNITIES

PROMOTING SMALL AND MEDIUM ENTERPRISES IN THE EU

WITH EVIDENCE

Ordered to be printed 2 November 1999

LONDON: THE STATIONERY OFFICE
£14·40

HL Paper 115

CONTENTS

ORAL EVIDENCE

WRITTEN EVIDENCE

Note: Pages of the Report and Appendices are numbered in bold type; pages of evidence are numbered in ordinary type. References in the text of the Report are as follows:

(Q)   refers to a question in oral evidence
(p)   refers to a page of the Report or Appendices or to a page of evidence

TWENTIETH REPORT

2 NOVEMBER 1999

By the Select Committee appointed to consider Community proposals, whether in draft or otherwise, to obtain all necessary information about them, and to make reports on those which, in the opinion of the Committee, raise important questions of policy or principle, and on other questions to which the Committee considers that the special attention of the House should be drawn.

ORDERED TO REPORT

PROMOTING SMALL AND MEDIUM ENTERPRISES IN THE EU

PART 1: INTRODUCTION

1. This Report considers ways in which the development of "Small and Medium Enterprises" (SMEs) might be better promoted in the EU.

2. There are over 18 million individual companies in the EU, of which the large national and multinational companies, whose activities tend to dominate the business headlines, comprise only 0.2 per cent. Under the standard EU definition[1], the remaining 99.8 percent of businesses are classified as SMEs, principally by having fewer than 250 employees. The typical SME is much smaller than that – on average, having only four employees. Nevertheless, SMEs provide nearly two thirds of employment in the EU.

3. The business world is undergoing a revolution. The development of globalisation and the spread of e-commerce have radically changed concepts of the firm, manufacturing, services and general trade that were familiar a generation ago. The driving forces of rapid technological change, freer international financial exchange and the reduction in barriers to trade are found across the world. The transformation they have brought so far seems bound to continue – and no less rapidly. In addition to those global trends, businesses in the EU are subject to further dynamic changes in the development of the European Single Market and the introduction of the Euro.

4. The concept of employment is also changing. This is facilitated by changes in the business environment, but is also driven by choice – to promote a preferred lifestyle (working for oneself and home-working) – or by necessity as a result of unemployment (often through downsizing by large companies).

5. SMEs, particularly the vast majority of micro and small enterprises, are not potted versions of large businesses. Their size allows them a speed of action that big businesses struggle to match. The opportunities for entrepreneurs have never been greater and, in many respects, SMEs are entrepreneurs' ideal base. At the same time, SMEs' small size means that they can face particular challenges in tackling businesses opportunities.

6. SMEs play a vital part in general wealth creation and in employment, in some cases giving rise to new large businesses. They also have a key role in the provision of a wide range of goods and services, often working closely with large enterprises. It is therefore not surprising that the EU and Member States regard SMEs as requiring special policy attention. The question is what form such policy attention should best take in the transformed business and employment environment.

7. Against that background, the Committee considered that a study of the measures available in the EU to promote SMEs would be both timely and useful. However, the importance of the topic is matched by its potential size and complexity. Rather than launch straight into what would be a major full-scale enquiry, we saw the need first to clarify the questions that needed to be pursued in depth. Accordingly, we undertook a short enquiry into what, within EU policies, the European Commission, national governments and their agents were doing to promote SMEs, and what they should or should

---

[1] Discussed further in paragraphs 11 and 12, although it should be noted here that this excludes agriculture, fishery, horticulture and forestry – as does the discussion of SMEs in this Report.

not be doing for such enterprises. This report sets out our findings, and concludes with our recommendations on the issues that merit more detailed study.

CONDUCT OF THE ENQUIRY

8. The enquiry was carried out by Sub-Committee B (Energy, Industry and Transport), whose members are listed in Appendix 1.

9. The call for evidence set out in Appendix 2 was issued in early July 1999. Given the nature of the enquiry, this was deliberately open-ended. Those who gave evidence are listed in Appendix 3.

10. We are grateful to all those who gave oral and written evidence for their thoughtful contributions to our deliberations. We also thank our Specialist Adviser, Dr Shobhana Madhavan, Director of the Centre for Business and the Environment at the University of Westminster, for her able assistance in guiding us through the complications of wide-ranging issues relating to SMEs in the EU.

PART 2: BACKGROUND

THE DEFINITION OF SMEs

11. The European Commission adopted the present classification of SMEs in its Recommendation of 3 April 1996[2]. Although the number of employees is a key – and the best known – criterion, there are financial issues as well. The full criteria are summarised in Table 1.

Table 1: EU definitions of SMEs

	Micro	Small	Medium
i. Number of employees	Up to 9	10 to 49	50 to 249
ii. Independence	less than 25 per cent owned by one or more enterprises falling outside the definition of an SME		
and at least one of the following			
iii. Maximum turnover (in million ECUs)	–	7	40
iv. Maximum balance-sheet total (in million ECUs)	–	5	27

12. The definition excludes enterprises in primary sectors of agriculture, fishery, horticulture, forestry etc. Such enterprises are not explicitly covered by the discussion in this report, although much of its content is also relevant to them.

NUMBERS, EMPLOYMENT AND TURNOVER

13. The main indicators – numbers, employment and turnover – for SMEs and large scale enterprises (LSEs) within the EU are set out in table 2 below. By definition, these figures exclude the informal or underground economy. In the UK, for example, that has been estimated[3] as contributing some 6-8 per cent of the Gross Domestic Product.

Table 2: Enterprises in the EU – main indicators 1996

	SMEs				LSEs	SMEs & LSEs
	Micro	Small	Medium	All SMEs		
Number of enterprises (000)	17,285	1,105	165	18,555	35	18,590
Employment (000)	37,000	21,110	15,070	73,180	38,220	111,410
Employees per enterprise	2	20	90	4	1,035	6
Turnover per enterprise (m ECUs)	0.2	3.0	16.0	0.5	175.0	0.8
Value added per occupied person (000 ECUs)	30	40	50	35	55	40
Source: ENSR[4]						

14. As shown, there are over 18 million individual enterprises in the EU, over 99 per cent of which fall within the definition of SMEs – indeed, well over 90 per cent are categorised as "micro". SMEs account for two thirds of the EU workforce and 55 per cent of business turnover.

SECTORAL DISTRIBUTION AND PERFORMANCE

15. Small enterprises are more common in the service sector than in manufacturing, although we recognise the increased blurring of these boundaries under the impact of flexible manufacturing

[2]   *Official Journal* 1996 L 107/4.

[3]   *Inland Revenue,* House of Commons Treasury Committee 6th Report 1998-99 HC 199.

[4]   European Network for SME Research in *The European Observatory for SMEs, fifth annual report, 1997, ISBN 90-371-0643-9.*

techniques and information technology. In the EU, approximately 70 per cent of the jobs in the service sector are in SMEs. The trend towards increasingly knowledge-based economies is likely to favour service sector SMEs. The flexibility of SMEs makes them well suited to an economic system characterised by co-operative and synergistic alliances, as advances in telecommunication technology and data processing capabilities, discoveries in science, and social changes have transformed the business environment. Table 3 illustrates the 1996 sectoral distribution and performance of SMEs in Western Europe.

Table 3: Sectoral SME comparisons, Western Europe (European Economic Area plus Switzerland), 1996

	Average number of employees per enterprise	**Labour productivity** (SME value added per occupied person as a percentage of sector average)	**Relative profitability** (SME average minus sectoral average, measured by value added minus labour cost, as a percentage of value added)
Extraction	33	84	-7
Manufacturing	14	88	-4
Construction	4	97	-1
Wholesale trade	6	89	-5
Retail distribution	4	95	-1
Transport, communication	9	72	-8
Producer services	5	78	-7
Personal services	5	96	-2
All SMEs	**6**	**84**	**-6**
Source: ENSR			

16. As shown, the average size of enterprise is much smaller in the construction, retailing and service sectors than in manufacturing. In all sectors, the overall performance of SMEs, in terms of labour productivity and profitability, is below the average (although SMEs are of course extremely diverse in this, as in other, respects).

TRENDS IN VALUE ADDED, EMPLOYMENT AND TURNOVER

17. Over the decade to 1998, SMEs grew more slowly than LSEs in the EU as a whole, although in the UK there was no difference. In the EU and – especially in the UK – employment generally declined, but less in SMEs than in LSEs, while the change in profitability was the same for SMEs and LSEs. These trends for the larger EU Member States and the EU as a whole are shown in table 4 below.

Table 4: Changes in SME and LSE value added, employment and profitability, 1988 to 1998

	Value added (Average annual percentage change, adjusted for inflation)		**Employment** (Average annual percentage change)		**Profitability** (Average annual percentage points change)	
	SMEs	LSEs	SMEs	LSEs	SMEs	LSEs
France	1.3	2.0	-0.1	0.0	0.4	0.4
Germany	2.6	3.2	-0.1	-0.6	0.6	0.6
Italy	1.4	1.9	-0.7	-0.7	0.5	0.6
Spain	1.9	2.3	0.5	0.3	0.5	0.6
UK	1.7	1.7	-0.4	-0.9	0.1	0.1
All EU	**1.9**	**2.3**	**-0.2**	**-0.5**	**0.4**	**0.4**
Source: ENSR						

18. The divergence in growth rates in value added began in 1993, possibly because LSEs were the main beneficiaries from export-led growth as the economy recovered from the recession of the early 1990s. Similarly, the greater decline in employment in LSEs was concentrated in the recession years 1990-93.

GENERAL CHARACTERISTICS OF SMEs

19. Size is the only feature that SMEs have in common. The sector displays great diversity in the motivation for starting up businesses; the nature and volume of effort deployed to achieve success in business; aspirations for growth and for market penetration at both home and abroad; and in internal organisation – all as illustrated below.

- There are among SMEs some "dynamic" businesses (including some future large enterprises), and – at other extreme – "lifestyle" businesses, where the proprietors' main priority is job satisfaction rather than expansion of the business.

- While some SMEs are long established enterprises, business start-ups have a high failure rate.

- Entrepreneurs manage their own enterprises. Other businesses are mainly run by managers on behalf of the owners.

- Where the potential market is very large compared to the size of the firm, there is scope for expansion, but vulnerability to competition. Where the market is smaller, the firm faces limits to its growth although, in some instances, specialisation in niche markets may give protection from competition.

- A firm with a large number of customers is not over dependent on individual customers – but relationships with individual customers may be weak. Conversely, a small customer base allows relationships to be strong – but with a danger of over-dependence.

- A firm selling consumer products requires customer awareness, whereas suppliers to other companies may have problems with technical specifications.

- Specialised and "hi-tech" operations employ highly skilled people, and need to ensure that their skills remain marketable. It is difficult for businesses with low skills to stand out from the competition.

- High profitability may be an indicator of success, or of failure to spend adequately to ensure long term success. Low profits may indicate failure, or a transitional phase on the way to success.

- Where turnover and profits are prone to fluctuate over time, the business has high risks and – possibly – high rewards over the long term. Where fluctuations are less, the risk is lower.

20. As a very broad generalisation, SMEs tend to have lower wages, higher insecurity and poorer working conditions than LSEs. Compared to LSEs, SMEs also employ a higher proportion of women and younger workers, and their workers tend to have lower educational attainment.

KEY POLICIES AT EU LEVEL

21. The purpose of enterprise policy at the EU level is mainly to enable businesses (including SMEs) to take advantage of the competitive opportunities offered by the European Single Market. The Single Market programme, formally completed in 1992, was designed to facilitate free movement of goods, services, capital and labour. Technical barriers to movement are diminished by harmonisation of standards at EU level or, in the absence of harmonisation, by mutual recognition of national standards. VAT levies and refunds at national frontiers have been superseded by a system of EC sales declarations.

22. Governments of EU Member States have been concerned to limit the impact of "harmful" tax competition in the Single Market. A Code of Conduct was agreed by the ECOFIN Council in December 1997, which restricts tax concessions which affect the location of business activity. In principle, tax concessions for SMEs could come within the Code of Conduct, although, as was noted in our recent report on taxes in the EU[5], the implications of the Code of Conduct are not clear.

---

[5] *Taxes in the EU: can co-operation and competition co-exist?*, House of Lords Select Committee on the European Communities, 15th Report, 1998-99, HL Paper 92.

23. The Commission has noted[6] "a perception ... that the principle of mutual recognition is not operating satisfactorily" and proposed a number of remedies, including:

- monitoring of the application of mutual recognition;

- dialogue with citizens and businesses;

- training;

- quicker responses to individual complaints; and

- action by Member States to facilitate mutual recognition.

24. The cornerstone of EU policies for SMEs are the Multiannual Programmes (MAPs). The third MAP (1997-2000) is now well under way. This has an overall budget of €128 million to pursue the following main objectives[7]:

- to simplify and improve the administrative and regulatory business environment;

- to improve SME policy instruments;

- to improve the financial environment for enterprises;

- to help SMEs to Europeanise and internationalise their strategies, in particular through better information and co-operation services;

- to enhance SME competitiveness and improve access to research, innovation and training;

- to promote entrepreneurship[8] and support target groups.

25. The MAP was the subject of a recent evaluation report by Deloitte & Touche[9]. This concluded that "DG XXIII[10] has a committed leadership ... continuing to keep SME and Enterprise issues at the forefront of the Union's agenda" and that "the real gains for DG XXIII often come from expert policy work", rather than pilot projects or provision of information. The cost-effectiveness of the Commission's activities under the MAP was characterised as "broadly acceptable", although "in some cases, there are grounds for concern, that the results of some of the pilot actions will be inadequately analysed and/or that the results will not be disseminated in a timely fashion".

LEGISLATION

26. Administrative burdens are estimated to cost European businesses 540 billion ECUs/year (3 - 4 per cent of GDP) and SMEs are particularly hard hit[11]. To meet these concerns, the Commission procedure for developing legislative proposals includes a Business Impact Assessment (BIA). The Deloitte & Touche evaluation report concluded that the BIA system "does not work optimally, but the fact that BIAs must be done gives DG XXIII some leverage over the other DGs and scope to influence their activity ... the procedure is still cost-effective".

27. The EU has established the SLIM (Simplified Legislation in the Internal Market) project, to identify ways in which Single Market legislation can be made less burdensome for business. The Commission has also produced an action plan for SMEs, based on the recommendations of the Business Environment Simplification Task Force (BEST), which reported in May 1998[12]. BEST was established to propose measures to improve the quality of legislation and eliminate unnecessary burdens on enterprises. Its recommendations included the establishment of an EU Better Regulation Unit.

---

[6] *Mutual recognition in the context of the follow-up to the Action Plan for the Single Market,* EC Communication COM(99)299.

[7] *9th Annual Report on the Structural Funds, 1997,* European Commission (1998).

[8] New measures to foster entrepreneurship have recently been proposed in the *Global Entrepreneurship Monitor,* London Business School and Apax Partners & Co, 1999.

[9] *Report on the evaluation of the third Multiannual Programme (MAP) for Small and Medium-sized Enterprises (SMEs) in the European Union,* European Commission (1999), COM(99)319.

[10] The then European Commission Directorate General with responsibility for SMEs. This role has been taken over by the Directorate General for Enterprise. Although DGs are no longer referred to by number, this Report makes a number of references to DGXXIII where it was the relevant DG at the time.

[11] *The Report on Regulatory Reform* OECD (1998). The report recommended that regulations should be subject to rigorous appraisal, both when introduced and at regular intervals thereafter (a process known as "life cycle management of regulations").

[12] *Report on the evaluation of the third Multiannual Programme (MAP) for Small and Medium-sized Enterprises (SMEs) in the European Union,* European Commission (1999), COM(99)319.

EU STRUCTURAL FUNDS AND OTHER ASSISTANCE

28. EU institutions make only limited use of financial instruments to assist SMEs. There is no organisation comparable to the US Small Business Administration (SBA) which has an extensive programme of support through loan guarantees. A European mechanism was established in November 1997 to finance high technology projects in small firms, with the collaboration of EU financing institutions including the European Investment Bank and the European Investment Fund[13].

29. Between 1994-99, 15-20 per cent (€23-30 billion) of Structural Fund resources were earmarked for measures to stimulate small firms and improve their productive facilities and economic environment. This was particularly targeted on SMEs in regions whose development is lagging behind, areas undergoing industrial conversion, rural areas and very thinly populated areas. Structural Fund financing supports[14]:

- aid for capital investment through direct grants or financial engineering measures;

- part-financing business start-up areas;

- training, including management training;

- advisory and information services;

- measures to promote research and technological development;

- measures relating to the information society;

- assistance for internationalisation.

COMPETITION POLICY

30. Competition policy at EU level has two facets: first, cartels, abuse of market dominance and mergers; and, second, the regulation of state aid. SMEs are unlikely to be constrained by the rules, because their scope for anti-competitive practices or abuse of market power is necessarily limited by their size. The Commission has acknowledged this: "agreements entered into by independent SMEs whose annual turnover and balance-sheet total do not exceed ECU 40 million and ECU 27 million respectively and which have a maximum of 250 employees will not in principle be investigated by the Commission"[15].

31. State aid to industry is regulated by the European Commission under Article 93 of the EC Treaty. The Commission has issued guidelines on state aid for SMEs[16] and, under Council Regulation (EC) No 994/98, may exempt aid for SMEs from the notification requirements of Article 93. In the period 1995-97, state aid targeted at SMEs accounted for 7 per cent of the total amount of state aid payments for manufacturing industry in the EU[17]. There is considerable variation between countries: the highest figure (for Finland) was 19 percent, while Greece had no state aid in this category. The UK figure was 9 per cent.

KEY POLICIES AT NATIONAL LEVEL

32. The monetary, fiscal, trade and other policies that bear on business generally also have an impact on SMEs. There is a general recognition that SMEs have a unique contribution to make towards the development of local economies, the promotion of technological change and the evolution of new industries. At the same time, it is also acknowledged that SMEs face particular problems as a result of their size and consequent circumstances.

33. Those problems, together with SMEs' potential for enhancing economic well-being, have led the governments of EU Member States to seek to create a favourable business environment through specific policy measures. These include general legislative measures (company law, bankruptcy and insolvency laws) together with the creation of relevant government bodies with specific responsibilities for regulation and promotion of SMEs. Table 5 gives a brief summary of the types of policies existing or proposed in a selection of EU Member States as of 1997.

---

[13]   *9th Annual Report on the Structural Funds, 1997*, European Commission.

[14]   *9th Annual Report on the Structural Funds, 1997*, European Commission.

[15]   *XXVIIth Report on Competition Policy*, European Commission.

[16]   *Official Journal* 1996 C 213, European Commission.

[17]   *Seventh Survey on State aid for manufacturing industry (1995-97)*, European Commission.

Table 5: Summary of measures designed to assist SMEs in larger EU Member States 1997

	Finance	Innovation	Late Payments	Labour	Internation-alisation	Information	Admin. Burdens
Germany	●	●			●	●	●
France	●	●	●	●	●	●	●
Italy	●	●	●	●	●	●	●
Spain	●	●		●	●	●	●
UK		●	●	●		●	●
Source: ENSR							
● indicates implemented or planned action							

34. In the UK, the national network of Business Links was completed in 1996. These are designed to provide a "one stop shop" for SMEs seeking advice and services. In 2000, a new Small Business Service (SBS) will be established in England[18]. It will have a budget of £100m, and, reporting directly to the Secretary of State for Trade and Industry, the right to scrutinise draft legislation. The SBS will act as an advocate for small businesses, and also take over responsibility for Business Links and the UK's Enterprise Fund for high technology companies. The SBS draws on the model of the US SBA, established in 1953, which provides financial, technical and management assistance to SMEs in the US. With a loan portfolio worth more than US$45 billion, the SBA is the largest single financial backer of small businesses in the United States. There is also an Advocate for Small Business who directly advises the President on the impact of proposed legislation.

---

[18]   *The Small Business Service: a public consultation*, DTI 1999, URN 99/815.

PART 3: VIEWS OF WITNESSES

DEFINITIONS

35. The Commission's 1996 definition of SMEs as having fewer than 250 employees (with certain caveats about turnover and financial independence – see paragraph 11) appeared to be generally accepted (QQ 5, 34). Deutscher Industrie- und Handelstag (DIHT – the organisation representing German SMEs) had sought to persuade the Commission to revert to the higher cut off point of 500 employees, on the grounds that it led to unjustified exclusion of some companies from EU programmes (QQ 271, 276). Even under the more restrictive definition, the vast majority (99.8 per cent) of enterprises in the EU were categorised as SMEs (Q 224).

36. Professor Blackburn emphasised the extreme heterogeneity of SMEs, with variation by business sector, location, age, size and owner-managers' characteristics (p 72). DIHT favoured the use of qualitative criteria, to "differentiate between entrepreneur and mere manager". Distinctions could also be made between "growth oriented" and "lifestyle" businesses, and between "start-ups" and established enterprises (Q 271).

POLICIES FOR SMEs

37. The Minister for Small Firms observed that "small firms are critical to the health of the economy" (Q 182). However, Professor Blackburn warned against looking to SMEs as "a panacea for the cure of the ills in the economy and society" (p 72). As the CBI acknowledged, new businesses have a high mortality rate (Q 71).

38. Professor Storey stated that "most of the businesses which start do not want to grow" (Q 27). The Minister agreed that many enterprises – for example so-called "lifestyle" businesses – were consciously averse to expansion (Q 189). Moreover, successful enterprises do not necessarily increase employment proportionately as the business expands: we were told by the Federation of Small Businesses (FSB) that "most small businesses want to improve their profits", which may actually reduce employment (Q 22).

39. According to the Department of Trade and Industry (DTI), "statistics on job creation speak for themselves: between 1970 and 1995, the EU added 8.5 million jobs or 6 per cent of its workforce. In the same period the US increased its workforce by 46 million or 65 per cent" (p 43). The Commission representative said that "we need a culture of enterprise" (Q 250).

40. If job creation were the main objective of SME policy, then Professor Storey felt that "only a few firms matter": about half the new jobs in the SME sector were created by a very small minority (approximately 4 per cent) of firms (Q 13). The focus should be "on comparatively rapid growth businesses which are seeking to grow, and not upon lifestyle or start-up businesses" (Q 28).

41. Policy measures intended specifically to assist SMEs are very common across the EU. Policies and practice with respect to SMEs vary between Member States: Denmark, Ireland, the Netherlands and Germany were cited by the Commission as providing examples of good practice in aspects of SME policies (Q 244). The various schemes in EU Member States were summarised in the evidence from Professor Scobie (p 95).

42. The objectives of EU SME policy were summarised by Professor Blackburn as: "reduction of red tape; better involvement of SME organisations in the decision making process; help with finance; [reduction of] market distortions and inefficiencies; action to promote research, innovation and training; and [enhancement of] competitiveness and internationalisation". However, inadequate performance measurement was "a major weakness in UK and EU SME policy" (p 72).

43. The Commission was seeking, in conjunction with Member States, to promote an environment favourable to SMEs, by the "Concerted Actions" Programme – events which bring together relevant speakers and practitioners, in order to identify and disseminate best practice in support services for SMEs[19] (Q 251).

44. With respect to subsidiarity, the Minister urged that "we should be careful that European initiatives ... are complementary to national initiatives" (Q 186). The Commission representative stressed that the EU should act only where this provides "added value at the European level" (Q 222). DIHT emphasised that "it should only be the task of the European Community to set the framework", and EU programmes needed to be both transparent and consistent with activities at local level (Q283), and should focus on cross border co-operation (Q 291). Professor Blackburn identified "a number of

---

[19] The "Concerted Actions" Programme, on which a report was due in October 1999, is not formally part of the EC's MAP.

gaps in SME policy which may be assisted by EU initiatives ... [specifically] entrepreneurship education; assistance with business exit and entrepreneurial recycling; and support for middle layer businesses" (p 73).

45. However, according to the DIHT, "the typical entrepreneur says 'the best policy would be if the State leaves me alone'" (Q 289). Similarly, Professor Blackburn reported that "UK business owners are sceptical of Government initiatives", seeing the Government very much as "a regulator and 'taxer' of their activities" (p 72).

THE IMPACT OF LEGISLATION

46. Both the CBI and the FSB expressed concern at the cumulative burden of legislation (Q 89, 49). With respect to the implementation of EC measures, there can be a tendency – as in the UK – to 'gold-plate' the transposing legislation, and to include extra measures not required by EC Directives: as an example of this, the CBI cited the UK legislation implementing the Working Time Directive (QQ 92, 93).

47. There were few instances of SMEs being explicitly exempted from regulatory compliance (Q 201), although there were many legislative provisions (for example in the environmental field) where thresholds effectively removed SMEs from the scope of the regulation (Q 241). The Environment Agency stated that, in implementing the Integrated Pollution Prevention and Control Directive, the Agency would "regulate industry in proportion to the risks involved, and will therefore take account of the smaller businesses" (p 80).

48. The Minister considered that regulations should be designed for ease of compliance by all enterprises, irrespective of their size. He also expressed concern that exemptions for SMEs might inhibit enterprise growth (Q 202). The Commission representative suggested that exemptions could be justified at levels where the burden of the regulation outweighed its benefit (Q 242). The CBI urged that any exemptions should be on a "case by case" basis, emphasising flexibility (Q 89). The TUC observed that "allowing too many exceptions and exemptions adds to the complications involved in applying regulations" (p 98). The US had few regulatory exemptions, although there was strong support for them in the small business community (Q 114).

49. In some instances, SMEs wrongly believed that they were exempt from regulations: a study[20] of the implementation of the 1989 Health and Safety Directive found that many SMEs were under a misapprehension "that the Directive was not applicable to them or that they were not obliged to undertake an assessment [of risk]". In similar vein, the Environment Agency reported that "many [UK] SMEs are unaware of their environmental responsibilities, but are apprehensive about contacting regulators for advice in case they are found to be in breach of ... legislation" (p 80).

50. The DTI expressed strong support in principle for measures to ease the regulatory burden. However, support for deregulation was not unqualified: thus "we need to make sure that regulation impacts in the right way on small business ... some [regulations] are very helpful in opening up competition" (Q 189).

51. The Commission representative said that, in the formulation of legislative proposals, the Commission consulted widely with business organisations (QQ 237, 246); he also expressed a preference for informal consultative procedures (Q 237). He cited social legislation as an area in which DGXXIII (the then Directorate General for Enterprise Policy) had influenced the policy process to take account of the interests of SMEs (Q 241). The CBI felt that DG XXIII had not been "powerful or authoritative enough and therefore could not influence other Directorates who were putting forward proposals for legislation" (Q 92). Similarly, DIHT judged that DGXXIII had been "a reliable partner" for SME organisations "but not a strong partner", since its position in relation to other DGs was "very weak" (Q 287).

52. Commission legislative proposals generally included a statement of the regulatory impact on SMEs, although the DTI claimed that this procedure "has not really worked" (Q 184); DIHT characterised it as a "paper tiger" (Q 289). The US had both procedural and institutional mechanisms (in the form of the Advocate for Small Business, who could advise the President to veto legislation) to assess the prospective impact of proposed legislation on small businesses (Q 113). The UK Government have supported the establishment of a "European Better Regulation Unit", as proposed by the EU Business Environment Simplification Task Force (BEST) (p 42), although the Commission representative judged that almost all the other Member States were resisting (Q 233).

---

[20]   ENSR – see footnote 4.

53. The Commission representative drew attention to the danger that amendments put forward by the European Parliament could make legislation more complex (Q 237).

54. The FSB drew attention to the difficulty for the non-expert in understanding and implementing complex regulations concerning – for example – environmental protection, employment, and health and safety (Q 49). They pressed for the business community to be given sufficient time to acquaint itself with new regulations, and for even enforcement of EC regulations, to ensure that there was a "level playing field" (Q 55). The US had sought to convert regulations into "plain American English" (Q 113), and also made limited use of self appraisal (accompanied by spot checks) as a means of easing the burden of enforcement (Q 114).

55. The CBI had little evidence that "voluntary" standards disadvantaged SMEs (QQ 91, 94). CEN, the European Committee for Standardisation, acknowledged that "ISO 9000 for quality systems has been seen by some as a burden, by others as a benefit to exploit claims for quality ... ISO 14001 for environmental auditing has a similar image" (p 75). The British Standards Institution (BSI) acknowledged that SMEs "have historically been under-represented within the standard–setting process", a problem which it was seeking to address through improved mechanisms for consultation with SMEs (p 74).

ACCESS TO FINANCE

56. The CBI said that British SMEs' relationships with banks were "much improved" (Q 73), and that the UK had "a much better developed ... small firms finance and capital market ... than in other parts of Europe" (Q 69). However, KPMG said that there remained "gaps ... in the provision of finance", particularly for smaller firms and high risk ventures (p 88). The Inland Revenue stated that "Member States are encouraged to tackle the problems that SMEs face in obtaining finance [and] incorporation of businesses" (p 85).

57. The CBI called for faster progress towards a single financial capital market for Europe, and the liberalisation of national restrictions on cross border pension fund investments. There were 33 stock exchanges in the EU, and there was no European equivalent of the US NASDAQ where high risk start-up ventures obtain equity finance (Q 86). Some SMEs in the US also received support from the SBA, which had leveraged a commitment of $200m to generate a loan guarantee portfolio of US$ 38 billion (Q 107).

STRUCTURAL FUNDS

58. Professor Blackburn found low awareness of EU funding in the UK, due in part to a lack of take-up and promotion by the UK Government (p 72). Nevertheless, Professor Storey said that "much European money is focused in the SMEs area on Objective 1 and occasionally Objective 2 regions[21], particularly in southern Europe and Ireland" (Q 17). DIHT said that the EU structural funds were important for SMEs in eastern Germany (Q 289). The Department of Economic Development for Northern Ireland outlined the benefits for SMEs in the Province from EU structural funds and Community Initiatives (p 78). The DTI emphasised that UK Regional Development Agencies should exploit synergies with the new round of ESF programmes "to have the maximum impact on eligible areas" (p 44).

TRADING WITHIN THE EUROPEAN SINGLE MARKET

59. The Minister said that "the Single Market is a fantastic opportunity for our small companies" (QQ 204, 205). The Commission representative outlined EU action to promote contacts between SMEs in different Member States (QQ 263, 264). German SMEs saw great opportunities in the prospective enlargement of the EU and the Single Market (Q 296).

60. CEN stated that standards provided "a common passport throughout Europe" (p 76). Nevertheless, SMEs could face difficulties in getting their products accepted elsewhere in the EU. The CBI saw this as "the biggest single barrier that we face in terms of the Single Market" (Q 97), and evidence from the BSI acknowledged that "SMEs can suffer if the results of an accredited test body, for instance the BSI in the UK, are not accepted in other countries" (p 74).

61. For example, UK suppliers of pressure vessels found that "virtually all" European countries did not recognise the BSI standard as sufficient, and required imports to meet their own procedural

---

[21]　Specific priority areas for Structural Fund expenditures are defined in Council Regulation 2081/93, Article 1: Objective 1 focuses on the development and structural adjustment of regions whose development is lagging behind; and Objective 2 focuses on assistance for regions or parts of regions seriously affected by industrial decline.

requirements for standardisation (QQ 77-79), the costs of which could be very onerous for SMEs (Q 84). The Commission representative's response was: "where there is no [EC] legislation, mutual recognition applies. That is the law as it stands. In all cases where a problem arises because of non-conformity with the law then you have to make a complaint so that the law can be implemented" (Q 232). The Minister noted that the recent Commission Communication on mutual recognition contained suggestions for improvement[22], which the Government were "treating ... as a matter of priority within the Internal Market Council" (p 54).

PUBLIC PROCUREMENT

62. The CBI said that many of its members, large and small, "feel that markets in other Member States are often difficult to penetrate" (Q 96). On the other hand, the Commission representative felt that SMEs were too often disadvantaged by their own attitudes that "it is too complicated" or "it is too big for me" (QQ 255, 256).

63. The CBI suggested "unbundling" of calls for tender would make contracts more manageable for SMEs. Electronic invitations to tender could also ease market access (Q 96).

64. The CBI was cautious about quotas for SME participation in public procurement contracts, fearing that it might compromise value for money, although it was extremely interested in the US Small Business Information and Research scheme (SBIR) – which sets quotas for SME participation in research contracts – because of its impact on development of new technologies and hi-tech enterprises (Q 96).

65. A freelance consultant drew attention to the bureaucratic nature of the Commission's own procedures for the award of contracts, and called for their simplification to increase accessibility for small enterprises (p 89).

TRAINING

66. Professor Blackburn pointed out that "many training initiatives have been qualifications driven (eg NVQs) despite the absence of a market for qualifications driven training in SMEs" (p 72). Professor Storey commented that there was no clear evidence that publicly subsidised management training enhanced the performance of small firms (Q 21). Similarly, KPMG commented that most SMEs "are not well served by current publicly provided courses" (p 89). The FSB pointed out that the available training, which sells skills, was often unsuited to the requirements of SMEs who needed to buy tasks. Training geared to the "plan, manage, monitor" model of large enterprises was not appropriate for SMEs which "buy, produce, sell" (Q 54).

AVAILABILITY OF INFORMATION AND COMMUNICATION NETWORKS

67. Provision of information and advice, by various means including electronic media, constitutes a major component of the EU programme of support for SMEs. According to Professor Scobie, UK Government assistance had frequently been "in the form of consultancy or advice which often SMEs do not find very useful" (p 95). The FSB said that "getting information in a usable form that [small businesses] understand is the single biggest problem" (Q 41). Mr Bichard of the Co-operative Bank National Centre for Business and Ecology noted that, in some instances, EU–funded environmental advice schemes for SMEs had been discredited by the poor quality and lack of focus of the advice offered (p 91). Miss Soden of HSBC noted that banks and accountants were often SMEs' first port of call for advice (Q 167).

68. The FSB observed that application procedures for EU support were characterised as exceedingly complicated, and SMEs often required the assistance of a consultant whose fees could amount to a considerable proportion of the grant obtained (Q 42). One possibility was a "one stop shop" for SMEs to deal with the multiplicity of EU programmes, although fears were expressed that this could amount to a "one stop choice" (Q 41).

69. The Minister saw an important role for the EU in the sharing of best practice among European partners (Q 186). The Commission has acknowledged that it was difficult for SMEs to be effective when they were faced with an exploding information market: it considers that *Euro Info Centres* should provide advisory and counselling services to SMEs.

70. Professor Blackburn was highly critical of the present Business Links network (p 73), while the CBI characterised its performance as uneven (Q 19). KPMG characterised UK SME support

---

[22]   See paragraph 23.

services as "fragmented ... with Business Links often existing alongside Enterprise Agencies, Regional Supply Offices and Innovation programmes" (p 89). The Minister expressed a concern that "Business Links only reach a very small proportion of the people they should be reaching and also by definition they are reaching the wrong people". He was "looking at ways in which we can make things more accessible—not just to give worthy documents out" (Q 195).

E-COMMERCE

71. The Minister saw e-commerce as affording opportunities for SMEs to go beyond the limits of their local markets (Q 191). The Commission representative identified three key issues: training, business confidence, and the cost of telecommunications (which was "far too high" in Europe). Since e-commerce was a global issue, there was a need for EU dialogue with the United States (Q 239). DIHT saw a key role for the EU in disseminating information on best practice (Q 306).

TAXATION

72. In 1992, the VAT regime was modified to permit the removal of frontier controls in the Single Market. According to HM Customs and Excise, this has benefited SMEs to a greater extent than large businesses (p 82). However, the FSB told us that "most small businesses do not know if it made a difference" (Q 56).

73. HM Customs and Excise also noted that, while "the UK has chosen to allow non-established taxable persons the option to take responsibility for their own VAT affairs ... some [EU] Member States insist on the appointment of a tax representative in all circumstances, and take financial guarantees that can be bureaucratic and burdensome, for SMEs in particular" (p 83).

74. The UK annual turnover threshold for VAT registration, currently £51,000, is among the highest in the EU: discussions were proceeding on distortions associated with the threshold (p 82). According to the CBI, the level of the threshold was not a major constraint on the growth of SMEs (Q 87).

75. The EU is concerned with direct taxation insofar as it affects the smooth functioning of internal market. The Inland Revenue noted that Member States were encouraged to mitigate the administrative complexity of taxation systems; and that tax concessions for SMEs fell within the EU state aid regulations and "are also potentially within the scope of the Code of Conduct on business taxation" (p 85).

LATE PAYMENTS

76. A proposed EC Directive on late payments had been agreed by the Council of Ministers, and referred to the European Parliament (Q 235). The FSB was unenthusiastic about such EC legislation (Q 59). DIHT noted that "the State is the worst payer" (Q 308): Germany had a system of interest payments to discourage late payment, and similar regulations should be considered at EU level (QQ 308, 311).

BANKRUPTCY

77. The FSB commented that "if we are to encourage the entrepreneur ... [we] have to look at the bankruptcy laws"(Q 56). The CBI observed that "there is a difficult balance ... between the interests of creditors and of those who fail" (Q 75).

THE EURO

78. Miss Soden said that many UK SMEs wrongly believed that, because the UK was outside the single currency, their business would not be affected (Q 136). She expected the Euro to have the greatest impact on medium sized companies, which did at least half of the UK's trade with the Euro-zone (Q 139), but were too small to have a treasury department to manage foreign exchange and interest rate risk (Q 132). Those SMEs that foresaw an impact apparently perceived it as negative: the FSB told us that its members believed the Euro would benefit large companies and impose additional costs on small enterprises (Q 63).

79. Miss Soden judged that "Euro-creep" (whereby the use of the single currency gradually increased in the UK, even in the absence of UK membership of the Euro-zone) was "very likely to happen", although the rate of change was uncertain (Q 166). She cited the tourism sector as a possible instance, suggesting that "companies who are arranging tours of Europe will say 'most of Europe is in the Euro so we would like to trade with you in the Euro'" (Q 136).

80. If the UK were to participate in the Euro, there would be no more movement in interest and exchange rates vis-à-vis the present Euro-zone countries. According to Professor Scobie, "SMEs have suffered from ... [recent] appreciation of the pound" (p 93). Ireland's participation in the single currency had led to an appreciable lowering of interest rates. If the UK adopted the Euro, the impact would depend on the relative levels of sterling and Euro interest rates at the time (Q 163).

CULTURAL AND PSYCHOLOGICAL ASPECTS

81. Several witnesses noted the importance of perceptions. The FSB claimed that "most small businessmen are actually very positive towards Europe" (Q 49). The DTI noted that most SMEs perceived EU social legislation as a constraint (p 44).

INTELLECTUAL PROPERTY

82. The Commission was seeking to improve SMEs' access to information and advice on defence of their intellectual property (Q 237).

INSTITUTIONAL STRUCTURES

83. The FSB expressed strong opposition to mandatory membership of local chambers of commerce as in Germany (Q 52).

84. The Minister stated that the new Small Business Service (SBS) should "bring together, streamline and make more coherent the delivery of business support services" (Q 181) and also lighten the burden of compliance (Q 189).

85. Within the European Commission, responsibility for SMEs was being taken over by the Directorate General for Enterprise. The DIHT representative commented that "we do not know what the effect will be. We are always asking for a reliable partner we can keep in contact with" (Q287).

86. The US SBA assisted 200,000–300,000 businesses per year, mainly through loan guarantees (Q 107), and had a loan guarantee portfolio of some US$38 billion (Q 105). When asked whether there might be an EU version of the SBA, both the Minister and the Commission representative expressed opposition (QQ 183, 247, 248).

PART 4: OPINION OF THE COMMITTEE

POLICIES – GENERAL PRINCIPLES

87. Most of EU industry and commerce consists of SMEs. To ensure that their contribution is fully realised, well-directed policies are needed to promote general competitiveness while giving appropriate support to SMEs so that, as far as possible, they can operate on a like for like basis with LSEs.

88. All EU Member States have policies to support SMEs. The EU has initiatives which are specifically targeted at SMEs – in the framework of its third MAP[23] – and also policies in various areas which affect SMEs. Policies at EU level have a significant role in facilitating the participation of SMEs in the European Single Market, through dissemination of best practice, promotion of co-operation between enterprises, and support for infrastructure development. The activities of the EU should, in accordance with the subsidiarity principle, be complementary to action at national level.

89. SMEs thrive on self-help and, at the level of both the EU and Member States, care needs to be taken that this is not stifled. SMEs should be subject to the minimum necessary regulatory burdens. There is a balance to be struck between the interests of individual SMEs and the wider interests of the economy and society.

90. Policies need not be only regulatory. SMEs seem particularly likely to benefit from imaginative schemes for providing information or other non-financial assistance.

DEFINITIONS

91. Over 99 per cent of EU enterprises come within the current definition of SMEs. Although the definition includes sub-categories of micro, small and medium enterprises, we found little evidence that such differentiation was observed by policy makers. We accept that there is some argument against such differentiation in that it may create barriers to growth: for example, an SME might decide against taking on an additional employee if this took it into the next category with additional burdens. However, the same arguments do not apply in respect of non-regulatory matters such as non-financial assistance.

92. In any case, SMEs do not vary only in size. A "lifestyle" micro business not geared to expansion is very different from a dynamic growth-oriented one. A service enterprise may have very different needs from one involved in manufacturing. The concerns of new SMEs (the failure rate of which is high) will not be the same as those of established ones. We found minimal evidence that policy makers took account of these variations in developing their policies.

THE IMPACT OF LEGISLATION

93. The Commission consults representative business organisations (although not normally with SMEs themselves) when formulating legislative proposals. Various efforts have been made to ease the regulatory burden. The Commission has a procedure for screening legislative proposals for their impact on SMEs, although doubts are expressed about its effectiveness. The US has a free-standing Advocate for Small Business, who advises the President directly on the effects of proposed legislation. The Committee endorses the UK Government's strong support for a "European Better Regulation Unit" to help assess the likely burden of initiatives for SMEs against the expected benefits.

94. Although the EU is often blamed for the effects of regulation, part of the blame attaches to the governments of Member States through the practice of "gold plating", where measures ostensibly implementing EC Directives go beyond the requirements. Employment legislation and Health and Safety measures are often cited as areas where this has happened. Member States should generally resist the temptation to extend or "gold plate" EC requirements in domestic legislation. Where such extension is intended, they should consult carefully and, if and when proposals are pursued further, distinguish more clearly between EC requirements and national supplementary provisions.

95. There are few instances where legislation explicitly exempts SMEs, although in some cases (for example, environmental legislation) impact thresholds effectively exclude many smaller enterprises. There are possibilities for substituting regulatory enforcement with a system of self appraisal, and for achievement of policy objectives through voluntary measures. While these may not necessarily ease the overall burden on SMEs, there may be a case for further examination of voluntary measures which substitute for, or supplement, regulation.

---

[23]   Multiannual Programme – see paragraph 24.

ACCESS TO FINANCE

96. SMEs in the EU face difficulties in raising finance due to risk aversion on the part of banks, fragmentation of the capital markets and general shortage of venture capital. While the EU's capital markets are likely to become more unified as the European Single Market develops, there is a place for greater EU and Member State pro-activity in eliminating the remaining obstacles to free movement of capital within the Single Market. The Commission's effort to diversify SMEs' access to finance are welcome.

STRUCTURAL FUNDS

97. Structural funds account for a large proportion of the EU budget and offer the prospect of significant support for SMEs. The UK (apart from Northern Ireland) has not been a big recipient of these funds to date. While the Committee welcomes the Government's emphasis on synergies between European funding and the activities of UK Regional Development Agencies, more work should be done on developing individual SMEs' awareness of the availability of European Funding and refining the targeting to provide best value for money in supporting SMEs.

TRADING WITHIN THE EUROPEAN SINGLE MARKET

98. SMEs should have unfettered access to the markets in other EU Member States. Under European law, many standards for products and services are harmonised. Where there is no such harmonisation, the doctrine of mutual recognition applies so that a product meeting the standards of one Member State can be sold throughout the EU. In practice, SMEs face considerable difficulties: for example, compliance with the UK BSI standard does not guarantee acceptance in other EU markets. This problem may be most acute in the case of "intermediate" goods which are used in further stages of production. The Single Market cannot be effectively completed while SMEs are disadvantaged in this way[24].

PUBLIC PROCUREMENT

99. SMEs are disadvantaged in public procurement by invitations to tender which specify volumes which are beyond their capacity. In addition, the relatively high turnover rate of SMEs can make it harder for them to meet requirements for an established track record. While these restrictions may have administrative convenience, the effective exclusion of SMEs from major procurement exercises may mean that procurers deny themselves the possibility of innovative solutions. We welcome the efforts of the Commission to increase SMEs' awareness of the possibilities for collaborative participation in procurement tenders and to encourage dissemination of information by electronic means. While we share the reservations in some quarters about the suggestion of quotas for SMEs in procurement, we consider that general tendering procedures should be reviewed to ensure that they do not unnecessarily preclude SMEs. In particular, the scope for unbundling and, as appropriate, decentralising large contracts should be examined.

100. Consideration should also be given to the more explicit use of government research contracts to promote the growth of high technology SMEs.

TRAINING

101. Given the obvious need for SMEs to keep up to date – particularly those involved in innovation – we were concerned to learn that public funding for current training initiatives in the SME sector may not represent good value for money. The way training support is provided to the sector should be re-examined to ensure that public resources are used to best effect in benefiting SMEs.

AVAILABILITY OF INFORMATION AND COMMUNICATION NETWORKS

102. Much of the present support for SMEs takes the form of information and advice. It was disappointing to hear widespread doubts as to its effectiveness given the limited capacity of many proprietors of small businesses, in the midst of all their preoccupations, to take up and absorb what is available. The Committee believes that advice should be more closely geared to the specific requirements of individual businesses, and we welcome the Minister's willingness to consider alternative ways to deliver information and advice to SMEs. We also look forward to the

---

[24] According to *The Single Market Scoreboard* (European Commission, No 3, October 1998), 41 per cent of LSEs thought that the Single Market had benefited them over the last two years, compared to 28 and 23 per cent respectively for medium and small companies.

Commission's forthcoming initiative on improving SMEs' access to support programmes. Careful consideration should be given to identifying the varying information needs of SMEs and the most effective means of drawing up and delivering the necessary advice and information. We welcome the suggestion that *Euro Info Centres* should provide advisory and counselling services to SMEs.

E-COMMERCE

103. E-commerce, where transactions are not constrained by the distance between the parties, allows businesses to overcome the geographical limitations of their local markets. There is a general perception that this affords great opportunities for SMEs, but they must be in a position to take advantage – and the costs of telecommunications must not be excessive.

TAXATION

104. Our recent report *Taxes in the EU: can co-ordination and competition co-exist?*[25] looked at the ideas floated by the Commission for fundamental changes to the VAT regime. We noted (in paragraph 245) that the canvassed "single place of taxation system":

"is presented as having significant advantages for business – in particular for small firms wishing to export, which would have to grapple with the bureaucracy on only one Member States. We were initially attracted to it for this reason, but then found that in fact small firms would benefit only in rare circumstances, and the proposed system for redistributing revenue might well lead to more rather than less bureaucracy."

105. Some EU Member States (but not the UK) require exporters based in other EU countries to appoint a tax representative and give financial guarantees to the tax authorities. The Committee is concerned at the burden that this imposes on SMEs, and urges that initiatives be taken at EU level to promote liberalisation and thus increase SMEs' market access.

LATE PAYMENTS

106. The EC is planning legislation on late payments. The Committee awaits this with interest, and hopes to see monitoring arrangements built in to ensure that it is effective in achieving its objective.

BANKRUPTCY

107. Inevitably, a number of SMEs will fail. The consequences of failure influence the willingness of entrepreneurs to take risks. While creditors need some protection in the case of bankruptcy, and society needs appropriate protection from reckless or duplicitous businessmen, it is possible that bankruptcy arrangements are too harsh, particularly in the case of "fault-free" failures, such as those resulting from changes in the market. Consideration might be given to whether the current bankruptcy and insolvency laws strike the right balance between safeguarding creditors and promoting entrepreneurship among the SME sector.

THE EURO

108. The merits of UK participation in the single currency are outside this Committee's terms of reference. Nevertheless, it is clear that the Euro affects UK businesses, including SMEs. Some of them compete in Euro-zone markets and may have to quote prices in Euros (which may affect pricing structures and manufacturing/packaging options). Furthermore, even with the UK outside the Euro-zone, there will be increasing use of the Euro within the UK. The Government should give particular attention to the position of SMEs in its assessments of the impact of the Euro and, whether or not the UK decides to join the Euro, ensure that SMEs receive adequate support in Euro matters.

CULTURAL AND PSYCHOLOGICAL ASPECTS

109. In doing business in the European Single Market, some SMEs appear to be constrained by linguistic, cultural and psychological barriers. They have difficulty in understanding EU institutions and legislation. The Committee supports the Government's efforts to overcome these problems, and to make use of varied channels of communication to get the message across to SMEs.

---

[25] House of Lords Select Committee on the European Communities, 15th Report, 1998-99, HL Paper 92.

INTELLECTUAL PROPERTY

110. The Committee shares the Commission's concern that SMEs are not well placed to defend their intellectual property rights, and supports the Commission's efforts to strengthen the position of SMEs in this respect.

INSTITUTIONAL STRUCTURES

111. Both in the UK and at EU level, changes are being made in responsibilities for formulation and implementation of SME policy. It remains to be seen what the effects will be. There appears to be no support for an EU counterpart to the US SBA, which provides assistance to SMEs in the context of a nation-wide capital market. At present, the capital markets in the EU, particularly for the financing of SMEs, are extremely fragmented. Nevertheless, as the European Single Market develops, they are likely to become more unified; and arrangements for SME support may also need to change. In the light of the various other points made throughout this Part of our report, the need and scope for institutional structures at EU level to support SMEs should be reviewed.

CONCLUSION

112. SMEs make a substantial contribution to wealth creation, employment, and the provision of goods and services across a very wide range. The nature of SMEs means that they can react quickly to exploit new opportunities. As a result of revolutionary changes to the general business environment and the development of the European Single Market, opportunities (and challenges) for SMEs are greater than ever before. While large national and multinational enterprises in the EU may be seen as the major players in modern economies, we are clear that the vital and sometimes unique roles of SMEs need also to be clearly acknowledged and appropriately fostered.

113. Such support is not an optional extra. The development of the international marketplace that offers opportunities to EU-based SMEs also offers opportunities to other businesses in the EU and elsewhere. We believe that future EU prosperity will, in large measure, rely on entrepreneurs in SMEs being helped to make the most of those opportunities.

ISSUES FOR FURTHER STUDY

114. Previous paragraphs have discussed and commented on the various themes emerging from the evidence received. None of that is the last word. As indicated in the introduction, the main purpose of this short enquiry was to identify issues that merit more detailed study. In our view, those key aspects of promoting SMEs in the EU are as below.

(a) **The nature of the modern business environment**. The environment for business is being revolutionised by a fresh wave of rapid technological change, the development of globalisation and, within the EU, the gradual implementation of the Single Market. The traditional methods of and geographical limitations on doing business are being swept away. The culture of entrepreneurship has been transformed. Only if this context is well understood will it be possible to frame effective policies to support SMEs.

(b) **The role of e-commerce.** One of the most exciting components of the transformed business environment is e-commerce: in many cases, distance is now absolutely no object. E-commerce is in its infancy in the EU. It is growing very rapidly, but with little regulation. To ensure that it can continue to develop, measures may be needed to promote confidence and to ensure the proper functioning of markets. It will be important to understand more about the growth of e-commerce so that its further development can be appropriately fostered.

(c) **An improved classification of SMEs.** SMEs vary in ways other than size as measured under the present EU definition – not least in their capacity and appetite for growth. Unless SMEs are classified meaningfully, policies affecting them can be neither appropriately tailored to their circumstances nor framed to accommodate the various types. This means wasted time and effort by the EU and Member States, as well as frustration for SMEs for which certain policies may be inappropriate. Might different ways of classifying SMEs do better justice to their diversity?

(d) **Operation of the European Single Market.** As far as SMEs are concerned, the Single Market seems still far from complete. What changes are needed to ensure that SMEs play a full part in the operation of the Single Market?

(e) **Harmonisation and mutual recognition of standards.** Standard-setting is one of the key components of the Single Market. SMEs are obviously disadvantaged by unfair conditions on standards. What more could be done to ensure that the principle of mutual recognition is respected? When things go wrong, SMEs can be deterred from pursuing legitimate complaints by both cost and the slow pace of the available remedies. Could the remedial procedures be improved?

(f) **Access to finance.** Finance is a key issue for SMEs, particularly if they wish to expand. What further steps are needed to simplify and extend SMEs' access to sources of finance? Is there a need for an EU equivalent to the loan guarantee portfolio system of the US SBA?

(g) **The regulatory burden on SMEs.** The balance between the interests of SMEs and the wider interests of the economy and society needs careful thought. In each case, there must be a clear test of necessity (rather than administrative desirability) and an assessment of the financial and opportunity costs of compliance. It might be useful to consider whether there would be merit in developing clearer general guidelines for policy makers and, more generally, a stronger culture within government of compliance cost assessment. Furthermore, it might be useful to examine the concept of "life cycle management of regulations"[26].

(h) **Information for SMEs.** Accurate and timely information is essential for sustained business success. SMEs seem swamped with well-intentioned but often unhelpful material. What should be the main components of an SME information policy in terms of value for money, role, quality, targeting and general availability?

(i) **Institutional structures.** What structures at European level are needed to provide the best support for the development of SMEs? For example, is there a case for a European Small Business Agency? Should there be a dedicated advocate for SMEs?

115. In pursuing any of those points further, it would be important to take fuller account of non-UK perceptions than was possible during the present short enquiry.

116. The Committee considers that the promotion of SMEs in the EU raises important questions to which the attention of the House should be drawn, and makes this report to the House for information.

---

[26] See footnote 11.

APPENDIX 1

Sub-Committee B (Energy, Industry and Transport)

The members of the Sub-Committee which conducted this enquiry were:

L. Berkeley
L. Brooke of Alverthorpe
V. Brookeborough
L. Geddes (Chairman)
L. Haslam
L. Howell of Guildford
L. Methuen
L. Montague of Oxford
B. O'Cathain
L. Paul
L. Sandberg
L. Skelmersdale

The Sub-Committee's Specialist Adviser was Dr Shobhana Madhavan, Director of the Centre for Business and the Environment at the University of Westminster.

Members of the Sub-Committee declared the following interests in relation to this enquiry.

L. Berkeley —   Chairman of Rail Freight Group and Adviser to Adtranz, both of which may have dealings with SMEs .

L. Brooke —   Non-executive director of an SME in the finance sector.

V. Brookeborough —   Owner/director of a micro business involved in agriculture and tourism in Northern Ireland.

L. Geddes —   Non-executive chairman or non-executive director of a number of private SMEs in the service and finance sectors.

L. Montague of Oxford —   Non-executive chairman or non-executive director of a number of public and private companies engaged in manufacturing, home development and display equipment, some of which are SMEs.

L. Paul —   Chairman and beneficial owner of the Caparo Group, some subsidiary companies of which may fall into the category of SMEs.

L. Skelmersdale —   Director of a family-run mail order micro business in the horticultural sector.

APPENDIX 2

Call for Evidence

The following call for evidence was issued at the beginning of July 1999, with a request for material to be submitted by the end of the month.

> Sub-Committee B of the House of Lords Select Committee on the European Communities is undertaking a short exploratory enquiry into the opportunities and challenges for Small and Medium Enterprises (SMEs) within the European Union's structures.
>
> Evidence is invited on what, within EU policies, the European Commission, national governments and their agencies are doing to support and promote SMEs, and what they should or should not be doing for such enterprises.

APPENDIX 3

Witnesses

The following witnesses gave evidence. Those marked * gave oral evidence. Those marked ** gave written evidence which is not printed, but is available for inspection at the House of Lords Record Office (020 7219 5316).

     Professor Robert Blackburn, Director of the Small Business Research Centre, Kingston University
     British Standards Institution (BSI)
     Comité Européen de Normalisation (CEN), Brussels
*   Confederation of British Industry (CBI)
** Confédération Generale de Petits et Moyens Enterprises, Paris
     Department of Economic Development for Northern Ireland
** Dirección General de Política de la Pequeña y Mediana Empresa, Madrid
     Environment Agency
*   Federation of Small Businesses
*   Herr Hans-Herman Jürgensmann, Head of Department for Industry, SMEs, Start-ups and Consultancy, Deutscher Industrie- und Handelstag, Bonn
     HM Customs & Excise
     Inland Revenue, Business Tax Division
     KPMG, Owner Managed Business Group
*   HE Mr Philip Lader, US Ambassador to the Court of St James's
*   Mr Lorimer Mackenzie, Director of Enterprise Policy and SMEs, European Commission
     Mr David Milborrow, Freelance Energy Consultant.
     National Centre for Business and Ecology, The Co-operative Bank
     Professor Hannah Scobie, European Economic and Financial Centre
*   Miss Margaret Soden, Senior Manager for EMU Planning, HSBC
*   Professor David Storey, The Business School, University of Warwick
     Trades Union Congress (TUC)
*   Mr Michael Wills MP, Parliamentary Under-Secretary of State, Department of Trade and Industry

MINUTES OF EVIDENCE

TAKEN BEFORE THE EUROPEAN COMMUNITIES COMMITTEE (SUB-COMMITTEE B)

THURSDAY 8 JULY 1999

Present:

Berkeley, L.
Brooke of Alverthorpe, L.
Brookeborough, V.
Geddes, L.
   (Chairman)
Howell of Guildford, L.

Methuen, L.
Montague of Oxford, L.
Paul, L.
Sandberg, L.
Skelmersdale, L.

Examination of Witness

PROFESSOR DAVID STOREY, Centre for Small and Medium Enterprises, Warwick Business School, called in and examined.

Chairman

1. Professor Storey, good morning. You would be welcome in any circumstances, but you are particularly welcome for having come at very short notice indeed. We are really very grateful to you for that. As you know, this enquiry is very much a paving enquiry with a view to our successor Committee looking at the subject of small and medium enterprises in depth. I think it is important to set that scene. On behalf of every Member of the Committee, as it happens except Lord Methuen, I also declare a general interest: we are all, to a greater or lesser extent, involved in business, which may or may not involve small and medium enterprises. We have discussed this just now and we came to the conclusion that if we were to go round the table and actually declare every single nut and bolt, you would have no time to give evidence at all, which would be rather detrimental to the idea of the session. I hope that is sufficient. Would you like to introduce yourself, tell us who you are, where you come from, what your background is in this context, and then, if we may, we find very often we get the most benefit in these sessions from a question and answer situation rather than a long monologue?

Professor Storey) Thank you. My Lord Chairman, I am genuinely grateful for your giving me this opportunity to make a few opening remarks. I will seek to provide you with an idea of where such expertise as I have may lie. The crucial point for me is that I am an applied economist. I am interested in the subject of small firms and I often feel that my expertise as a witness to Committees like this lies in the fact that I have been around studying the subject for an awfully long time. Indeed, I gave evidence to the House of Lords Select Committee on Unemployment in 1980 when I was asked about job creation in small businesses. So I sat down and reflected on what has happened and changed over those 20 years. Given that you are concerned with a scoping enquiry, I concluded that the five issues which were of concern to small businesses about public policy 20 years ago are pretty much the same five issues that are of concern to them today: taxation; bureaucratic burdens; access to finance;

getting good workers out of the education system; and, finally, getting a satisfactory macroeconomy, which I have taken to be low inflation, low interest rates and steady growth. So those five issues are the same five issues which were around 20 years ago. If you turn it on its head and ask, "What in some senses is the Government interested in from the delivery of public policy?" there is a strong overlap but the overlap is not perfect. The Government is also, I genuinely believe, interested in minimising bureaucratic burdens but it has a wider perspective on what constitutes bureaucratic burdens. It is also interested in ensuring access to finance, but it is much more interested than small businesses are in the area of the provision of information, advice and training, both for workers and managers in small businesses, and in recent years it has become much more concerned with what might be called creating positive attitudes to enterprise. So that, in some senses, is the public agenda. What I now want to do is to make three points, again related to the applied economist's perspective. As an applied economist I am interested in what businesses do and not interested so much in what they tell me. So I am interested in their actions and not necessarily in what they say. The second is that I am interested in the United Kingdom economy and society as a whole and not just in small firms. So if we have a policy initiative which benefits small firms but disbenefits either large firms or their labour force, then I do not necessarily regard that as a wholly good thing, and I am interested in the trade-offs between those two. But you are interested in public policy and so am I. I am interested in what impact that public policy has upon the economy as a whole as far as public policy towards small firms is concerned, and I have to say that assessing the impact of public policy in this area is extremely difficult, primarily because the objectives of public policy are rarely specified. In other words, there are lists of intentions, lists of initiatives, but there is rarely a specification of objectives or targets. I can do no better than quote to you a document which I gather you have, which is the Sixth Report of the Select Committee on Trade and Industry[1]. Its

---

[1] *Small and Medium Enterprises*, House of Commons Trade and Industry Committee Sixth Report, HC 774, Session 1997–98 ISBN 0 10 238 798 2

Chairman *contd.*]

conclusion says: "We are convinced that a coherent SMEs policy framework, with clearly defined and measurable objectives and targets, is essential, but remains lacking. We recommend that, as a matter of urgency,"—this is 1998—"the Government define the objectives of SMEs policy. The objectives chosen must be accompanied by measurable targets, with a timetable for their attainment." The most recent document to emerge from the Department of Trade and Industry is *Small Business Service: a Public Consultation*[2]. I have looked pretty closely through that document and I have not seen the word "objective" appear and I also have not seen the word "target". It may be hidden away but I could not pick it up. I have to say this is not unique at all to the British Government. The same principle applies in the European Union.

2. Professor Storey, could I interrupt you for a second there because already time is against us? The focus from which we are coming is that of the European Union rather than just the United Kingdom and what we are trying to get in our paving report is what is it that the European Union is doing for SMEs, what should they be doing and, just as important, what should they not be doing that they are? I think those are the areas on which we would like to concentrate.
A. I understand.

3. Could I then perhaps probe the first of your very interesting list of five (I think it was) and that is taxation. What are they doing—and I am talking Europe-wide now, not just the United Kingdom—and what, in your opinion, should they and should they not be doing?
A. My silence indicates the difficulty of responding to that question, because I come back to my point, which is that if you look at the stated objectives of enterprise policy as presented in the EU integrated programme, you see that they are in five categories. There is not a single objective or target within any of those five categories—so it is very difficult for me to sit here and make a judgment about what it is that they are supposed to be doing when I in fact do not know what the targets are. There are no targets specified. Just to give you an illustration of the first one, and I realise we are very tight on time, but the types of objectives are to simplify and improve the administrative and regulatory business environment. That is not a target.

Lord Howell of Guildford

4. I wonder whether targets and objectives are the right currency in this area at all or whether it is not more a question of the EU authorities and the national governments seeking to create an environment in which the discovery and innovation process which creates small businesses, which might create large businesses, takes place. Sorry about the gardening analogy, but is it not a question of creating the flowerbed rather than running around trying to plant the seeds? If we cannot define the objectives

between us, which we probably cannot, what do you think is the EU vision or grand strategic thought? Do they today see, as the Americans do, that really all the jobs will come from small business, that big businesses are downsizing and cutting jobs by the thousand and that thousands and thousands of new small businesses have to be created, or do they rather see it as a sort of exercise in bourgeois protection and middle-class comfort, keeping a lot of traditional businesses? Which do you think is the vision, in your view, which comes from Brussels?
A. There are two questions there. Your first was, "Don't let's worry about targets; it may be that we are becoming too detailed." My reply to that is that most certainly I do not agree because, for example, the EU, as one of its five objectives, has to promote entrepreneurship for specific target groups. That is a specified objective as far as the integrated programme is concerned, and it mentions women and young people. You can very clearly have a target there. If the target is to say, "Our purpose is to increase the stock of businesses owned by females by 10 per cent in the next five years", I would then know what the target was, so I can very clearly formulate targets out of woolly objectives. I therefore do not agree that you cannot formulate targets; you most certainly can. Let us deal with the second question, "Does the EU have a vision of the importance of SMEs in job creation comparable to that of the United States?" and most certainly it does. It clearly has observed what has happened in the United States. It is interested in job creation, but the work that I have done for the EU also suggests that it is more concerned than the United States about what it perceives to be the quality of those jobs. Essentially, it is perceived that, in the United States, many are "McDonald's jobs"; they are poor quality, low skill, low pay, low job satisfaction types of employment. The EU is more concerned than the United States to ensure that, if it can, it would prefer better quality jobs and possibly fewer of them, rather than more jobs of lower quality.

Chairman

5. Professor Storey, just for the record, what are your definitions of "small" and "medium"?
A. I am happy to take the EU definitions, and the EU definitions broadly are that 250 employees or less constitutes an SME, and an "S" is less than 50; you will also hear a lot of talk about micro-enterprises which is ten or less, so those are the types of definitions which we are talking about.

Lord Berkeley

6. One of the five issues you mentioned, Professor Storey, was access to finance, and on page 312 of your very interesting and important book[3], you note that the first objective must be "to encourage the bank to give greater weight to the merits of the trading business, and rather less weight to the value of the collateral", and it is a story that one hears

[2] *Small Business Service: a Public Consultation*, URN 99/815, Department of Trade and Industry 1999

[3] *Understanding the Small Business Sector*, D J Storey, Routledge 1994 ISBN 0 415 10038 0

Lord Berkeley *contd.*]

repeated again and again here. In the UK is that still the case? Are the banks even more difficult when it comes to businesses which seek to trade outside the UK and other Member States and, most particularly, how does it compare with the attitude of banks in other Member States and what is the EU doing about it, if anything?

A. Again, there are various questions there. The first question or the implied question is, "Has it changed in recent years in the UK?" and I think it is unquestionably the case that, for whatever reason (and I might offer you a couple) there has been an improvement in the relationships between the banking sector and small businesses in the UK. There are two obvious reasons for this. One is that the macroeconomy has considerably improved and, therefore, the pressures are less. Secondly, greater efforts have been made by the Bank of England and the Government to bring these various parties together, so I see that there has been a quite significant shift. Whether it would continue if macroeconomic circumstances deteriorate, I am not sure, and that would be the test. The second question is about how it differs within EU countries. Well, the country that I know best, as we have been looking at it in some detail, is Italy. I do know that there the relationship between banks and small businesses in terms of ease of access to loans is much easier in the UK than it is in Italy and particularly in the south of Italy, so I think that, by European standards, the UK relationship is pretty good. The third part of your questions related to cross-border transfers and whether that has eased.

7. Business as opposed to transfers.
A. I honestly do not know. I have never seen any careful research on that and I really would not like to comment.

Lord Paul

8. Professor Storey, you have just read from the House of Commons Trade and Industry Committee's Report when they were looking for a coherent policy on SMEs by the Government. Tell me one thing: is it really possible to have a coherent policy for such a wide range of industry which we have lumped together, small and medium industries, when above 250 you can be a big industry nowadays instead of medium? Is it really possible or are we talking of just pie in the sky?

A. Number one, it is not pie in the sky. Number two, you are entirely right to reflect the heterogeneity of the small firm sector, so what you do is to have appropriate policies for groups within the wider group. It is not a justification for woolly statements; in fact precisely the reverse. If you have a policy, let us say, to develop business sectors owned by different ethnic origins, you have that as a clear target. You specify that you are seeking to enhance either the performance or numbers of jobs created by businesses in those sectors. What you do not do is to say, "We are trying to do our best to help ethnic entrepreneurs" because we have no idea whether we are succeeding or not. So you are quite right, that you need to segment the policy areas so that you have different policies appropriate to different groups,

whether it is high technology businesses, whether it is female-owned businesses, whether it is exporting businesses, whether it is micro-firms or whether it is rapidly growing medium-sized firms.

Lord Skelmersdale

9. Is not that last point a difficult one because surely governments and the Commission expect a natural progression from strong micro-firms?
A. Yes.

10. And many firms just do not want to do that.
A. Yes.

11. Is this an inhibition either on the firms or, indeed, on the Government?
A. I do not think any government ever believes that firms are born, start as micros, move on to smalls, intermediates and then, by some linear process, become multinationals. That is not the reality. The reality is, particularly in the small firms sector, that most people who have businesses do not wish to grow. What you do is you formulate appropriate policies for the different groups.

12. Could I stop you there? My point is that governments on the whole, in my experience, do not recognise that particular phenomenon. Would that be a true or false statement?
A. They have been told it!

13. That is not the question.
A. If I may just respond to it, Lord Howell talked about job creation. If we believe our objective is job creation, then a key statistic for government is that, in terms of job creation, although the small firms sector as a whole is creating jobs and large firms in general are shedding jobs, job creation takes place in a tiny proportion of firms. Crudely, 4 per cent of small businesses end up creating 50 per cent of the additional jobs in small firms. Therefore, if you have policies and you are interested in job creation, then you target your policies towards enabling those businesses that want to grow to grow that bit faster. You do not focus upon the 96 per cent who actually have a perfectly legitimate objective, to run a family business or to pass the business on to the next generation, or to offer customer satisfaction. That is your objective, but you have to be clear on what your objective is. If your objective is job creation, then only a few firms matter. If you are interested in encouraging large numbers of people starting businesses, which is a different objective, then you have different policies. You have to specify the objectives first before you specify what policies flow from those objectives, and there is a great reluctance on the part of governments to specify what their objectives are, otherwise we would not be having this discussion.

Chairman

14. Professor Storey, taking that point up and broadening it slightly, what is your feeling about existing European legislation regarding SMEs and, without going into minutiae, what part of that

Chairman *contd.*]

legislation do you consider to be positive and which parts do you consider to be negative?

A. I have a feeling this is very similar to the question you asked me earlier.

15. I did not quite get an answer.

A. I have a feeling that my answer is going to be pretty similar to what I gave last time. I do not know what the objectives are. How can I comment upon the effectiveness of legislation unless I know what it is trying to achieve?

Chairman: Okay, let us leave it at that.

Lord Montague of Oxford

16. I have listened to you with very great interest, particularly your statement that you believe that most small businesses do not wish to grow. Those were your words?

A. Certainly.

17. As one who started his business in a garage some 40 years ago and ended up with a multinational company with 25,000 people, I have met a lot of companies on the way, and despite the fact that people will think I am playing the violin, I can identify with a lot of companies particularly on that. I wanted to ask a very narrow question. One of the things Europe has got is money, and money talks. To what extent, in your personal experience, are small businesses aware of the money that is available, or are they unaware of it?

A. I think I can answer a question on awareness. What I would not want you to do is to interpret awareness as equal to good and non-awareness equal to bad. So I am not saying necessarily that if you demonstrate that a particular policy initiative has high awareness, then that is necessarily a good policy initiative. That would be getting close to the question I refused to answer from the Chairman. Awareness of European funding is low, there is no question about it. Partly that reflects the fact that much European money is focused in the SMEs area upon Objective 1 and occasionally Objective 2 regions, so it is geographically concentrated. That is making a statement from a United Kingdom perspective. If, however, you look at this from a wider European perspective, what you see is that the countries who are most appreciative of, and most aware of, European money for the SMEs area tend to be Southern European countries and Ireland. Because their awareness is very much greater, the amounts of money are more substantial than they are, let us say, in the United Kingdom or in the Northern European countries. So I think awareness tends to equate to money. What I would emphasise again to you, though, is that you cannot judge the impact of a particular initiative purely in terms of whether people are aware of it. What you have to do is to say, "Does it make a difference to that business if you get the advice, assistance, money?" whatever it is.

Chairman

18. Are you saying then, Professor Storey, that the size of the available pots is greater in Southern Europe and Ireland than it is in Northern Europe?

A. That is my interpretation.

19. And your premise is that that fact creates a greater awareness?

A. Yes, but I emphasise to you that awareness is not the only criterion for judging the impact of the initiative.

Chairman: I heard that the first time round. It just shows the quality of your evidence. I have a huge list of members of the Committee wanting to ask questions. Lord Brooke?

Lord Brooke of Alverthorpe

20. If I may, Lord Chairman, return to your first question, the one about objectives, specifications of targets, have you, Professor Storey, done any work in this area and, if you have, could you endeavour to enlighten us on the work you are doing, particularly in the context of Europe? If you have not done so, is there anyone you might recommend we should seek evidence from who might be able to help?

A. May I deal with the last question first and then a little bit with the first one. There is an SMEs observatory document[4] which is produced annually. It is somewhere around 5-600 pages and it provides information upon SMEs in Europe and is produced for DG XXIII by a consortium of research institutes throughout Europe. Should you be interested I have some copies in my briefcase. I would very strongly suggest that you invite the Secretary of the Observatory Group, whose name is Rob van der Horst from EIM in the Netherlands, to give evidence to you. EIM have been producing these reports for five years. We at Warwick are the United Kingdom partners but Rob has the big picture. As far as my own work is mainly at the level of the United Kingdom rather than Europe and I could talk to you about that but I think, given the time constraints that we have, I would be happy to—

21. If we have the time I would like to hear a bit more.

A. May I say two things on that very quickly. You have seen my 1994 book. There are statements in there which are controversial about the impact or lack of impact of management training in small firms. In the last five years I have seen nothing to contravene those statements, so I do not believe that there is clear evidence that the publicly subsidised management training enhances the performance of small firms. However, what I do believe is that training for workers in small firms benefits the workers, but not necessarily the businesses. Yet we insist on delivering our training through workplaces, and I do not think that that works in the case of small and medium enterprises. That is one crucial area of uncertainty which I would like to bring to the Committee's attention.

4 *The European Observatory for SMEs: Fifth Annual Report 1997*, co-ordinated by EIM Small Business Research and Consultancy. ISBN 90 371 0643 9

Viscount Brookeborough

22. Just to go back to objectives for one moment, it seems extraordinary that the main objective is not simply to create more jobs, although you talked about the quality of jobs, but surely that should not be the concern of the increasing numbers of small businesses in employment when European legislation on minimum wage, pensions and so on should be taking care of the welfare. Surely from our point of view what we wish to do is to increase the number of jobs. Can you comment on why this is so? Also on page 304 of your book, you actually mention that it leads to welfare improvements and I am not quite sure why that should be the concern of this particular part of business promotion.

A. It clearly was not the objective of past UK governments simply to maximise the number of jobs created in small firms.

23. But you said you could not find those objectives anyway.

A. I can speculate as to what the objectives are and are not. What the objectives could be are: the creation of jobs, they could be the reduction in unemployment, which is not the same, they could be the creation of large numbers of enterprises, they could be reductions in the death rates of enterprises, they could be the more rapid growth in small firms, they could be the increased competitiveness of small businesses. All of these are implied objectives from parts of the legislation; you can infer these objectives. If your objective quite simply is the creation of employment, then you will be focusing almost exclusively upon encouraging and enabling growing businesses to grow faster and yet the Government is clearly saying in its recent Small Business Service consultation document, "We are putting £10 million aside for the creation of new start-ups". That frankly is not going to create jobs. It may enable individuals to enter businesses, it may create an enterprise culture, but it is not focused upon job creation. Governments have to be clear as to what their objectives are. The objectives have to be inferred and are very rarely specified.

•

Lord Berkeley

24. I have two quick questions, Professor Storey. We are talking about the awareness of new funding, particularly in Objective 1 status, and I just wondered, reverting to my last question, whether there was any connection between a greater awareness and the availability of funding in southern Italy with the lack of availability of funding from banks. Perhaps there is not actually a need for it in Italy. I am interested in your comments about the management and workforce training that you mentioned just a few minutes ago, saying it had not achieved very much in terms of either growing a business or making it more profitable. What do you think should happen—or is more training unnecessary in SMEs?

A. No. I am not sure that I understood the question about southern Italy. Could you repeat that?

25. You mentioned that you have done some work in Italy and that the availability of finance from banks for SMEs was more difficult there than in this country. I wondered whether businesses setting up in an Objective 1 area could get enough money to set up from Objective 1 funds and probably then would not need to go to the banks so much or is that too naive?

A. I think that, even before EU funding became available on its current scale for the SME sector, it was always a problem for southern Italian businesses to obtain bank funding. If anything, I think that the EU funding has eased that problem rather than in some senses made it worse. As far as the workforce issue is concerned, I believe that the previous Government and to some extent the current administration have set the workforce training agenda to be delivered by—well, enterprises essentially set the agenda. Small and medium enterprises—and the smaller you are, the more true this statement is—are less committed to workforce training and to management training. This means that, if you are going to upskill the people who work in small businesses, you actually have to focus the attention upon them as individuals rather than getting it organised through enterprises. That is the strategic change that I would like to see. It will not work through small enterprises.

Lord Paul

26. You have talked about objectives and whether the objective is job creation or setting up new businesses or creating enterprises. In the end it all boils down to an objective of wealth creation for the country.

A. Okay.

27. Now, taking that as the objective, can you come back to the Chairman's original question which was are the EU laws helping that or are not helping that? You have written a wonderful book, but that is what I think I would like to hear. What is it in those laws which prohibits the creation of wealth, irrespective of what the ordinary media says is job creation because in the end it is always the creation of wealth or not the creation of wealth?

A. I have to say that I have to retain my position on this, that I do not believe that it is possible to make a generic statement about wealth creation. What is easier for me, and I believe more appropriate, is to talk about the various components of that which you talked about in terms of job creation, starting businesses, competitiveness, and I am happy to talk about those particular elements. If then you are gradually forcing me for the third time to answer the Chairman's question, I believe that there are major differences within Europe from country to country, so if you now push me into saying what I think from the UK's perspective, which is how I interpret what you are saying, where would I place my emphasis in terms of policy? I believe that it is very difficult in the area of bureaucratic burdens to assess the impact of policy. I believe it is important but it is very hard for somebody like me to do anything on that. As to the second area in terms of improved financing, I believe that, in the United Kingdom, the market for finance works well—with two exceptions, and they are high-technology businesses and some forms of ethnic businesses. So I do not believe that new initiatives in the financial field are appropriate in the context of the United Kingdom. As far as better information is concerned, which is the third part of the integrated

Lord Paul *contd.*]

programme, I am also rather sceptical as to the extent to which this is used and benefited from by small businesses. No. 4 in the integrated programme is to enhance competitiveness through access to research and training: training, potentially but not as it is currently delivered; research, possibly, and finally, to promote entrepreneurship for target groups I believe is important.

Lord Howell of Guildford

28. I do not understand, Professor Storey, your divorce between the job creation aspect and the new business start-up. Surely it is the thousands of new businesses that start up every day, and have started since we began this hearing, which create one, two, three jobs—all this adds up eventually whether they grow or not. You say it does not?

A. No, we should talk about this on a separate occasion. Let us assume we have two pots of money. Pot of money one is for start-ups and pot of money two we can put into growing businesses. The analogy is a horse-race. What we can do is we can put our money on at the start or after the race has started. We have a very stupid "bookie" and the bookie says, "I do not really mind if you put your money on at the start of the race—which is the start-ups—or you can put your money on when the horses have jumped 14 fences and the water jump and have got the sprint to home." Naturally you put your money on later on in the race when it becomes clear, because we have observed that actually most of the businesses which start do not wish to grow. The vast majority of the jobs which are created are created in a tiny proportion of firms. The history of putting money into start-ups is that you encourage essentially unsuitable people to enter businesses, to subsidise and knock out the unsubsidised, so you get no more

jobs in the economy. You might get an additional job in the one that starts but it knocks out the one which is there. The focus has to be, if you are interested in job creation, on comparatively rapid growth businesses which are seeking to grow and not upon lifestyle or start-up businesses.

29. It sounds to me like picking winners.
A. What it is doing is avoiding losers.

Chairman

30. It takes me back 40 years to economics lectures at Cambridge but that is another story. Professor Storey, if I could hold on to the horse-racing analogy, and hoping that you have staying power, I wonder if you would be kind enough to send us a written memorandum, of whatever length you would like, really going back to the fundamentals I opened with of what is it that the European Union should be doing and what is it they should not be doing to promote SMEs, remembering that this is a paving enquiry, not an enquiry in depth? We want to try and get a broad feel within the European Union, frankly, what is worth it and what is not. Could you do that for us?

A. I am currently on study leave and this is my first visit outside my back garden in four months. I will try to produce you something. I do, however, feel that it may tend merely to reiterate what it is that I have said. So I will look carefully at what the transcript says I said and whether this calls for any expansion or clarification.[5]

Chairman: In all the circumstances, Professor, more than that we cannot ask. Thank you very much.

---

[5] In the event, Professor Storey concluded that his oral evidence needed no supplimentation.

Examination of Witnesses

MR BRENDAN BURNS, Chairman, Policy Unit, and MR STEPHEN ALAMBRITIS, Head of Press and Parliamentary Affairs Division, Federation of Small Businesses, called in and examined.

Chairman

31. Mr Alambritis and Mr Burns, welcome. I think you heard me say just now, whilst you were listening to Professor Storey, that we are undertaking a paving enquiry into the pros and cons of existing European Union legislation as far as SMEs are concerned, and frankly, what the European Union could do, should do and should not do in that context. I think you were not here at the beginning of Professor Storey's evidential session, so I will repeat a general declaration of interest, which one is obliged to do. It is not quite as simple as normal in that all Members of this Committee, including myself but other than, as it happens, Lord Methuen, are to a greater or lesser degree involved in business which may or may not involve small and medium-sized enterprises. I think beyond that we really cannot go other than occupying the entire evidence session. We prefer to proceed with questions and answers rather than long

statements, but if you would like briefly to set the scene for us as to the origins of the Federation of Small Businesses and what it does, that would be very helpful.

(*Mr Alambritis*) Yes, thank you, Lord Geddes. Thank you for inviting us to give evidence. My name is Stephen Alambritis, I am Head of Parliamentary Affairs at the Federation of Small Businesses and I was involved with a family-owned business for about ten years based in the West Midlands, up until 1995.

32. As a matter of interest, what did that do?

(*Mr Alambritis*) That was a restaurant, a Greek restaurant. On my right is Brendan Burns, who is the Policy Chairman for the Federation of Small Businesses.

(*Mr Burns*) I have run several businesses in the last 30 years and am presently in forestry harvesting. I was previously in the hotel/catering/restaurant

Chairman *contd.*]

industry. I have had experience also of running a small business in relation to exporting.

33. You should perhaps have been a witness for us in our previous enquiry into renewable energy, but that is rather beside the point.
(*Mr Alambritis*) The Federation of Small Businesses was started in 1974 and is non-party political and currently has a membership of around 135,000 members. Their complexion is the truly small business—as Napoleon called us, "a nation of shopkeepers". The vast majority employ fewer than ten people.

34. What is your definition of small and medium?
(*Mr Alambritis*) The European Commission got it wrong for a number of years in calling them SMEs. Now both the DTI and the European Commission talk of a micro-business, one layer below small, which is 0 to 9 workers; you then have 10 to 49 workers, which is your small business, then you move to 50 to 249 workers, which is the medium-sized business. We agree with this latest definition from both the Commission and the DTI, but under the old regime the European Commission used to talk about SMEs employing up to 500 workers. That is where you had good money going really to quite wealthy businesses through their support of SMEs but now it is more targeted.

35. I have just one more question, if I may, to set the scene. Your Federation is entirely UK-based, is it?
(*Mr Alambritis*) Yes, it is. We have some members in Jersey and we have some friends in Gibraltar, but it is UK-based.

36. And, anticipating Lord Brookeborough, does that include Northern Ireland?
(*Mr Alambritis*) Yes, Northern Ireland as well.

37. Could you just tell us whether, in your opinion, you are adequately informed about what is happening throughout the rest of the European Union in this context?
(*Mr Alambritis*) The Federation of Small Businesses is informed through its membership of the European Small Business Alliance. As to whether our members are aware of what is happening in Europe, we try to get as much information out to them as possible, but I do not think they are as aware as we are. There are two types of information. One is the old-fashioned information through the Euro info centres and these are in most major towns and the small business needs to visit or to phone or sometimes to pay a small fee. Increasingly, small businesses and we are encouraging both the Commission and the DTI in the UK to post information on websites. The Commission has set up a website about two weeks ago on access to grants and to services and to legislation in Europe and that is receiving some 11,000 hits a day. Yesterday, Lord Simon of the DTI announced a website for government and business on contracts in business and grants in Europe and so on. Increasingly, we are looking to electronic commerce and to electronic mail to get information as to what is happening in Europe.

38. To your knowledge, are there similar organisations in all the EU countries?
(*Mr Alambritis*) Yes, there are similar organisations in other EU countries. Some EU countries have what is called public law status which forces the business to join its local chamber of commerce or local business club, so in France, for example, you would have the national statutory business body, but you would also have independent private bodies like the Federation of Small Businesses, but yes, there are similar bodies. In Germany you would have the German Federation of Independent Businesses, for example, and in Italy you would have the Confederation of Artists and Craftsmen, so yes, there are and we liaise quite closely with them.

39. Is there a pan-European association?
(*Mr Alambritis*) Yes, there are two main ones. There is ESBA, which is the European Small Business Alliance, of which we are members, and there is one called EUAPME and the rough translation, I would imagine, is the European organisation for small and medium-sized enterprises.

40. Where are those two based?
(*Mr Alambritis*) Both are in Brussels.

Viscount Brookeborough

41. We have heard previously that there are no well-defined targets and objectives. When I asked the Northern Ireland Small Business Agency what systems there were for supporting small businesses, they came up with a large number of different funds within the system, for instance, INTERREG, which is cross-border, KONVER II for deprived areas because of reductions in armed forces post the Cold War, LACE TAP (linkage across communities in the EU) and so on. It seems that, first of all, we do not have well-defined objectives, but, secondly, there is a myriad of little segments that they wish to promote. Do you feel that this is the way forward or should there be a single system for promoting small businesses throughout the EU? There does seem to be a lack of knowledge amongst small businesses that they can even tap into.
(*Mr Burns*) I think it depends what you mean by supporting small businesses. The big problem as far as the average small business is concerned is that there is a lot of information and there are a lot of people wanting to help. The hard brutal fact is that, as far as most small businesses are concerned, getting that information in a usable form that they understand is the single biggest problem. A simple example would be where you go to one agency, you are diverted to another one, and you are then diverted to another one and by the time you get to the end of the list, you are quite clear that you have been pushed around with all good intentions to try to get help, but nobody in the initial stage was clear with the businessman as to what help he actually wanted. There are proposals to bring in the one-stop-shop approach, but that could also be a one-stop choice and that does give us a considerable amount of concern.

Viscount Brookeborough *contd.*]

42. But at the moment people are not using all these funds correctly because they are not aware of them anyway.

(*Mr Burns*) That is correct. We have two problems with the funds and I have actually attempted to try to get some of these funds, so this is very much from a practical end of it. I worked it out that, by the time I had actually got a consultant to help me apply for the funds and got all the other professionals in, my £40,000 grant would probably look like £2,000, with £38,000 worth of consultancy costs. Our other big problem is language. Very many times the information about getting money is presented to us in a complicated language. It has got terms and conditions which require a considerable amount of research. As a small businessman, I am really likely to come to the conclusion at the end of this that it really is not worth the salt in trying to get the end product. We would actually far prefer to have low per cent interest money rather than any grants.

(*Mr Alambritis*) The previous definition of SMEs up to 500 employees meant that there was no pressure on the Commission to make the language easier, to target the grants and the help because the applicants in the main were fairly well-off businesses that could appoint someone to apply for the grant, or in fact they have a department, so you have businesses employing 100 people, 150 people, qualifying for the grants. So the civil servants, the Commissioners in Europe, became *laissez-faire* about whether it was meeting its true target. Because it is the fairly medium-sized companies taking advantage of the monies and the grants over the years, the impression amongst the small business community of grants is rather like someone asking you to give them money for them to get you a Christmas present, but that Christmas present being worth less than the money you had given them, so there is an acknowledgement that the money is there in the first place, that there is taxpayers' money swilling around. Our preferred option is that if businesses can retain their own resources a bit more with proof of expansion or job creation, a lot of these grants and schemes can actually be cut away.

Lord Methuen

43. Looking at your paper[6] which you submitted to the Trade and Industry Committee, the majority of these businesses, these micro-businesses, is something of the order of 3.4 million businesses, which you say is 90 per cent of the 3.8 total. My impression is, and I had a different impression initially because I was thinking in terms of small engineering firms, but my impression is that most of these are things like back-street shops and small back-street garages which have absolutely no desire to expand: I cannot imagine the local corner shop wanting to expand. A whole lot of what we are talking about is totally irrelevant to this. The relevance of this is actually to a very small number or

a relatively small percentage of the firms we are considering. Is this true?

(*Mr Alambritis*) Yes, that is true.

44. Is my definition of these firms correct anyway? For me, small represents some "back street" shops, small "back street" garages doing a bit of spraying or car repair.

(*Mr Alambritis*) But they are also bombarded with information leaflets. There is a plethora of grants, schemes and moneys there. There are consultants that are "cold calling" companies and small businesses saying, "There are billions of ecus out there and all you need do is this". Some of the small businesses have been stung for fees and consultancy fees. There are some fairly brazen "cowboy" companies out there. But we agree with some of the points made by Professor Storey in so far as, in terms of marketing, the Commission and the DTI and institutions need to acknowledge the needs of some 3 to 4 million lifestyle businesses or what I call "candy floss" businesses, because once you get into them there is not much there but they are quite happy to be where they are and trying to target some of these grants, schemes, help for businesses, if DTI can identify businesses as having the potential to grow. But yes, you are right, in so far as the vast majority of small businesses, both in Europe and in the United Kingdom, are small and they are very tiny, they will not be interested, but they are made well aware that their taxpayers' money is funding Europe and that when they are told there is some money around they are tempted to apply to see if it works, and if it does not work, again they are alienated and they resent Europe even more.

(*Mr Burns*) There is also the question of what you mean by "expand". I would like your definition as to what you mean by "expand" in as much as you are wanting small businesses to expand.

45. There is an awful lot of them who are not interested in expanding. Lord Montague's business has obviously expanded. You can say, yes, some of these "back street" firms that have been building computers or something then end up as a software house and the turnover has gone rocketing up, but I have a feeling an awful lot are totally uninterested.

(*Mr Burns*) My reason for making that particular point was that it is the expansion of profit, not the expansion of employment. Listening to the tail-end of the previous conversation, most small businesses want to improve their profits. That to them is expansion, but obviously if we are talking about extra employees then there is a problem there. I put in a new piece of machinery not long ago and did away with four men. That was good expansion. I have four employees fewer and an awful lot more owed to the bank in the process, of course, but I am producing an awful lot more now. So my company is now more guaranteed, it is more stable and is in a better position. So there is this vocabulary aspect, that when organisations talk about expansion or improving the viability of businesses, we do get a slightly different view as to what we mean by this. It would be socially unacceptable this statement, I accept that, but I would be delighted if I could run my business with no staff. I cannot. They are required to run machines, but if I could I would reduce all my

[6]Memorandum by the Federation of Small Businesses, *Small and Medium Enterprises*, House of Commons Trade and Industry Committee, Sixth Report, HC 774, Session 1997-98 ISBN 0 10 238 798 2

Lord Methuen contd.]

liabilities and I would have less of a problem with legislation relating to employees. It is impractical but that is where I would like to be: to have sustainability, to be able to guarantee the men I have employed greater sustainability in their jobs.

Lord Sandberg

46. We have heard a lot today about workers and creating jobs and this, that and the other. What sort of encouragement do especially medium-sized businesses have for exporting? Their finance becomes much easier but in England you have the ECGD, in France you have COFACE etc and this is a much easier way to get finance. So what encouragement in the United Kingdom and the rest of Europe are you getting to support export business?

(Mr Burns) You mentioned medium companies and support for the medium companies is really quite good but the support for the smaller companies and the micro-businesses is really not good at all. You write in to a man in the trade area and there is an automatic assumption that I have an export department in my company. I have; it is me. There is also an expectation that there is a finance department and we know where that is, too. So the accumulation of the legislation, the accumulation of the advice, means that eventually I have to try to decide which I am going to deal with today. If today it is going to be dealing with environmental stuff and getting my books done and my VAT finished, I am not going to have time to do anything else. One of my businesses is a very small exporting business that could grow quite considerably—and I mean by "growth" sustainable growth. I could employ three, possibly four people but when I have gone and asked for that help, I suddenly discover that I am back with this problem of language. They are expecting me to do an awful lot more research than would be expected. I would also like to raise the particular issue that there are one or two good examples of agencies that have done a lot of good work in getting round small businesses. The Highlands and Islands Development Board—I am not just touting that because I am from Scotland— have some good advice and show some good practice and so has Rural Forum. So there are good examples out there of how to help the small businesses.

(Mr Alambritis) Could I raise one issue? The Government has a £99 package to encourage small businesses to export and we welcome that. We have also approached the Export Credit Guarantee Department to put real small employers on to their advisory council. We are talking to the chief executive there, nominating people to get them working. Our main lobby to government on exports is our embassies throughout the world. We feel the commercial attaché should actually be the most senior person in the embassy rather than the ambassador or the diplomat. I am not saying that literally. What I am saying is that there needs to be a change in the emphasis, rather than this anxiety amongst our diplomats to get promotion from one embassy to another so they are there for three years or two years. We need them to grow the business contacts. Business contacts can be easily won and easily lost. If we had commercial staff who have the seniority and can stay there for ten or 20 years and create these contacts, so that it is tweaking the influence amongst our embassies, and have fewer diplomatic receptions, fewer champagne receptions and more commercial receptions.

Chairman: The FCO might have views on that. Sadly, we do not have any retired ambassadors on this Committee.

Lord Paul

47. First of all, your definition of a medium enterprise was from 50 to 249. Is that accepted all over Europe or is it still a question mark?

(Mr Alambritis) No, I think it is accepted.

48. Both of you are the kind of entrepreneurs the country needs who can build small businesses. Do you think it might be better if small businesses were classified absolutely separately from micro- and medium sized businesses, in separate groups? From certain things you are saying, they are completely separate. I have had occasion to visit a lot of foreign offices as ambassador for British business. There is a lot of cultural change in the embassies and they have made commercial attachés fairly independent and the No. 2 is always a local man who is more permanent. So are you seeing an improvement or what aspirational thing would you like to see? I am not sure I fully share your view on the champagne parties. The poor ambassadors work very hard.

(Mr Alambritis) I will take that last point first. There is still a long way to go and His Royal Highness Prince Charles is very keen to get our embassies working more commercially. There is also a snob element within the country desks at the DTI. The civil servant manning the country desk for Mexico or for Brazil is more at ease dealing with a large company enquiry than a blunt, handwritten, opinionated enquiry from a small business, because it is virtually the civil servant, where the enquiry is from, say, GEC's buying or exporting officer and the country desk with the DTI person in Mexico rather than a small builder, say, who has got an idea that morning, has woken up with that idea, and puts in a call to the country desk. It is fairly poignant: the small businesses have the view that they are the taxpayer and the civil servant is there at their beck and call, at their bidding. It is for the civil servant to be patient and more tolerant in dealing with some very genuine enquiries. Once that telephone call is not followed up or the enquiry is not followed through, the small business aspirant drops it and will not go back to it, so it is a case of getting the genuine nature of small businesses in the UK who do have potential for growth, for getting our civil servants, our embassies not to expect that high profile, big business reaction and approach which is very professional and very reassuring.

(Mr Burns) To take up the point about separating it out, as far as we are concerned, it will not make any difference really. I think that is really a question that it might be very useful, or as far as the Federation is concerned it would be very useful actually to get more accurate data and information. The only problem that I have about it, whilst initially saying, "Yes, that might be a good idea", is that we could

Lord Paul *contd.*]

ghettoise the whole process, you know, "You are in the micro lot and you don't matter". We have seen this too often where it is a lot of hard work to help me to get my products into my marketplaces and it will not be half as much hard work to help GEC or a company like that.

Lord Howell of Guildford

49. Going back to overall impressions, is it possible to draw views from the majority of your members about their attitude to the activities of the EU? You were reminding us earlier that the EU small business policy activities are not just grants, but we have lots and lots of regulations as well. Does this produce overall a negative view about the EU and a wish that it would go away or a positive view that something good is coming from Brussels?

(*Mr Burns*) I think most small businessmen are actually very positive towards Europe. They will moan to me in the bar and tell me all the wrong things, but if you actually sit down with them and start talking to them about what it means to their business and the potential and the possibilities—well, there is an old saying that if there was a nuclear war tomorrow, you could guarantee the day after on some corner, somewhere, some small businessman is going to be selling something. We are not sure what, but he will be in there. Concerning the legislation aspect which actually does cause us considerable concern, and the volume of it, the accumulated effect of it, we constantly use the terminology, "It is only this bit of legislation that we are worrying about because that is what the civil servant at this particular time is working on, but it will be quite easy to comply with". Now, it might be. That bit of environmental legislation might be very easy to comply with, but when you add the health and safety and the other stuff and the staff employment and all the rest of it, there are only 24 hours in a day and I am the one that is going to have to understand this. I will quote something that I said to the Environment Committee about an environmental Directive. What I said was that it was written by highly educated, highly qualified academic administrators to be interpreted by the environmentally dyslexic. That is the situation. I do not understand some of these Directives. If it was not for something like the Federation, I am not really too sure what I would do other than try to ignore them, which I have a sneaking suspicion is what is happening in a lot of cases. It is not intentional. Most businessmen are law-abiding and they want to comply if they could just understand what it was that people were trying to tell them and hopefully give us enough time to actually understand what it is that we are being told.

Lord Berkeley

50. We were discussing earlier the access to information on EU programmes and funds and you were saying how difficult the language was. I tried to complete an application several years ago with a French company and that leads me to my question. My impression there was that whereas there was no help at all in this country that I could find apart from

phoning up friends in the Commission which I was able to do and other people could not do, in France, there was a mechanism through local authorities to help businessmen complete these forms and translate the language into idiot's speak, if you like. I am just wondering have you got any information about what assistance other Member States' governments or local authorities within those Member States give to small businesses in applying for funds and helping them get away from this consultancy problem that you mentioned?

(*Mr Burns*) You may note that we actually have identified France as one of the areas. I was talking to a student who is doing a reciprocal over in France about the idea of her looking at exactly this point, so yes, we have identified it, but no, we do not have the evidence. Unfortunately that student is not going to be able to do that project with us, but we will in fact be going down that route to look at it.

(*Mr Alambritis*) What has happened is that our local authorities have not moved with the times and they are still wedded to the economic development units. Every local authority has an economic development unit which is still obsessed with property register, giving business rate holidays, start-up businesses, business centres, so local authorities have not put aside funding for help for small businesses to access Europe. I think they have sat back and said, "Well, the Government has set up Euro Info Centres or Business Links or the TECs", so local authorities which have a big interface with the small business community are lacking the resources and the systems in place to directly help their local businesses to access European funds. If a local authority is helping in any way, it is in helping to gain funding overall throughout perhaps for the area.

51. That is my perception, but many local authorities now have representations in Brussels and you would think that that would be an ideal opportunity from which to dump down, if you like, to unload information to help the micro businesses, but you have said this does not happen.

(*Mr Alambritis*) No, it does not because many local authorities still view the small businesses just as business ratepayers and the link between the business rates and the businesses is taken completely away, so there is no incentive on either side to help each other or to be warm to each other. Business rates are now set centrally, they are collected by the local authority, handed to the Exchequer and then the Exchequer hands it back on the basis of how many council taxpayers there are, so there is a lot of resentment amongst local authorities of small businesses in particular, so there needs to be a lot of working to get them closer together and to get local authorities to set up officers purely to help businesses with European regulations or with European schemes.

Lord Montague of Oxford

52. I would like to probe you a bit further on this communication issue in relation to whether your members would get greater help if the trade associations were stronger or if there was any other aspect of trade associations in this area, and also the

Lord Montague of Oxford *contd.*]

chambers of commerce. After all, I think I am right in saying that in Germany you have to be a member of the local chamber of commerce and that is part of the structure. Would you care to comment on how we might use trade associations and chambers of commerce to better advantage to assist your members?

(*Mr Alambritis*) Yes, you are right about Germany, that they have public law status and businesses do have to belong to their chamber of commerce. There was some talk at one stage that Michael Heseltine, then as Secretary of State for Trade and Industry, was looking at this area of chambers of commerce because, when he became Secretary of State, he asked the civil servants, "How many businesses are there out there and how many do we know of?" and they came back and said, "We are only aware of 40 per cent being registered with a business organisation, with the CBI, with the Federation of Small Businesses or with a chamber", and he was appalled at that. The deregulatory train of thought meant that he could not go down the public law status route which was to force companies to join their chamber of commerce. What has happened since and what the present Government has also accepted and is working on is the move towards lead trade associations. There is a trade association forum under the auspices of the CBI to boost trade associations to have a lead model for trade associations and yes, you are right, there are too many associations in the UK, ill-researched, under-funded, under-resourced, very local, and that is why the British Chambers of Commerce are putting together core chambers. So if you go to the North-East you will not see a Teesside Chamber of Commerce or a Middlesborough Chamber of Commerce or a Darlington Chamber of Commerce. What you have in the North-East of England is the North-East Chamber of Commerce. So there is a route we will be going down of making the representation of the business community more enhanced without forcing businesses to join the organisation. We are a pluralistic society. Each organisation has its view and it has the right to put its view forward. But you are right, there has always been a debate since Lord Devlins' report on the representation of the business community in the United Kingdom about how to make it much clearer and more supportive of its business community. We are not there yet. There is talk of a merger between the chambers of commerce and the Confederation of British Industry. Some years ago there was talk of a merger between the CBI and the Engineering Employers Federation. That is not happening but I think we are getting to the stage where business organisations are working much closer together.

(*Mr Burns*) I would have to ask the question, why should I be forced to join anything because that is what the situation is in Germany? If you speak to our German business friends over there, their attitude is, "This is just a tax. We are forced to pay it. We are forced to join. We do not even get what we want." As soon as you remove from our Federation and from our civil servants the fact that he has to go out there and work really hard to make the money to pay his wages, then we remove the incentive. We are good and we are the biggest Federation in this country

because we give our members something. But if they once had to join us, we would be dead against the idea of them having to join the Federation or the Chamber or anybody else. We will go out there as a business and fight it. I do not want to be forced to join anything.

Lord Berkeley

53. But one could argue that you could give advice on how to fill in forms and everything to your members if that was a service they wanted?

(*Mr Burns*) Yes, if that was a service the members wanted and which the members were willing to pay for. Again we have to be careful here because, as a business ourselves, we are out there pitching our membership fee at the level our members want. What they have asked us to do, we provide. We can do that. This is wider than just the Federation. This is an issue, as I have mentioned, for councils, who in theory should be interested in developing their own area. Therefore, they have a vested interest to ensure that those businesses are helped. So the choice aspect is the bit that we would always wish to keep.

Chairman: I am very conscious of the time, as always, and we have four Members of the Committee still wanting to ask questions, indeed, I have one at the end, too. So perhaps we could try to be as short as we can. Lord Skelmersdale?

Lord Skelmersdale

54. Before you came in, Professor Storey gave us a hit list of the targets for small businesses: low tax, minimal bureaucracy, access to finance, the ability for the education system to provide good workers and a stable economy, to which you have added understanding Directives. Is there anything else that you would like to add to that hit list?

(*Mr Burns*) I would certainly like to take up the issue of education because I think the Professor made a very valid point without necessarily seeing it from the businessman's side. To put it simply, when education is presented to us it is correct that the real winners in an education system are the employees, and I would even go so far as to say that is how it should be. If you want to help businesses in the development of management and to help us to be able to get the most out of the education, we have an absolute fundamental problem in the way that education is sold to us. When you look at any of the training, it is clearly based on what we would classify as a "plan, manage and monitor" approach. All the training courses are laid out as "plan, manage and monitor", because that is how big businesses work: if they did not work that way they would not succeed and survive. When you look at how small businesses run and how they perceive things and how they want information fed to them, it is on a "buy, produce and sell" model. There is actually a fundamental change between a small and a medium business that is something to do with a change between "buy, produce and sell" to "planning, managing and monitoring". Now in the "buy, produce and sell" model "plan, manage and monitor" is obviously in it but it is scattered throughout. Therefore, you get, for

Lord Skelmersdale *contd.*]

example, a receptionist who, in fact, does three or four other jobs at the same time. When we want her to be trained, then we have to be clear of the tasks that she does. Education is about selling skills; we want to buy tasks. There is a fundamental difference. I was the chairman of the small firms lead body many years ago and landed up in a situation where the Government did not want to hear this message, but this message is still the same message ten years later, when, in fact, we are saying, "There is a problem in the education system. Please will somebody listen to us."

Lord Brooke of Alverthorpe

55. I was interested in your observations about what local authorities are not doing and what you would like them to do. Could you make some comments on what you would like to see the European Union doing for small businesses, as an example?

(*Mr Alambritis*) I think getting the Government drive here on better regulation may be useful; I think not regulating in an area where the national government is best able to regulate, so the Commission should stay away from being tempted into areas where national governments are best looking at the area, giving as much time as possible to the business community to acquaint itself with regulations and making sure that regulations are enforced evenly throughout the whole of the European Union. We have no exploitation of workers, or very little, in the United Kingdom. We have no child labour or sweated labour in the United Kingdom, or very little. There are some elements of that in places like Spain, Portugal and Greece, and it is for the Commission to ensure that when it puts forward Working Time Directives and social legislation like that, it monitors that to make sure all the Member States follow it through so that there is a level playing-field on that score. Also it should be no embarrassment to the Commission to go one year or two years without any Directives. I know that it has to justify itself by having Directives but what businesses do from time to time is exactly that, ie they may not expand for a year. They will consolidate, they will solidify, they will look at the systems, they will take a breather, they will sit back and see how it is all going. Why do there have to be Directives year on year on year? So if it can do even that for one year I think businesses would be very pleased.

(*Mr Burns*) On the personal side again, the last regulation, is it needed? There is a tremendous amount of legislation out there. As I said, small businesses are law-abiding. We are members of our society; we employ our friends and our relatives. We are not some sort of great hairy monster out there. So we live within our society and we keep asking ourselves when we see this coming from Europe, why? Why did anybody waste our time even going down this route to regulate? Boiler regulation is covered perfectly well by our own regulation. It could have been transferred over quite simply. Another issue, we are listening to ideas. There is an attitude that small business are small, insignificant, not important, stupid, do not have any ideas. I obviously

resent that because that comes through when speaking to Europe. They do not like talking to small businesses. They are genuinely trying to reduce the representation of small businesses to less and less organisation. That is a concern because it means that it will literally come together into bigger organisations, which will then be funded by bigger companies, which means that at the end of the day they will not be getting the opinion of the smaller businesses.

Chairman

56. Could I put a couple of questions, getting slightly more specific on regulations, one on the VAT regime on trans-frontier transactions. Has the change that was made in 1993 been helpful or not, and can you comment on the harmonisation of bankruptcy laws?

(*Mr Burns*) The VAT across frontiers, for certain businesses there is no doubt that it has proved to be very useful, but in many cases those were the more established, the slightly bigger businesses anyway. From the evidence that we can see, most small businesses frankly do not know if it made a difference at all. As to the harmonisation of bankruptcy laws, we had a look at this and we cannot really see good bankruptcy laws anywhere in Europe that we would classify because what it does across the board is it seems to say, "You have been a naughty boy. You have failed. You have gone bankrupt. Therefore, there is a penalty issue". If we are going to encourage the entrepreneur, then what we have to do is look at the bankruptcy laws. I would not say that there is a good example out there, but yes, we would like it tidied up.

57. In your opinion, it needs attention?
(*Mr Burns*) It would be beneficial.

58. So you listened with welcome ears, if one can have such a thing, to the rumoured proposals that were I think around last week for a change in the bankruptcy laws?

(*Mr Burns*) Depending on the outcome.

(*Mr Alambritis*) We have been lobbying Stephen Byers to improve the opportunity of those who have started up in business, but went bankrupt through no fault of their own, no deceit, no dishonesty, no fraud, may not have been paid by a big company, or they are a grocery store and Tesco opened next door, that they should then get back into the commercial world within six months say, not within three years as it is at the moment, What the Secretary of State is suggesting is that if there is a pot there, then perhaps £10-20,000 can be set aside that they can use when they get back into the economy, so we have no truck with cowboy directors, rogue directors, and in fact as a balance perhaps the disqualification period could be increased for those people whilst reducing the disqualification period for those who have gone bust through no fault of their own.

59. A final question on late payments. Everybody has problems with late payments, and small businesses even more because it is so crucial. Can you see any pluses or minuses of harmonisation across the EU in that respect?

Chairman *contd.*]

(*Mr Alambritis*) They are all negative in terms of harmonisation. The way to improve late payment is through the credit management of each business within each Member State. It is not for the European Union to draft a Late Payment Directive to get payment terms agreed throughout the whole of the European Union. It is all about credit management. We do not feel excited about the right to interest legislation. It is there and we will be monitoring it to see if it will work, but at the end of the day it is about the businessman not being tempted into leaping into a contract and then thinking about whether they will get paid. An order is not an order until the business has been paid and that is what we tell businesses and that is what they should stick to.

Viscount Brookeborough

60. We have heard about many organisations this morning and agencies and your own in particular, but we have not heard about governments' small business agencies. In Northern Ireland we have LEDUs and in England we have the Business Links and the TECs and in Wales and Scotland the local enterprise companies. Why have we not heard anything about them? Are they not doing the correct job or are they not important?

(*Mr Alambritis*) In England you have the Small Firms Division of the DTI which is basically the predecessor of the proposed Small Business Service which the Government is intending to bring in. I think the Business Links and the Training Enterprise Councils again perhaps have a bit too much bureaucracy for the liking of a lot of the business community. We are hoping that the Small Business Service will be genuine and that the proposed chief executive will act independently, and that the Enterprise Council will act as an honest broker between the proposed chief executive of the new Small Business Service and the business community. In terms of the south-east of England, it is Business Links and TECs in the main, and we have not had an agency as such, so the Small Business Service may plug that hole.

61. So it is too fragmented at the moment?

(*Mr Alambritis*) The fragmentation is too great with the Business Links vying with each other, competing with each other, having glorified lunches with celebrity speakers like Will Carling and charging businesses £200 to attend. This kind of thing does not go down well with the business community and that is because they need to finance themselves.

(*Mr Burns*) It also is worth saying that there are some TECs that have worked reasonably well and there are some TECs which just have not. The general consensus of opinion in England is that the TEC structure is not acceptable. If we look at the Scottish example, it is not really much better. We have got Scottish Enterprise dealing with the bigger companies and it does not deal with the smaller companies. The result is that the small business issues are ghettoised. I would again be concerned about the Small Business Service in that we are very willing for it to work, but is this another ghettoisation that is going to be dumped down or is it actually going to be

given the kind of people that are going to drive it and be able to help small businesses and argue the case at the level so that when I disappear, because I have to go back out and make some money, this agency is going to do its job when speaking to government? That is a big question.

Lord Paul

62. You are working very closely with Brussels and your counterparts in Europe. Would you like tax harmonisation in the whole of Europe and a single currency?

(*Mr Alambritis*) We have no problems with tax co-ordination downwards, so if there is a European Member State with a very attractive tax rate, it should be up to each individual State if they want to co-ordinate downwards, but there should not be any tax harmonisation that leads to taxes being hiked up.

Chairman

63. What about the common currency?

(*Mr Alambritis*) Our members see the costs of the euro rather than the benefits. They see the benefits accruing to the large companies and the costs passing their way. We have done countless surveys amongst our members and they are still asking a lot of questions. They are fairly opposed to the euro. We have the latest survey and we are trying to be impartial and independent with our members, but at this moment in time they have got grave concerns. They would rather the European Commission got the Single Market right first before moving on to this next stage of the single currency.

64. Are you going to publish that survey?

(*Mr Alambritis*) That will be out in September[7].

65. Would you be kind enough to make sure that we get a copy?

(*Mr Alambritis*) Yes.

Lord Skelmersdale

66. Is the VAT threshold still an issue for your members?

(*Mr Alambritis*) Yes, it is. They are fairly divided. The UK benefits from the highest threshold throughout the whole of the European Union. We have members who would rather everyone paid from £1 so that there was a level playing field, and there are some members who ask for it to be up to £200,000. There is a current debate within Customs & Excise as to how to go about it. Our preferred option is to leave it there and allow it to wither naturally on the vine. It is of some help to a lot of small businesses, hairdressers and cafés, but it does not cause a lot of concern. What we would rather see is that registered traders, when dealing with each other, should be able to cancel out their VAT transactions, so zero rate VAT transactions between registered VAT traders, so when a restaurateur is buying chairs from a chair

---

[7] *Survey on Members' Attitudes to the Single Currency,* Federation of Small Businesses, 1999. Copies available from the Federation at 2 Catherine Place, London SW1E 6HF.

Lord Skelmersdale *contd.*]

manufacturer which is VATable, he has to pay the VAT to the chair manufacturer and the chair manufacturer has to hand on the VAT to Customs & Excise. If they could cancel each other's transaction out, that would be the best way forward in terms of cutting back on VAT regulations. What that would also cut back on is thousands of VAT personnel and I do not think they like that.

Chairman: Mr Alambritis and Mr Burns, we have kept you much longer than we should have done and for that I apologise. But I also thank you most sincerely, both of you, for a very, very interesting session of evidence. It has got us off to a very good start. Thank you.

THURSDAY 15 JULY 1999

Present:

Brooke of Alverthorpe, L.   Methuen, L.
Brookeborough, V.   Montague of Oxford, L.
Geddes, L.   O'Cathain, B.
    (Chairman)   Paul, L.
Howell of Guildford, L.   Skelmersdale, L.

Memorandum by the Confederation of British Industry

The enclosed evidence was submitted to the Trade & Industry Select Committee enquiry into SMEs conducted in March[1]. In our recent European Elections business manifesto the CBI highlighted four key areas where EU action could help SMEs:

— SME access to the Single Market must be improved;

— All Community activities and proposed Directives should be framed with SMEs in mind: an SME impact assessment should be applied to all new legislative proposals;

— Financial services must be liberalised and conditions for an effective pan-European risk capital market created;

— Good practice on encouraging technology-driven growth SMEs must be spread.

The CBI's general approach in deciding whether or not action at EU level is appropriate is to support the clear principles of subsidiarity and proportionality set out in the Treaty of Amsterdam, which specifies that:

— Community action shall be as simple as possible and the Community shall only legislate where necessary;

— As much scope as possible should be left for national decision as well as for long-standing legal and other arrangements at national level which reflect citizens' aspirations. This will become even more important as the European Union admits new member states;

— Community action should only be taken where there is a clear "added value" and where it can be shown that a Community objective can be better achieved at European rather than national or regional level. All proposals for Community action must in future satisfy the test of subsidiarity and proportionality;

— To show that action at the European level is justified three guidelines should be met:

    — First, that the issue in question has trans-national aspects that cannot be satisfactorily dealt with by Member States alone;

    — Second, failure to act by the Community would conflict with the Treaty;

    — Third, that Community action is of clear and substantial benefit.

July 1999

Examination of Witnesses

MR PETER AGAR, Deputy Director General, MR COLIN PERRY, Chairman of the CBI's SME Council, Confederation of British Industry, called in and examined.

Chairman

67. Mr Agar and Mr Perry, you are most welcome. May I thank you for coming at remarkably short notice. Believe me, the Committee and its Chairman are very appreciative. Before we start may I just make two comments? Firstly, it is now common practice for members to declare interests. To a greater or lesser extent all members of this Committee are involved directly or indirectly with SMEs. It would take up most of the evidence session if we were to go through every single one. We do, however, have a printed sheet. It is being updated at the moment. If you wish to have it, you are most welcome. Secondly,

may I apologise on behalf of Lady O'Cathain and Lord Paul. They have another meeting which clashes with this one and they will have to leave in the middle of your evidence session. No offence is intended whatsoever; I hope none is taken. We have your brief introductory memorandum and the evidence that you gave to the House of Commons' Committee very recently and found those extremely helpful as background. I am going to lead you deliberately now by saying I hope you do not want to add anything to that so that we can get straight into questions and answers, but if you do feel that you should, please do.

(*Mr Agar*) My Lord Chairman, I am perfectly happy to go straight into the questions.

[1] House of Commons Trade and Industry Committee, Thirteeth Report, HC 330, Session 1998–99, ISBN 0 10 5564 13 3.

Chairman *contd.*]

68. What a tactful man you are! Could you just explain to us how the CBI is set up in the context of SMEs? Are you—and forgive my ignorance—heading up a specific section on SMEs and, if there is a separate section, how watertight is it from the main thrust of the CBI?

(*Mr Agar*) My Lord Chairman, we do not attempt to segment our SMEs in quite that way. There is sometimes a misconception that the CBI only represents very large companies. Of course it is true that most of, for example, the FT-100 are members of the CBI, but a large number of our members, both businesses in direct membership of the CBI and, of course, indirect members who are represented by their trade associations, are SMEs. We do have an SME council, of which Colin Perry is the current chairman, whose job it is at the centre of our policy making machinery to take an overview on all those policy areas that impact on SMEs significantly and to ensure that the SME voice is properly reflected in policy discussions. We also have SME members sitting on all of our major policy committees dealing with economics, dealing with the environment and so on. Colin, as Chairman of the SME Council, sits on our Presidents' Committee and a significant number of members of the National Council, which is the ultimate governing body of the CBI, are also from the SME sector. We have a small staff group which supports the SME Council, recently named the Enterprise Group, since enterprise is the word of the moment. Their job is both to develop specific SME policies, for example they will drive forward our response on the Government's proposals for the Small Business Service and also to ensure that the other 80 policy staff that I have in the CBI who are dealing with things such as environment, health and safety or other areas of employee relations, are fully aware and taking account of SME interests in everything they do. I am Deputy Director General and have overall management responsibility for all our policy work in the CBI and the SME unit, what is now called the Enterprise Group, reports directly to me amongst all the other policy directors who also report to me and so part of my job is also to ensure that our SME members' views and interests are properly reflected in the work that we do.

Chairman: Thank you.

Lord Paul

69. The SME sector is really becoming quite a wide field and most of them have to compete now with Europe and the EU. In what way are there problems for the SMEs in Britain so that the Europeans are making far more progress in SMEs than Britain?

(*Mr Agar*) I am not sure that I would agree, my Lord, that other European countries are making more progress with SMEs or the growth of small businesses than the UK. We have a very good record in terms of start-ups relative to many countries in the rest of Europe. We have a much better developed, although it is imperfect, small firms finance and capital market, particularly risk capital market, than in other parts of Europe.

70. But the mortality rate in Britain is far higher than, let us say, Italy or Germany.

(*Mr Perry*) I do not think that is true, certainly not in my experience. You may be referring to the *mittelstand* in Germany which, of course, is a much longer standing phenomenon, but in terms of new start-ups, new technology companies in areas like biotech and so on, I think the UK is actually leading in many cases.

71. With normal manufacturing and other small businesses in the UK, the failure rate is definitely higher from my information.

(*Mr Perry*) You get a higher mortality with start-ups, of course, but that is the case everywhere. I think in Germany you have these *mittelstand* companies which were largely founded after the war and of course they have got through the start-up phase and therefore there is a lower mortality rate.

72. Comparing like with like, with the new start-ups in the last five years, according to reports that one gets, the mortality rate is higher in Britain. Have you done any research on that?

(*Mr Agar*) I do not think we have any recent research, but I would be happy to reflect on that question[2]. Given that we have not had time to provide you with a custom-made piece of evidence, if questions come up that we cannot address we can look at our information and send some more material to the Committee if that would be helpful.

Baroness O'Cathain

73. I am just wondering if you have got any evidence or have you done any work which compares the attitude of the banking community on Continental Europe towards SMEs compared to the attitude of the banking community in this country towards SMEs because most of the problems that you hear about SMEs are their relationships with banks, at least at start-up and in the early stages for those who see such relationships as an excuse for the high mortality rate.

(*Mr Agar*) We have not done any systematic comparative analysis so I cannot answer that question in the way you put it. What we have been involved in over the past years is working with others to improve the relationships between banks and small companies in the UK and particularly working with the Bank of England who have taken an important and lead role in improving the relationships between SMEs and banks. You will be aware that the Governor, Eddie George, has taken a particular interest in this area. When we talk to SMEs, most of our members would feel that

---

[2] Mr Perry subsequently added the following:
Statistics on this subject are quite unreliable. In fact, as part of the DTI's Company Law Review, they have commissioned special research into it, since there are no known figures which can usefully be relied upon. The results of this research are expected to become available to the Company Law Review Steering Group (of which I am a member) during the next few weeks.
It can be said however that closing a company is a much faster and simpler process in England than it is in Germany, where it can take several years of court procedure. Thus the German statistics may also be misleading, in that there may be many businesses which have effectively ceased to operate but have not officially closed.

Baroness O'Cathain *contd.*]

relationships have improved and that banks have a better understanding than they had perhaps at the beginning of the decade about SME issues. Since Colin is chairman of several SMEs perhaps he should answer too.

(*Mr Perry*) You are quite right, one did hear a lot about those problems five or six years ago, in the early 1990s, in the depths of the recession. Today it is no longer true, at least not to the same extent. The relationships with the banks are much improved. The banks have a much better understanding of SMEs, they work more closely with SMEs. The problem area on finance today is more on the equity side. There are gaps in the equity market for small companies, but there are many fewer problems on the banking side than there used to be.

74. Can I just make two points on that? Your first answer about the Bank of England, that does not really help SMEs on the ground, that is just trying to do something about the culture and say, "SMEs are great", but the Bank of England cannot really influence the banking relationships with SMEs. On the second point, is there any case for suggesting that the larger banks that have got merchant banking wings should become more involved with SMEs or do they still have this culture of just going for huge merger and acquisition and transaction finance of that type rather than helping with small scale finance to get these SMEs off the ground or help them over a particular temporary problem?

(*Mr Agar*) On the first part of your question, I disagree, I think the Bank of England in that rather peculiarly Anglo-Saxon way does have quite a lot of influence on the way that the large banks think. It has been very noticeable that in a sense by peer group pressure and by reporting annually on the financing of small companies (and the Bank of England reports once a year on performances at a very large conference which Eddie George chairs and which brings the banks and representatives of small firms together). It has in fact had an impact, plus normal commercial and competitive pressures. The banking system itself has become more competitive and you will see that a number of the banks have done a good deal more on the ground in terms of setting up special units so that they can advise their lending managers on, for example, technology, because when a company comes in with a particular issue on financing which is technology-based the local bank manager may have no understanding of that. So there is a back-up service. There are a lot of individual things that banks have done in the purely competitive mode of trying to win business against the background of pressure to understand and support the SME sector more effectively. I think the Bank of England has played a role even though it is a behind-the-scenes role. Having been involved in this myself, I started out cynical and have become less cynical about the effectiveness of the Bank using those methods. The second point about whether Credit Suisse Boston or anybody else get more involved with SMEs is a more difficult issue. The big investment banks are on the whole not structured to deal effectively with small companies. Their economics are not structured so that they can deal with small sized transactions. That is where in practice part of the problem which Colin referred to in terms of the gap in small amounts of risk capital arises, but I do not think the answer is necessarily to make the biggest players in the City start small firm practices. The answer is to fill that gap in other ways with specialist funds, with a better "business angel" network and with the right incentives in the tax system to encourage private equity investment which is the great strength of the United States economy.

Lord Howell of Guildford

75. In your very interesting exchange with Lord Paul on more deaths of SMEs, you were saying more births and therefore more deaths, there is a higher turnover generally here. One does hear the allegation that, nevertheless, it is more difficult in this country having gone bust or failed to start up again than in America or in some other EU countries. Have you heard that allegation and is CBI giving a lot of attention to revising the bankruptcy laws to make it a bit easier to start up when you fail?

(*Mr Agar*) Clearly, Ministers have put that issue into the policy domain and the DTI are currently looking at the revisions to the bankruptcy and insolvency laws. Stephen Byers has spoken about this, he spoke about it again a couple of weeks ago at a conference organised by Philip Lader and we are in discussions with DTI and we will obviously respond to any consultation paper that they put out. There are difficult balances to be achieved here between the interests of creditors and the interests of those who fail, not because of a lack of due process or criminal activity but because the market goes against them.

(*Mr Perry*) In terms of being entrepreneur friendly, in this country we sit somewhere between the US and the other European countries. I would say that in many ways we have a more entrepreneurial culture here than in some European countries. On the other hand, we are way behind the United States in that respect and that is the mark that we should be looking to reach.

(*Mr Agar*) Part of this is about law, but I think what came through quite clearly, for example, at the conference in which the United States Ambassador Philip Lader brought across 75 entrepreneurs, venture capitalists and so on from the United States, is that it is also about attitude and culture as much as it is about legal frameworks. It is about how people are treated if they fail and then come back for more; if they come back with a new business plan, a different idea, how they are treated by equity and banking investors and financiers. The sense that I got was that on the ground in the United States the culture of "if you fail once you should try again" is just as important as any differences between the bankruptcy and insolvency framework.

Chairman

76. You may be aware that Ambassador Lader is giving evidence immediately after you.

(*Mr Agar*) I am sure he will be most erudite on that point.

Lord Montague of Oxford

77. In your evidence you state that there are "four key areas where EU action could help SMEs" and I would like to try and tease this out a bit in two areas. One is that "access to the Single Market must be improved". I would like a closer understanding of what lies behind that. Also, "financial services must be liberalised and conditions for an effective pan-European risk capital market created." I think the latter one probably relates to companies irrespective of size, but maybe there are some special factors relating to SMEs. When you say the Single Market must be improved, in what way? I have heard what you said already about the financial market.

(*Mr Agar*) Could I ask Colin to answer the first question partly from his own experience of operating in the Single Market.

(*Mr Perry*) There are a number of ways in which the Single Market needs to be improved for SMEs. SMEs have a disadvantage compared with large companies in that they tend to be single establishment companies located entirely within this country. In other words they are not multi-national or transnational, so the frontier barriers can be real barriers for them. One of the unresolved issues that SMEs face—I face it in my own company and I know other companies do—is the harmonisation of product standards. I manufacture equipment for microbiological laboratories and one of my main product lines incorporates a pressure vessel. There is no common standard for pressure vessels across Europe. We have other examples, for example, of environmental monitoring equipment. Each country has its own standards for this. It is not a question of quality, it is a question of procedures. You cannot sell in Germany unless you have been approved by the German Standards Authority, they do not recognise BSI, for example.

78. That is a very big statement and an important statement to be tested and there may be something we can do about it. Did you say they do not recognise BSI?

(*Mr Perry*) They do not recognise BSI.

Chairman

79. Does that apply in other EU countries?

(*Mr Perry*) Yes, it applies in virtually all the European countries. We are painstakingly going through each country at the moment. In the last two months we got approvals in Finland, we got approvals in Sweden, but each country has its own process. Some will sort of recognise BSI and say, "Well, at least you are half-way there, but you have still got to go through these procedures before you can sell in this country." The Germans will not have anything to do with BSI at all, the French will not have anything to do with it and nor will the Italians. There is a new thing coming in, for example, in our industry, CE marking of products which supposedly gives you free entry, so legally you cannot be stopped in selling products into any European country, any Community country, if you are CE marked. You may be able to export the product there, but you cannot actually sell it there, you cannot install it there because then they get at the local buyer. You may have exported it but nobody can use it. In effect, CE

marking, which at one time one thought would give one entry to all the Community countries does not. You are still subject to the local standards.

80. Are you aware whether there is any reciprocal arrangement or agreement between other countries in the EU? For instance, you said Germany, France and Italy. I am equally picking those. Do you know whether Germany recognises France and vice versa?

(*Mr Perry*) I am not aware of bilateral arrangements of that type. What I can say, however, is that the standards authorities in each country differ in their approach. For example, British standards tend to be voluntary whereas German standards are written into the law. There is therefore a much greater inflexibility in Germany than there is in the UK. The UK will accept products that do not meet British standards because the British standard is voluntary, but the Germans will not accept British products because it is a question of the law in Germany.

Lord Montague of Oxford

81. Would other European states make the same criticism about access to the British market?

(*Mr Perry*) They might, but I am not aware of them.

Chairman

82. Does the UK recognise the German standard?

(*Mr Perry*) As far as I am aware we do not recognise it in any kind of formal sense, but a product can be sold in this country even if it does not meet British standards in many cases.

Lord Montague of Oxford

83. How did we come to harmonise plugs, although when you try to plug anything in they do not seem to be very harmonised, but they are harmonised.

(*Mr Agar*) There is a long saga over plugs!

Chairman

84. I do not think we should go into too much detail on this.

(*Mr Agar*) Before I go on to Lord Montague's second question about financial markets, can I just make a general point which Colin has been illustrating? The Single Market and the great Lord Cockfield initiative on the Single Market was based on the view that we were only going to get a Single Market if we had mutual recognition of standards as well as harmonisation in some areas. It was seen that the process of harmonisation which had been attempted through the 1950s and 1960s was so slow and complex and there are so many things to be harmonised that it was inhibiting the growth of the Single Market and the development of cross-border trade. The intellectual breakthrough was that the Single Market should be based both on harmonised standards and harmonised law in certain areas but also on mutual recognition. I think what we are saying is that—and we have said consistently to Government and Government also understands this

Chairman contd.]

and is as concerned as we are—the application of mutual recognition has been far from perfect and some countries, in particular Germany, have been extremely difficult markets in some technical areas to penetrate because there has not been mutual recognition of standards. It is a problem, of course, that affects all companies, but it is particularly onerous for small companies because of the fixed cost of getting approvals for a particular product type. If you are a small company and you are producing—I do not know how many pressure vessels you produce, Colin, but, not that many—it is pretty much the same cost to get approvals as it is for a very large company with scale manufacture. So the burden of independent standards is particularly difficult for small companies.

Lord Montague of Oxford: Is there any paper that we could have subsequently which sets out what the position is?[3]

Lord Brooke of Alverthorpe

85. What is the latest position on the initiatives from Cockfield?

(Mr Agar) The Single Market action plan which, from memory, I think was an initiative pushed forward and in part under the UK presidency got further on this track, but it is a constant process of attrition. The Finnish presidency has indicated that it wants to again put completion of the Single Market higher up the political agenda. The German presidency was not terribly interested in this for reasons perhaps that we have touched on. It is presumptuous of me to suggest who you should call in evidence, but I think that you would find Lord Simon extremely knowledgeable about this matter since he is responsible for internal market matters and sits on the Internal Market Council for the Government in the Council of Ministers and has been a champion of UK interests in this area during the period that he has been in office and I think would have much to say on this matter.

Chairman

86. Could you address Lord Montague's second point?

(Mr Agar) Your question was about financial markets and liberalisation. There are 33 stock exchanges across Europe all operating to separate standards and rules. We need width and depth in our capital markets. We have a market in economic terms slightly bigger than the United States, but we have a fragmented capital market particularly for equity and particularly for small companies' equity. It means that venture capital is underdeveloped in Europe as a whole because venture capital requires a proper stock market structure in order that it has an exit route. We do not have in Europe the equivalent of NASDAQ which has been a tremendous engine of growth in the United States because it provides early stage growth companies with the opportunity to float on NASDAQ. That in turn pulls through private equity investors to back high-risk start-ups. If you

are successful in three or four years from start up you can float on NASDAQ and exit at a proper reward for the risks that you have taken. The ability to do that in Europe is much more limited. In my view we need to move much faster in creating a single financial capital market in Europe. Some moves have been made. The Commission has published proposals for financial market liberalisation. For example, there are many constraints on the use of pension funds which are, in effect, protectionist. There are rules in other Member States about the proportion of pension funds that can be invested outside that Member State. All of those are constraints to creating a large and liquid capital market which will then draw in private equity which is of great benefit to small companies.

Lord Skelmersdale

87. I find the SME sector extremely puzzling because it contains firms, companies, call them what you will, made up of anything from one employee up to 500 employee, so by definition it includes all small shopkeepers. It is therefore bottom heavy. Even I was surprised to hear in evidence last week that only four per cent, as far as is known, of small and medium enterprises actually want to grow. You have talked about two inhibitions to growth emanating from the European Union. Would you say the VAT threshold was another one?

(Mr Perry) I would not have said that the VAT threshold was a major one. I think there will always be a large majority of small companies that do not want to grow because they are quite happy with their lifestyle and so forth.

88. Four per cent is a very, very small figure indeed.

(Mr Perry) But the proportion of companies that would want to grow would be increased if it was easier to grow, particularly in the field of employment and I think the amount of employment regulation that small companies have been hit with over the last two years is actually a severe inhibition on companies growing and taking on more employees. I would put that higher than the VAT problem.

Chairman

89. Would you propose exemption for SMEs as far as regulation is concerned and, if so, at what level?

(Mr Perry) I think it depends on the particular measure, of course. It is not that SMEs are bad employers or anything like that, it is the amount of regulation, it is the amount of form filling you have to do, it is the records you have to keep and I think an SME is typically run by a single owner manager who has not got time for all of that stuff.

90. That does not quite answer my question.

(Mr Agar) Our view on exemptions is that you do need to look at them on a case-by-case basis rather than having a blanket principle that all small companies under ten employees should be exempted from any piece of regulation or legislation. When we talk to SMEs we find that they are nervous about blanket exemptions because, particularly if they are

[3] See supplementary memorandum on p 23.

Chairman *contd.*]

ambitious, they do not want to be faced with the problem of thinking about the costs that they will take on in going from an exempt to a non-exempt category. Secondly, if you are ambitious and you are trying to attract good staff it is not terribly attractive to say, "Join me, work for me as a small company, but, by the way, I do not have to obey health and safety regulations". But there are particular areas where the burdens of compliance can be very high. So for a small company dealing with issues such as maternity or paternity leave, for example, it may be much more difficult in practical terms. If you have only got three or five employees as opposed to 1,000 and one person goes on maternity leave it is extremely difficult to cover for them. In the CBI I have 220 and so if someone goes on maternity leave it can be awkward, but I can usually shuffle the pack in order to cover for people who are taking their legal term. So there are areas where, if not through exemption, greater flexibility and recognition of the practical nature of small firm life needs to be included in the design of legislation.

Lord Skelmersdale

91. Does what you have said also apply to "voluntary" measures? There are a number of them, environmental, eco-labelling, auditing, non-statutory auditing. Do you find if SMEs cannot or do not go along with such voluntary measures they are put at a disadvantage?

(*Mr Agar*) I think it depends on the particular issue, my Lord Chairman. I think it is hard to generalise on that. I do not think we have a great deal of evidence that they are put at a disadvantage. Clearly, some forms of self-regulation, voluntary schemes of the kind you have described, can be actually pretty onerous in terms of what you have to do to comply—and some of those burdens would be particularly significant for small firms. In other cases my policy colleagues at the CBI have told me that where business has, perhaps encouraged by Government, taken the initiative in areas such as waste management and recycling, those schemes have consciously taken account of the particular issues that small firms face and been designed so that it is easier for small firms to join and be members. We would obviously encourage our larger members involved in setting up those kinds of schemes to take the small firm interest into account.

Lord Methuen

92. Do you think that the EU could do more to help lift the administration burden on small firms, particularly the micro firms which you have already commented on who have probably one managing director who is attempting to do all the bumph?

(*Mr Agar*) I think the EU could do more when Directives are being considered. I think greater consideration of their impact on small firms of different kinds needs to be explicitly taken into account. In the past we have been very critical of what was DG XXIII, which had the small firms mandate. We felt that they were not powerful or authoritative enough and therefore could not

influence other Directorates who were putting forward proposals for legislation. I think there is a need for European rule makers to become much more sensitive to the ultimate impact of what they do, on business in general as well as small businesses in particular. It is often in the implementation of EU Directives, which themselves have to be translated into national law and national regulation, where the detailed compliance burdens arise. We have seen this recently in the Working Time Directive. That is a Directive which we in the CBI opposed in general at the European level as an unnecessary burden. Once passed, the initial way in which it was implemented in the UK by Parliament was particularly onerous. As you will know, over the last couple of weeks, the Secretary of State for Trade and Industry has announced revisions to the regulations which meet at least in part some of our objections to the amount of bureaucracy and compliance burdens that fall on small firms in that area. He is able to do that. He is not rescinding EU legislation, but has in fact quite a lot of flexibility. The Government of the day has quite a lot of flexibility within most EU Directives to design the detailed implementation. So much of the onus for reducing burdens even in areas of EU law rests with Member States rather than with people in Brussels, but Brussels needs to be sensitive to this too.

Lord Skelmersdale

93. Is he removing some of the "gold-plating" from the proposals or rather are they regulations of the last Government?

(*Mr Agar*) Gold-plating is a continuous problem. There is always a tendency, I suppose, amongst law-makers, when given the opportunity, to pull some favourite nuance or scheme out of a bottom drawer and attach it to a Directive. There is a famous example of revising the fire safety regulations, I think as part of the implementation of EU Health and Safety Directives. Quite unnecessarily and not required by Europe, the Government decided in its wisdom that if any self-employed person, for example a redundant manager who had set up at home as a one-man marketing consultant who used the spare bedroom as an office, entertained a client or a potential client in his house then that became an office and had to have illuminated exit signs at strategic places on the landing and in the hall. This is not on the whole a feature that would endear itself to estate agents when they came to sell the house. It was a completely unnecessary piece of gold-plating.

Lord Brookeborough

94. Nationally, do we make it easy enough for SMEs to gain access to help and information or, taking it one stage further, do we encourage them to look for that access? Are the SMEs adequately equipped to participate in voluntary measures, environmental, management and auditing, eco-labelling etc?

(*Mr Agar*) On your second question, I think it depends and really I come back to my original answer. If the schemes are designed badly and in a way that is complex then it is just another compliance

Lord Brookeborough *contd.*]

burden, it is like trying to cope with your tax returns. There are some schemes which are SME-friendly and there are some which are not. SMEs in general have limited management resource and administrative resource. The managers are focused generally on ensuring that they are delivering the right products at the right price at the right time to their customers and do not have a lot of time to do much else. On the first point about general advice and business support, we have been supportive of the Business Link, for example, and we feel that this has improved access to advice and support over the years in which it has been in place, but it is far from perfect and performance is very mixed across the country. There are very, very good Business Links that proactively have created a much greater awareness amongst the SME customers of advice and support that can be got and there are Business Links that are not terribly good. There has been inconsistency in performance. The Government's new proposals for a Small Business Service offer an opportunity, I hope, to make more of the best and to improve the ease of access to support and advice—particularly by delivering more effectively a single gateway, one place where you can go as a small business to find out everything you need to know, not necessarily delivered by that agency, but a single gateway that directs you very quickly and easily and simply to where you do get the advice and support.

95. Can you see that coming about in the near future? Can you see a time-frame for that?

(*Mr Agar*) The Government's objectives as laid down in the consultation document on the Small Business Service certainly recognise the need to improve the quality of advice and support and we are glad to see that recognition. The consultation finishes in September. We will be responding formally to it and I think the Government is hoping to begin to implement an improved Small Business Service in the spring of next year, but that is really a matter for them.

Lord Howell of Guildford

96. On public procurement, the Americans have made huge efforts to promote small business and minority businesses and so on and so forth. Does that go on in Europe or are there separate European Member States inclined to use procurement just to look after their own? How do you view it?

(*Mr Agar*) I cannot speak with authority about what other Member States do. You will be aware that there is a common framework for public procurement within the European Union: it is an important plank of the Single Market. It works imperfectly and I think that many of our members, large and small, feel that procurement markets in other Member States are often difficult to penetrate despite the principle that they should be easy to penetrate. The amount of cross-border procurement is actually very small despite this framework of procurement rules set down by the European Union which were supposed to encourage and facilitate cross-border procurement. The Commission is currently looking again and making a number of proposals to improve the effectiveness of the procurement framework to achieve that goal of more cross-border procurement where it makes economic sense and we support that. The Commission is also taking measures not to move to electronic procurement as such, but invitations to tender and so on which are currently in something called the "Official Journal" which is a rather daunting book that comes out every day or so and contains all of the notices of tender. A lot of that is now going electronic, so it would be much easier for SMEs right around Europe to access information about what the opportunities are, which is clearly one of the constraints. I am sure cases can be found where Member States are rather protectionist about favouring national companies, although legally they are not supposed to, but it is hard to prove that and to challenge it. I think the Commission is facing in the right direction on these issues. On the question of preferential treatment: the US Ambassador will be able to talk to you about US experience. We are cautious in the CBI about a generalised approach on public procurement of quotas for particular companies partly because we are also interested in best value for money in public expenditure and there is a danger that by imposing rigid quotas one might not be getting best value for money. What I think is important is that there is a completely open and transparent market in procurement and that the mechanisms of procurement are simplified so that it is easy for small firms who can compete effectively, and often they can, to get access to the kind of contracts that are available. The government also needs to look carefully at the way in which it makes up contracts, that it does not bundle up things into such large packages for convenience or lack of thought that it is difficult for small firms to bid. A small firm may not be able to bid to provide all the chairs in all of the social security offices across the UK were that to be the contract, but it may well be able to supply five offices in the local area. So the structure of contracting is important. However, there is one area where we are very interested in the US experience and that is a scheme run by the small business administration called the SBIR. This is a scheme on research contracts, particularly defence research contracts in which there is a quota and in which government establishments letting research contracts do have to ensure that a proportion of those contracts go to small firms that are properly qualified to carry out that research. I think there is quite a lot of evidence that in that area in particular it has had a very important impact on the ability of the United States to develop new technologies and to grow small firms into big firms in the high-tech area, but that is a very specific programme, as I say, to do with research contracts. It is something which Philip Lader again could speak about in much greater detail than I can, but it is something we are looking at with DTI. I know that they are also extremely interested in this.

Lord Brooke of Alverthorpe

97. This is for Mr Perry, a simple one but not an easy one. You can have one change from Europe. Which would you like?

Lord Brooke of Alverthorpe *contd.*]

(*Mr Agar*) You are on the record, Colin!

(*Mr Perry*) The product standard difficulty that I referred to earlier is a major problem, not just in my industry but in several industries. There are some industries where standards have been harmonised, but there are still many where they have not been and that is the biggest single barrier that we face in terms of the Single Market.

Lord Montague of Oxford

98. I just want to talk for a second about motivation in monetary terms because we are all motivated by money and I am thinking here about capital gains tax. With larger firms we have got share option schemes and that can work very well, particularly if the company is quoted and there is a market for the share, but with small companies that does not happen and we have got the new introduction of the taper for capital gains. I wonder if you have done any investigation in your taxation department about what exists in the rest of Europe and whether that is advantageous to us or disadvantageous and how our small businesses are thinking about it?

(*Mr Agar*) We have not done a comparative study across the rest of Europe but we do believe that capital gains tax has a very important impact on risk taking, particularly in the small firms area and not just for owner/managers but for encouraging what I have called throughout this evidence private equity investors, business angels, people reinvesting the gains they may have made from one small company in another company even though they are not necessarily the majority shareholder. We have argued strongly through our Budget representations for reform of capital gains tax. The taper that was introduced I think was a move in the right direction but there was one great error in it which was that it does not include rollover relief. The Treasury I think has got, sometimes, rather confused when it talks about the need for long term investment between the need for investors to be long term investors and the need to hold a specific set of assets for the long term. In this area of investing in small companies, particularly small companies that are growing and can then attract venture capital, and ultimately equity from the public markets, we want those individual business angels to keep on investing over a long period but we ought to accept that, after two or three years, if they have invested in a successful company as a business angel they may well want to get out again. It may be appropriate for them to get out because the company will have grown to such a size that it needs access to the kind of capital that, say, a well established venture capitalist can bring. We believe that there ought to be rollover relief, that if an investor reinvests the gains made from one company in another company then that should count within the taper. So it is being an investor for ten years rather than holding the same assets for ten years that should attract a lower rate of capital gains tax. Also, we fundamentally believe that capital gains tax, at least for these kinds of investments, ought to be at a lower rate generally. The evidence from the United States is pretty strong that cutting capital gains tax significantly has been a real engine of increased private equity investment, both from individuals and from venture capitalists and that is one of the engines that has driven American success. So capital gains tax I think is absolutely critical to growing a real entrepreneurial company and supporting those four per cent, and let us hope it will get to ten per cent of companies that want to grow because they are the real engine of wealth creation and employment creation.

(*Mr Perry*) Can I just add one point? You mentioned share options and that they are not taken up much by private companies, for obvious reasons. There is one major change that I think could help private companies develop share schemes for senior managers and employees and that is if you are taxed at the point of sale of the shares and not at the point of purchase of the shares. There are many situations where you are taxed at the point of purchase because the Inland Revenue says: "Well the shares are now worth more than you are paying for them and we are going to tax you on the difference". Since there is no market in a private company's shares you cannot immediately recover that cash outlay that you have to make. So one important principle would be that for share schemes in private companies you would only be taxed when you sold the shares and not when you bought the shares.

(*Mr Agar*) This might, for example, be when the company goes public, say two or three years after you have purchased the shares as a result of an options scheme. Again, we have made strong representations to the Chancellor, which have in part been included in the proposals for an Enterprise Management Initiative. Small firms need to be able—particularly again high tech and growing small firms—to attract skilled managers from large companies and/or from overseas. There are plenty of United Kingdom entrepreneurs in Silicon Valley whom we ought to try and get back here. Small firms have to have the capability of offering those kinds of share incentives that say: "If you come back, if you build this company over a three or five year period, it is high risk but if you are successful you can make a great deal of money indeed". That is the compensation, if you like, both for the risk and the fact that the company cannot afford to pay a very high current salary. The current way in which share schemes work is a significant constraint on companies being able to do that.

Chairman

99. Mr Agar and Mr Perry, thank you very much indeed. You were kind enough to say at the beginning that if there were points that you thought were worthy of follow up you would write to us.

(*Mr Agar*) Yes.

100. I would be very grateful if you would do that.

(*Mr Agar*) We would be happy to do so.

101. If indeed you think we have failed to plug a major hole in this particular dyke feel free to put the plug in. We may have missed something of which we are unaware. You are the experts, we are learning. Thank you both very much indeed.

(*Mr Agar*) Thank you very much, my Lord Chairman.

Supplementary Memorandum by the CBI

1. As requested[4], this memorandum expands on the oral evidence given by the CBI relating to the barriers that national product standards can present to a single market.

2. As the CBI has said before, the Single Market has already brought significant benefits to SMEs. However, barriers remain—particularly in the area of common standards and mutual recognition. SMEs do not have the resources to appeal against these barriers or to absorb the costs of complying with separate technical accreditations.

CASE STUDY: LTE SCIENTIFIC LTD

3. LTE Scientific Ltd is a manufacturer of equipment for microbiology laboratories. We employ 55 people and have a turnover of £3 million. We export around 30 per cent of our turnover to some 30 countries all over the world. However, our exports have been slower to expand in the EU than we would have wished, due to the greater difficulties in becoming established in EU markets compared with other parts of the world.

4. One of our major product lines is autoclaves, which are steam sterilisers. Ours are designed for sterilising instruments, glassware, media, clothing and other contaminated articles in laboratories in the pharmaceutical, biotech, food, healthcare, and research industries. The equipment incorporates a pressure vessel, into which the articles are placed before steam is injected under pressure.

5. Pressure vessels and boilers are subject to regulatory control in virtually all developed countries, in order to prevent accidents occurring if the vessel should fail in any way. Each country has developed its own standards, which differ from each other in respect of the inspection and approval procedures rather than quality. There has been a working party on harmonising European standards for pressure vessels which has been deliberating for nearly 10 years, but no clear date has yet been established for reaching a result. The British Standards Institution (BSI) is a participant in the harmonisation working party.

6. One of the difficulties is that in some countries, such as Germany, the pressure vessel standard is enshrined in primary legislation. Consequently British exporters such as ourselves cannot at present sell their product in Germany without obtaining approval from Rheinischer Westfalischer TUV (RW-TUV), a private sector testing organisation which appears to hold a government-backed monopoly on the testing of pressure vessels, and which therefore has a vested interest in maintaining the status quo. To obtain their approval for our pressure vessels we would have to pay RW-TUV to fly their inspection team to England, and we would also have to make a number of visits to them to discuss our drawings and specifications. They can then ask for modifications, so that in effect we would have to create a separate product for the German market. Only German standard materials can be used, so we could not use British standard steel in the fabrication. The cost of the approval exercise is estimated at £30,000, which would be a speculative expenditure since we cannot assess our market prospects in Germany until we have obtained approval and started to market the product. We have preferred to wait for the advent of a European standard, which has taken much longer to materialise than expected.

COMMENT

7. The importer of pressure vessels into England has an easier task. The British standard is administered by BSI and is not enforceable at law except on general grounds of health and safety. BSI supervises a system of certification for each pressure vessel manufactured, but it is not compulsory to obtain this. Provided that the user can show that he is not neglecting reasonable health and safety precautions, and provided that he can satisfy his insurance company (and production of a foreign standard certificate would be supporting evidence on both counts), there is nothing to stop him buying and installing equipment containing a foreign pressure vessel.

8. Early in 2000, CE Marking is due to be introduced for pressure vessels (although to date the BSI has still not got around to appointing notified bodies to approve companies for this purpose). CE Marking is a harmonisation measure which has been applied in several countries, and it permits goods to be sold across frontiers within the EU. However, local standards can still be enforced on the buyer, with the result that whilst it will not be illegal for a company to export a pressure vessel to Germany, it will still be illegal for its customer to install and use it.

9. As a further example, the German Authorities also require that all environmental monitoring equipment be tested to the TUV standard. To counteract this position the DTI recommended that an equivalent British scheme should be established. This has now been done and the testing authority is SIRA and the certification is known as MCERTS. Manufacturers of British environmental monitoring equipment now plan to use this body, however, we now understand that it is unlikely that the Germans will recognise

---

[4] See QQ 84 and 99.

this seal of approval. Approaches have been made to the DTI and through the trade body known as GAMBICA to rectify this position. Clearly this is an anomalous situation and requires rectification in order that MCERTS is acceptable throughout the EU.

10. If Sub-Committee B decides to pursue this aspect of their investigation, since it is a subject which is of vital interest to British exporters, it is recommended that the BSI is called to give evidence. In addition, Action Single Market sits within DTI and offers help on making complaints about breaches of single market rules. They could provide the Committee with some useful case studies of the difficulties British businesses are facing.

11. Looking to the future, the European Commission has recently adopted a Communication which looks at ways of facilitating and improving the application of the principle of mutual recognition in the Single Market. Under this principle, each Member State is required to accept on its territory products which are legally produced and/or marketed and services which are legally provided in other Member States. The Member States may only challenge the application of the principle in certain limited cases, for example where public safety, health or the protection of the environment are at stake, and the measures which they must be compatible with, the principles of necessity and proportionality. The Communication provides for a series of actions to improve the monitoring of mutual recognition, making citizens, economic operators and the competent authorities at all levels in the Member States more aware of it. This is a positive development which should be supported.

July 1999

Examination of Witness

HE MR PHILIP LADER, United States Ambassador to the United Kingdom, called in and examined.

Chairman

102. Your Excellency, you are extremely welcome. I do not know whether I am correct in this, I can only talk from personal experience, but we may be setting a bit of history this morning. I am not aware that we have ever had an Ambassador to the Court of St James's giving evidence in front of one of these Committees. I have no doubt somebody will correct me if I am wrong but certainly in my experience we have not. This is a first and I really am, and we are all, very grateful for the trouble you have taken to come and talk to us. Obviously we have asked you whether you would be so kind because of your huge experience on what, on this side of the pond, we call small and medium sized enterprises. You are very much the expert, we are trying to learn the trade and we are doing a very short enquiry, a paving enquiry for what we hope this Committee in the next session of Parliament will pick up as a major one. This is a huge topic. There is not sufficient time to go into it in depth between now and effectively the end of October. What we would hugely appreciate from you is your experience in the United States on this subject and where there are differences between the way that the United States Administration, be it Federal or State, approaches the subject and how the European Union is trying to relative to its Member Governments. I do not know whether that is too broad a brief to start with. We find in these sessions that by far the greatest benefit we get out of it is in the question and answer session that we get into. If you would like to make an opening statement, and if you could possibly even begin to cover my opening query, we would be very grateful.

(*HE Mr Lader*) My Lord Chairman, Members of the Committee, certainly it is an honour for me to have the occasion to be with you. I am comforted a little bit by the fact that last week I was privileged to be the first non-British subject to address the new Welsh Assembly. I began speaking in Welsh, today will be relatively easy by comparison I suggest. The

Presiding Officer there demonstrated great diplomacy when I finished, he said "Your Welsh is almost as good as the Prince of Wales's"! An exaggeration on his part but on the other hand certainly it was very flattering. Let me make it very clear at the start notwithstanding the success of business formation and growth in the United States, particularly in the last decade or two, we Americans have no monopoly on wisdom on this or any other subject. At the same time I hope that perhaps some insight into what has worked and what has not worked in terms of public policy affecting small and medium sized enterprises might be useful. It is in that spirit that I offer these comments. The success story in this regard is significant. Since 1993, 18 million new jobs have been created in the United States, 92 per cent of them in the private sector. 70 per cent of the net new jobs since 1990 have come from small businesses. A few interesting insights—on any given day in the United States in the past 18 months six per cent of the adult US population is at some stage of starting his or her own business. It is interesting that, in 1995, 13 per cent of the American workforce was employed by businesses which did not even exist in 1990. The numbers are astounding. I believe that the answer is not simply an entrepreneurial spirit, it is really more as to the infrastructure of enterprise in the United States. Some policy is conscious by design, others perhaps inadvertent which has made it possible to have this record of wealth creation and jobs creation in the United States. A final observation, with 40 per cent of the American investment in the European Union nations being in the United Kingdom, that number is greater than the aggregate American investment in all of continental Asia. With more than a million Americans going to work every day for British owned companies, though often they do not realise it when they go to work for Holiday Inn and Burger King and Pilsbury and the like, the real reason for our interest and I suspect yours in this is jobs, jobs creation on both sides of the Atlantic. So I would be very pleased to respond to

Chairman *contd.*]

your questions as to some elements of this infrastructure that has promoted jobs formation, business formation and growth.

103. That is a fascinating start. Can I ask an extremely fundamental question to begin with? How do you define small and how do you define medium in the United States?

A. The definition under the US Small Business Administration, which is only one demarcation of it, is this: firms employing 500 or fewer employees are termed small businesses. We do not use the term medium sized enterprises, SME is an unheard of term in the US though practically every other nation on the globe uses that. In terms of qualification for certain Government programmes or grants, the small business determination is not necessarily on jobs but is based on revenues. In that sense, a good guideline would be that anything with a turnover of 20 million dollars a year or less would be considered a small business. Now, in other countries obviously the threshold is considerably lower.

104. Is the thrust—and clearly I am sure the Committee will want to get into the detail of this a bit more of what assistance is given to small businesses—of that assistance at Federal level or at State level?

A. The answer, as in politics, you hear oftentimes is both. Let me explain it in a bit more detail. I would say as a prefatory note, as a former businessman I have a very strong conviction that it is the private sector that is generating these jobs but at the same time the public policy has played a very significant role. Not simply tax, regulatory and education policies, those are central foundations, but an enormous number of what we call public/private partnerships. Let me give you some illustrations, the most interesting of which in many ways is the Agency that was started in 1953 by President Eisenhower that I was privileged to head for several years under President Clinton, the US Small Business Administration. The US Small Business Administration has—I do not know the current number—a guaranteed small business loan portfolio of about 38 billion dollars.

105. Billion?

A. Billion dollars. It has another approximately eight or ten billion dollars of venture capital funds available. In addition to that, it operates 1,000 small business development centres in communities, colleges, universities around the country. It is the sponsor for what is called the SCORE, the Service Corps of Retired Executives, which is comprised of 13,000 retired executives who provide free consultancy services to small businesses. It administers a programme called the SBIR—Small Business Innovation and Research—grants whereby most agencies of the Federal Government are required by law to devote a certain percentage of their R&D grants to qualified small businesses giving rise to considerable innovation and bootstrapping by those small businesses and a host of other programmes. I should mention all of this is public/private partnership. Now as an illustration, that multi billion dollar loan portfolio is accomplished through a budget of only about 200

million dollars of public funds a year. How? 12,000 private banks in the United States participate in this Government guaranteed loan programme. The average guarantee is about 75 per cent and each private bank must certify that loan, that financing would not have been extended but for the Federal Government guaranteeing a proportion of it. The reason it is important to have a programme like this at a national level is those commercial banks then can take 75 per cent of a 100,000 dollar loan for example and sell the 75,000 dollar guaranteed loan portion into a secondary market. They will get back, let us say, 72,000 dollars for that and they can relend that 72,000, increasing their own liquidity. Since they charge points and their earnings are dependent on the points as well as the interest rate paid it encourages them to relend that money. You can see the rotation benefit and the liquidity to the lending institutions. Similarly, in the multi billion dollar venture capital portfolio, the Government's programme is that the Government will provide up to three to one leverage to private venture capitalists with the private venture capitalist's money at risk first, his or her investors then at risk and then finally the Government at risk. Through debentures or through subordinated debt that allows a venture capitalist who puts together three million dollars from investors to have a ten million dollar investment pool allowing greater diversification of his venture capital investments and therefore greater likelihood of the success of the overall portfolio. There again, though it seems like a huge Government expenditure, it is a relatively minuscule Government expenditure based on the leverage devices and the use of the private secondary market. A final observation on that. The loss rate when I was there for a two year period in 1996 to 1998 was less than 1.3 per cent of the overall portfolio which I would argue is more successful than the loss experience of most commercial banks' own portfolios. That is not suggesting only 1.3 defaulted, many more defaulted, but as you restructured and did work-outs of loans, the ultimate loss to the taxpayer was 1.3 per cent. The major cost to the Government, that 200 million dollars, was the guarantee, the reserve, for losses set aside that generated this huge amount of lending capacity. I go into such detail because that is a pre-eminent example of the public/private partnership to which I refer. Similarly, in State level, there are a great number of State programmes. I was an author of legislation in my home state of South Carolina creating what was called the Jobs Economic Development Authority that used some similar devices to help particularly minority entrepreneurs and rural entrepreneurs and inner city entrepreneurs, much as the Prince's Trust does here so successfully as a private venture capital mechanism securing finance for business growth and expansion. I have gone into much too much detail, excuse me, some of this you do know already but I wanted to give you some sense of the structure and of the volume that was involved. I hope it is helpful.

Lord Paul

106. Thank you for responding so quickly, Ambassador, to my request. I think all us were very keen that you should come.

Lord Paul *contd.*]

A. I have learned in London when you call I should answer!

107. I offer my apologies because after the answer to this question I will have to leave, but I look forward to reading the rest of the evidence. The Small Business Administration in the United States has been in operation since 1953, although it has only been high profile since 1993. At the risk of embarrassing you, is it the man behind the administration or the rules and laws which play the role?

A. I will be very quick to point out that the Small Business Administration, the SBA, is a relatively small part of the reason for the numbers I recited to you at the start. In the Reagan Administration, for example, the Head of the Office of Management in Budget, David Stockman, wanted to close down the SBA. I testified almost 40 times before our House and Senate as they considered closing down both the Commerce Department of the United States and the Small Business Administration. My argument as a businessman was simply the fact that it may well be that less than two per cent—I do not know the number—a relatively small percentage of the businesses in the United States have ever had direct support from the SBA, either in financing or in consultancy. The margin of businesses which were impacting were extraordinarily important to the families of those tens of millions of people involved. What do I mean by that? In any continuum of feasibility, financing or anything else, you will have those businesses which anyone can finance coming down to those which are marginal below which none of us, if we sat on the board of the bank, private commercial bank, would extend financing to. There is always a grey area. What the SBA and some of these State Agencies have done is allowed the commercial banks to dip lower into that grey area. It may be a very narrow slice of the overall entrepreneurship community that is affected but if you are talking about every year 200,000/300,000 businesses getting started in that narrow margin, that is that many families who have greater potential to realise their dreams, to create jobs, to pay taxes. I would not in any way suggest that it is a major force. Much more important, of course, in the United States has been the commercial lending practices and the access to early stage venture capital with active networks of angel investors which are not as well accepted or broadly active in this country, which is my observation, as in the United States today. They play a far more significant role in terms of financing businesses than any of the Government agencies.

Lord Montague of Oxford

108. We are talking really in terms of small business but actually I think, very strongly, we are talking in terms of entrepreneurs and entrepreneurial outlook. You have got a great number of American businessmen passing through your organisation here in London. I was wondering what you hear them saying about the differences for entrepreneurs in developing in other states in Europe and this country? You refer to this high percentage that are investing here, for example, but I am thinking of the smaller businessmen and their hearsay rather than the bigger companies.

A. Lord Chairman, I may be an amateur diplomat but I am not going to say anything critical of your sister European nations: at least I have learned that so far. I will say this, as Americans look to where they could invest in Europe, it is not an accident that 40 per cent of that investment is in the United Kingdom. The divergence of labour practices and environmental issues and other concerns between your sister European nations and the United Kingdom are very real considerations for American companies seeking to invest. As to the question of entrepreneurship, however, it is an interesting phenomenon that the Internet was essentially invented by a Cambridge graduate student, Tim Bernard Lee, and yet the explosion in wealth creation that has occurred in Silicon Valley, in the Washington-Dulles area, Route 128 around Boston in the Research Triangle Park, all these dot com companies has come about to a much higher degree in the United States. Professor Michael Porter, Harvard Business School, has indicated in his study of the development of intellectual capital into commercialised products that, measured in his study by patents and trade marks, Britain has not succeeded as well as other nations on the Continent, certainly not as well as the United States in that type of technology transfer from the well springs of new technologies, universities particularly, the institutes and laboratories to commercial application. That is Professor Porter's conclusion, not mine. I would simply say that that is noted by many American investors. It is changing. At the Enterprise Conference last week which I was privileged to co-host with Secretary of State Byers and Chancellor Brown, there was a relatively young woman entrepreneur who had started a company called Last Minute.Com. After eight months of being in business or so she already has a very flourishing business, not showing any profits but who knows if these dot com companies can or should be measured in that regard. Her suggestion was the extent to which some of this risk aversity in her culture—saying this as a resident of London, as a British subject—if the risk aversity could be changed—that is what she saw as the greatest barrier to the entrepreneurial spirit in her home country. What she was taking away from conversations with visiting Americans was that she perceived a very significant cultural difference in risk aversity.

109. Taking up your point about the universities, it is said, I think, from these studies also that the universities in America are much more liberal in their approach to letting their staff who work in this research possess the patents and take financial benefit whereas here patents and the rights are held by the universities and the universities not the individuals want to take the benefit. Do you think there is a great truth in that?

A. I will respond in several ways. I think you have some very good models, Sir Alec Brewers and others, he is at Cambridge, of course, have really been shaping ways in which the entrepreneurial appetites of dons can be stimulated to the self-interest of university and their own right. You see here in Silicon

Lord Montague of Oxford contd.]

Glen and elsewhere some genuine well springs of thought. The numbers in America though are astounding. If you take just—as an illustration—the market capitalisation of companies started by the faculty and alumni of just one university, MIT— Massachusetts Institute of Technology—the market capitalisation of those companies today would be the 24th largest economy in the world, larger than Thailand. When I said this to a trustee at Stamford he said it would not compare, that Stamford's were much bigger.

110. Almost zero in British universities.

A. Now you have put your finger exactly on an issue there. At the turn of the century Archbishop William Temple said—and I am always haunted by this—when he was Archbishop of Canterbury "government is the art of ordering life so that self-interest prompts what justice demands". What the American academic community has found is that if justice in the administration of university could be determined in recognition of the self-interest of the people in the laboratories, the individuals developing the new technologies, then they will both do better. I think there is an interesting model there on some of the American universities.

Lord Howell of Guildford

111. Ambassador, to what extent do you think American anti-trust policy helps this amazing growth and extension of small businesses in America? Then I have really a related question, to what extent is this present phenomenon, which is really more dazzling than anything else in American history, also a product of big firms unravelling and decentralising and downsizing as well as individuals stumping up the money?

A. Those are all significant criteria. There are a few others that I might add. Really I am not competent to address the subject of the extent to which anti-trust policy is affecting this for this reason. Some might suggest some different approaches in current anti-trust policy. I say this respectfully, the Head of Anti-Trust in our Justice Department right now is a law school classmate and close friend of mine. On the one hand you have some huge consolidations occurring in the telecom and other industries, as you know, at the same time you see what is happening with Microsoft and they are being taken to task in that industry. I am not about to suggest any competence in trying to distinguish what may seem to some to be divergent policies with agencies and different industries. On the other things though I think I can say some things which might be useful to you. One of the hidden secrets of that number is women in America and to a significant but lesser degree minorities in America. Women today in America are creating new businesses at three times the rate of the overall average rate. The downsizing to which you refer is a significant phenomenon as increased productivity has occurred. You should know that at a board meeting of an American company this morning at breakfast when they asked me to speak on the question of differences between the Continental European nations and Britain in this regard, what they kept coming back to was would the

European Continental nations achieve the same level of productivity as Britain might in following anything of the American model in squeezing out costs, middle management and the like. I deferred on that, just as I have deferred on you as I seem to be involved in a comparison, very undiplomatic of me. In the drive to greater productivity many people who have lost their jobs with big companies in America decided not just to get a job but to make a job. Through outsourcing, through access to capital and through a variety of the other things to which I have referred they have been able to start their own small businesses, some of which have grown enormously. The women factor and the minority factor is very important, the extent to which that has been helping to fuel our economy.

Lord Skelmersdale

112. You have described yourself as a learning but still somewhat amateur ambassador. I do not believe a word of it. I wonder if you would be inhibited in answering a question that I feel rather inhibited in asking? You have told us about the successes of the Federal Government so far as small businesses are concerned. There must be some things where the Government actually gets in the way. Can you tell us anything about those?

A. I could spend the rest of my time telling you that. Respectfully I might suggest that, at various points since 1953, even the Agency that I have described to you has had some very colossal blunders. I will give you an example of just one technical one. Frederic Maitland said that our common constitutions have come to us through the interstices of procedure, in that sense you see how a procedural thing has led to a major policy problem. In this venture capital pool that I talked about, the way it was set up with a three to one leverage, oftentimes with the companies under that policy the venture capitalist had to repay with interest a portion of those loans providing a leverage over a reasonable six or nine year period. But the portfolio companies, being relatively young and growth companies, were not paying dividends, were not going to public offerings and so were not creating the liquidity which caused many of the venture capitalists to have to declare bankruptcy. So there again a great concept but the way it was executed in detail was self-destructive. What we changed it to be was through a participating debenture or equity interest. So if the venture capitalist says "I want to defer repayment of that debt. I gave you the leverage", then through a formula it gives up equity in the portfolio companies for when the portfolio companies go public the American taxpayers are getting a piece of them. Now whether that works we will have to see but that is just two years old and seems to be working well. Other examples, through a great range of tax policies the continuing debate at any Parliamentary institution is of course what is in the best interest of the entrepreneur? You would find many small business people—witness the debate over health care policy in the United States which Mrs Clinton took the lead on. Some would suggest that the principal lobbying organisation, the National Federation of

MINUTES OF EVIDENCE TAKEN BEFORE THE

15 July 1999] HE Mr Philip Lader *[Continued*

Lord Skelmersdale *contd.*]

Independent Businesses—the NFIB—was most responsible along with elements of the health insurance industry for the defeat of that health care plan. I say that not in any defence of the plan or in advocacy of it but simply there is a matter where the small business community, rightly or wrongly, felt very strongly that that policy would be in their disinterest. Other illustrations, capital gains taxation, when there was very little variance between ordinary income tax rate and the capital gains tax rate—this was in the late 1970s if I remember correctly—there was enormous pressure and President Reagan and others responded to that and led in that in order to reduce the capital gains rate. It is a continuing debate as to whether the capital gains rate stimulates greater investment or motivates more entrepreneurs or simply gives a bigger pay out to those who made the risk. I will leave that to the mystic philosophers amongst you. Those are the kinds of issues which will always be major problems of things that have not been working. Many of the State finance agencies have not worked. There are as many reasons why they have not as there are different agencies. I would be very quick to say that while there are some successful public/private partnerships not only has most of the growth occurred because of the private initiative but also there have been some real—we would say—"bummers" in the public policy as well.

Lord Brooke of Alverthorpe

113. I would like to come back to the burden on business and wondering if in the time you have been here, as you have observed, angel investors are different in the States, the risk aversity is somewhat different, the transfer of R&D between universities and the private sector is somewhat easier in the States. Coming back to business and Government and compliance, do you see any difference there between the States and what happens here?
A. I suspect here, from what I hear from businessmen, and I know in the United States, that second only to access to capital when asked what are the major hurdles for business formation and growth, you would have cited the crush of regulatory burdens. I really cannot measure the extent of the difference. Every administration in the United States is committed to and works diligently to reduce the regulatory burden. We did things such as try to convert regulations to plain English, plain American English, so that small business people did not have to always hire lawyers to help them through the maze. At the SBA we thought we should set the example as we required other agencies to do it, what we did was cut our regulations in half. I suspect 90 per cent of the users of those regulations today would still complain that they are too burdensome, too complex, too incomprehensible. When I was a businessman and made reference to Federal regulations in the United States I had the same lament. I am not sure how much better we are doing that than you are. The second point though, finally, is apart from tax policy, the extent to which environmental anti-trust and other commercial regulatory policies take into account in their formation the impact of small

business is very important. We have two institutional mechanisms to address that. There is a Chief Counsel for Advocacy for Small Business in the Federal Government who is appointed by the President and confirmed by the Senate but is commissioned to stand only for the interest of small business, even if it is opposed to the Government, the administration's advocacy of a particular bit of legislation. So for every bit of legislation, the Chief Counsel for Advocacy makes an assessment of what the impact of that legislation would be on small business and that is taken into account by the Congress. Similar to that there has been legislation which takes into account in the regulatory process the impact of any new regulations by the small business. You would have active partisan debate in the United States today, as there always has been, as to whether that kind of counsel is really heeded by our Congress.

114. Could you say something on exemptions? As I understand it there are some areas in which you have regulatory exemptions, particularly for small businesses.
A. Yes.

115. Could you say how successful that is and the range of issues?
A. In a few areas such as—if I can remember the technical term—employee safety and the like, over the last six years some innovations were undertaken where there were self-appraisals by businesses with spot checks instead of audits that were done on a regular basis. This was reducing the amount of Government personnel, reducing the kind of "got you" spirit, as we call it, occurring. I think those have had good results in the United States. I say that with the knowledge that in a post luxuriant world there is a touch of the original sin with everyone, even small businessmen, and sometimes if one can get around the regulation one may be tempted to do so. Self-regulation, at some point it almost seems that there are so many violations in a self-regulatory environment that it requires more seemingly heavy-handed Government regulations. In terms of other exemptions, there are relatively few exemptions based on business size, that is a major political controversy in the United States in the small business community. They would like to be exempt wholesale. That has not occurred, particularly in the health and safety area and a payroll and tax area. They continue to be major sources of complaint, the lack of exemptions in the United States.

Viscount Brookeborough

116. Your Excellency, in 1998 your Small Business Administration came to an arrangement with Enterprise Ireland for co-operation and to promote strategic business alliance. Can you tell us how you became involved in that, what actually occurs in that arrangement and whether it is successful and has been perhaps a pilot model for arrangements with other European States?
A. Most things in life are just happenstance of individuals. President Clinton called, as you remember, an economic conference on the future of Ireland, whatever the specific name of it was. George Mitchell was the chairman of that, that is how he first

Viscount Brookeborough *contd.*]

got deeply introduced to the Northern Ireland issue. I attended the opening dinner of that and on my left and on my right were two businessmen, one from Northern Ireland, the other from the Republic of Ireland. They had complementary businesses. They had never met, certainly had never done business, and over dinner they did a deal. I was just watching as this was occurring which was fascinating.

Lord Montague of Oxford

117. I hope you got your commission.

A. I was just an observer at the dinner. I went back and discussed it with some of my colleagues and a wonderful assistant administrator, regional administrator, of the SBA who had New England, Patrick McGowan—who had a particular interest as you might expect in Ireland—he took the initiative and he is the one who really drove it to create that. As a result there have been a number of trade missions and some investments that I know of. There is a woman-owned business in Denver which is owned by Christie—I forget her last name. It is very interesting because she does waste treatment plants, not something you would necessarily associate with a female entrepreneur. She now has a flourishing business in the Republic and in Northern Ireland taking advantage of this connection. Whether that kind of thing can be helpful with other European nations, with the United Kingdom, I think it always depends on the commitment of the individuals involved. Because of the President's particular interest in the economic growth of the island of Ireland, in the interest of greater political stability and peace there, that certainly has contributed to more small business people and businesses generally in the States wanting to be helpful in that regard. It is a small step but I hope it has been significant. Again it was started by the initiative of one individual, Patrick McGowan, who wanted to push it.

Viscount Brookeborough

118. The experience of your small businesses in the North American Free Trade Agreement: are there lessons to be learnt out of that for Europe and trade within Europe?

A. You would find some dispute probably as to whether any segment of the American business community may have been affected in an unsatisfactory manner by NAFTA. Certainly what was alleged by opponents like Ross Perot, that it would cause a huge drain to Mexico and the like, has not occurred in a way that would in any way injure the American economy, looking at what has happened over the years since NAFTA was approved. I think you would still find in small business circles active debate about whether they have been hurt by NAFTA. I have not seen—it may exist, but I have not seen—any authoritative studies that demonstrate anything which has hurt the American business community or any segment thereof by NAFTA.

Chairman

119. We could go on for a very long time and indeed there are still Members of the Committee who wish to ask you questions. Could you give us a guide as to what your timetable is?

A. I am happy to respond to whatever you prefer.

120. You are relatively unpressed?

A. I have to do something with your Prime Minister in a little while but I am sure he would find this a very good excuse for my being late. I am one of many participating in that so I will not be missed.

Lord Methuen

121. To what extent do Federal procurement policies encourage and assist small businesses?

A. Certain agencies of the Federal Government do have not mandates or requirements or quotas but instead targets for small business procurement. This too is very controversial. It is argued by some that volume purchases, as you will soon learn from the advance of WalMart in the United Kingdom, reduce profit margins and therefore help the consumer, in this case the Federal Government. At the same time the attention to service, the availability of specialised items oftentimes is provided, some would argue, better by smaller firms. So there are targets, not quotas, of the Federal Government. There are audits of that done each year widely publicised and that becomes somewhat of a political issue. I will say, however, under Vice President Gore's leadership— and this is the kind of work I have to tell you about, having worked very closely with Vice President Gore in this reinventing Government effort—he has devoted himself to a whole range of—pardon the expression—"grunt" Government issues. He gets no political benefit, wins no votes in the Presidential election but improves the quality of Government. I am talking about financial management, procurement reforms, the everyday business of running the Government. He led this effort, which I work on, procurement reform to move to the greater procurement of truly commercial products. What do I mean by that? We had the insane system that if you wanted to buy a stapler and you worked for the Federal Government you had to do a requisition. The stapler may have cost four dollars but you needed ten dollars of time and people doing the paperwork for the procurement. Then you had to buy it in gross and maybe a further two thirds of the staplers were not used for two years. Essentially, the legislation that was developed and passed allowed more "off the shelf" purchasing by the Federal Government and the provision of credit cards to a much lower level of Government employee and a sense of "We trust you. We will audit you. The Inspector Generals will come and make sure you did not buy the stapler to use in your house or buy a picture to hang in your daughter's condominium or apartment at university" but at the same time, instead of having to go through all the paperwork, the issuance of Government credit cards to a much broader range of Government employees entrusted them with the opportunity to do procurement which ultimately saved the taxpayer enormous sums. How that works out again in the notion of original sin and

Lord Methuen *contd.*]

the like, we will have to see. But these procurement things have been very helpful to small businesses where individual Government people can go to the outlet down the street and buy that stapler, instead of going through three months of paperwork to buy it from the wholesaler.

Lord Howell of Guildford

122. Critics of the American models—and I am certainly not one of them, but there are lots around— say this is all terrific but it has created a more divided society. Real wages, real incomes have not risen in America for ten years, wealth is concentrated more, we are now in the top five per cent and so on. Give us, Ambassador, your rebuttal to that, which I certainly long to hear because I do not believe it but this view is very widely held.

A. My Lord Chairman, I feel very strongly on that and here I risk perhaps inappropriate comment. Lord Howell's comment is accurate in one sense. There has been a greater divergence of the very wealthy and the very poor in the United States and that is one of the real tests of our society, how we cope with that. It has been exacerbated over the last 20 years. That being said, we have the largest middle class in human history. I say that not from scientific observation but from having lived the example of the benefits, of a growth of the middle class, the level of jobs creation. It is very interesting to me when someone says "but is that job a job that really is good for the economy?" If that job is going to someone who has been on welfare or someone who has been unemployed for a sustained period of time, I think in that family's mind it is not a question of "is that job good for the economy?", it is "is that job good for that family?". I would argue that is the real question to be asked. We have had both an explosion in the services industry and some would claim that a high percentage of jobs is people making hamburgers for other people, I am not sure that is all bad. It is all bad if it is also occurring with this explosion of intellectual capital. You see in the information society, you see in the increase in productivity, you see what is happening in the increased growth of independent private utility companies across the board, greater productivity, more outsourcing and more jobs being created with a huge increase in the standard of living for the majority of Americans. My final observation: there may be one other element of truth in the argument that American society is too materialistic, is not focused sufficiently on quality of life, environmental standards or cultural issues and the like. I will leave that for the dons at the universities to debate. I would simply say the standard of living and the opportunity to provide for one's family is at a perhaps unprecedented level in the United States today and I cannot help but think in a very proud American sense that is good not just for our country but that is good for almost any society.

Lord Montague of Oxford

123. I just want to test your thoughts which are so very valuable, as society changes and there is more leisure. Leisure, of course, is a great creator of jobs. To what extent is that shown to be true in America?

A. It is very significant. Perhaps the fastest growing non-electronic industry of course is tourism. The reason I was late today is that London benefits so much from American tourism. I apologise again for that. More Americans come to London each year than live in my entire home state of South Carolina, three million people a year. The tourism and the leisure industry, which are irrevocably inter-twined, have provided countless new industries and jobs. I spent ten years in that industry in the development of recreational communities, 5,000/8,000 acres. People have a hard time understanding what that means. Hiltonhead Island, Amelia Island and Poanoke Island are some of the places my company was involved in. Hiltonhead is just one example. When I moved there in 1972 there were 2,100 residents, one major paved road on this island, today there are 50,000 residents. I think they have a million and a half or a million and three quarter visitors a year. It attracts people from about six surrounding counties who come in, most of whom live at very marginal standards. They are now employed in the service industry at hotels and retail shops and the like. Again I would hope that their children will have opportunities, with many of them themselves, to develop e-commerce companies or to become university dons. What is important is that they have jobs at this stage. So the notion of what was a resort, a recreational or tourism community, became a local industry. You see that here in Stratford, you see that in Cornwall, you see it elsewhere. The extent to which there is Government policy understanding in support of that has been very useful. Our Government has done several things in that regard. Every few years there is not only a White House Conference on Small Business but there is also a White House Conference on Travel and Tourism. That is a way to essentially garner together the political support of Democrats and Republicans in those respective industries to present policy agendas to the Congress and to the President. Some of it is taken, some of it is not, but I think it is a useful exercise. A final observation: in tourism and leisure industry, though all of us seem to be working longer hours and are more challenged by, more conflicts in the use of our time, the increasing alternatives to the use of leisure time are creating incredible new electronic and non electronic business opportunities. The wealth creation in that, just in the United States in the last 18 months, has been enormous. Cable & Wireless, BT, I can list other British companies, are very active in the United States now and in Asia in precisely this market. It is going to be very interesting to see where that all leads.

Chairman

124. Your Excellency, perhaps I could wrap this up with a couple of points. The witnesses immediately before you were saying—particularly one of them— that one of the big problems within Europe is non recognition of one European company to another's

Chairman *contd.*]

standard. That presumably does not apply within the United States? Is standard marking, recognition of standards, a Federal issue or is it a State issue?

A. My Lord Chairman, may I ask you, standards in terms of weights, measures?

Chairman: Yes, weights, measures, designs, safety issues.

Lord Methuen: Specification..

Chairman

125. Yes, specification.

A. It is preponderantly a Federal issue. However, there are specific State controls and concerns. I will give you a few illustrations. We continue in the insurance industry, for example, to have individual State Insurance regulators. The reason Sir James Goldsmith's effort to acquire BAT failed, as you may recall, with Jacob Rothschild was because the State Insurance Agency in California refused to approve their acquisition of Farmers Insurance which was a subsidiary of BAT. That is just one British only example of the role of these regulators. In most products it is the Federal regulations that control. That certainly would have to be seen as a difference between our Federal system and the system in Europe today.

126. So in that respect—and this does not surprise me—within the United States, the activities of small businesses would be less inhibited because the standards, the specifications, are relatively common across the whole of the USA?

A. I would prefer, as I trust you will appreciate, not to say something that would suggest I am critical of the European situation. What I would prefer to say is the fact of uniformity in standards—others not I might suggest uniformity in currency, we are getting into a very ticklish subject matter here, as you know.

127. Yes, I was trying to avoid that one.

A. As I have made clear that is not my point but others would say, certainly it is an advantage in overall commercial growth. At the same time what we see in the United States is you still have mini markets. I will give you the best illustration that comes to mind immediately. We have this huge aggregation of banks in the United States where you see the Bank of America, formally the Nations Bank, acquiring many others, First Union, what used to be the Chase, what used to be the Chemical combined. At the same time another generation of community

banks has been growing up in small communities and a group of entrepreneurs get together as I did some 20 years ago. The local bank was bought out and with a few of my friends we started another local bank, subsequently it was sold. Today it is part of the eighth largest bank in the United States and somebody who is 20 years younger than me is starting another local bank. I say all that because while the uniformity of standards and the like may be advantages, business is both national and local and entrepreneurs have taken advantage of both ends of that spectrum in the United States.

128. You have led me, your Excellency, beautifully to my last point. Would it also be fair to say that because of the size of the market within the United States there is less of a problem for small businesses in the USA to go international and therefore you are not perhaps within the USA coming up against the same barriers that SMEs, let us say within the UK for example, will come up against in trying to break into other countries, be they in the European Union or outside it? It is just the sheer scale of the market in the US gives such a bigger target that there is less incentive to go international. Is that fair comment?

A. I would believe it is a fair comment. I think it will be impacted by the Internet, how quickly I would not begin to guess.

129. Yes.

A. But sheer scale, the blessings of natural resources, population, markets and scale cannot be discounted in terms of the economic success story that I presented earlier. You have in Europe a market potentially of equal or greater size, so the experts tell me, whether some of the other characteristics of that market and the seeming fragmentation of it would jeopardise the securing of the advantages of scale that the United States has had is something all of you are going to be living out.

130. Your Excellency, may I again say how enormously grateful I am and we are for the fact that you have come and spent a lot of your time giving us extremely valuable evidence. I am going to advise my successor as Chairman of this Committee that he or she should choose a subject on which they can call on you again because clearly you are an expert witness and we are truly grateful. Thank you.

A. It is an honour to be with you today. Thank you very much.

TUESDAY 20 JULY 1999

Present:

Berkeley, L.   Howell of Guildford, L.
Brooke of Alverthorpe, L.   Methuen, L.
Brookeborough, V.   O'Cathain, B.
Geddes, L.   Skelmersdale, L.
(Chairman)

Examination of Witness

MISS MARGARET SODEN, Senior Manager of EMU Planning, HSBC, called in and examined.

Chairman

131. Miss Soden, good morning, and a very sincere thank you for coming at very short notice. I am sure you are aware of this, but just for the record I should like to make two comments. First, in this modern day and age we are obliged to declare our interests. We now have a piece of paper which I hope you have got which does declare our interests. Doubtless they will be added to but as a generalisation inevitably everyone on this Committee has some connection with SMEs directly or indirectly. I have said to other witnesses that, if we went through the whole lot, we would probably be here for the entire session and not get any evidence. The second point is that this is a paving enquiry to try to put down our views as to what Brussels or the Commission is doing, should be doing and should not be doing to encourage SMEs. Of course one of the problems we come up against almost immediately is the definition of an SME. Different people have different views on that. I am assuming, but please correct me if I am wrong, that you are coming to it very much from a banking background.
(*Miss Soden*) That is correct.

132. We want to avoid any in-depth discussion on the pros and cons of the euro. It is not the business of this Committee to get into the pros and cons of that. Having said that, we are interested in the overall context of the European single market and, to the extent that the euro or a common currency at a fixed parity is relevant, that is something that does interest us. Whether particular countries should or should not join is quite another matter. How important in your experience is the single market for SMEs within the European Union and to what extent is a common currency significant or essential for the workings of that single market in the context of SMEs?
A. SMEs span such a wide segment of the business community. For the smaller companies, the single market is probably not very significant; they are trading purely in their domestic market. For medium sized companies, I think it is important. If we look at the fact that between 50 and 60 per cent of United Kingdom exports and imports are to and from the euro zone, unfortunately we cannot get a breakdown of that by business size, bearing in mind the close geographic proximity I think it is very important. One of the advantages major companies have over medium sized and small businesses is that they tend to have a dedicated treasury function which can manage foreign exchange and interest rate risk. For a medium sized business and going down to the smaller size, you have probably a managing director who is trying to do a whole host of other things and that is one more thing for him to add. The single currency is not, in my mind, just a technical or operational issue. It raises very important strategic implications in terms of changing the market place into which a number of those companies enter and in which they operate. It is not just their exports but it could ultimately be their own home domestic market. What might be an opportunity in terms of the single currency opening up the rest of the euro zone to a medium sized company also works the other way: it opens up, let us say, the German market to a medium sized company in France. It is a two-way operation.

133. I said to begin with that there is a problem of definition. We have already discovered early on in taking evidence that the definition varies between the United Kingdom and the EU. Just in numbers of employees there is a difference of opinion. How do you define micro, small, medium and large?
A. It is a difficult one to answer, that.

134. That is why I have asked it.
A. Our definition of SMEs will involve anything from a self-employed electrician through to a company with several hundred employees and a fairly large turnover. Clearly within that range you have a very large range of needs. We are starting to see changes in the market place with the development of things like e-commerce and the Internet. A number of what we would define as smaller companies, probably with not very many employees, are now trying to sell to the retail customer base in countries other than their own. We are now starting to see them as having to take account of different currencies. A few years ago they probably would not have done because they would have been very much oriented to the domestic market. They are now using the new technology to say, "How can I expand my business?"

135. The message you are giving us is that the Internet is going to make a very big impact on our previously preconceived notions of what is micro, what is small, what is medium?
A. Yes.

Lord Skelmersdale

136. Miss Soden, you talked about exporting enterprises, but of course there is a vast range of micro and small enterprises, possibly even medium sized enterprises, who are not in the least interested in exporting but are interested in the growing home market. Would something like a common currency in your view help or hinder them, given that the tourist industry is very much part of all this?

A. The tourist industry is quite interesting because of course, while it is domestically based, not all its market is in the United Kingdom. We think a lot about the American tourist trade, the Asian tourist trade, and whether they will find that companies who are arranging tours of Europe will say, "Most of Europe is in the euro so we would now like to trade with you in the euro". The issue is that many United Kingdom small and medium sized businesses have taken the view, "We are not in the single currency, so it does not affect my business". We have been trying to encourage them for a long time to think outside the box and think about how they would react faced with those instances. There are also other issues related to the single currency in terms of what it does or does not mean in terms of low inflation, environment and stability, which it may or may not bring.

137. Surely the jury is still out on that one?
A. It is, very much so.

138. Which is why we are not going into it.
A. Precisely.

Lord Berkeley

139. Miss Soden, you mentioned that 50 to 60 per cent of imports from the euro zone were from medium sized companies or smaller. Do you have a similar figure for exports to the euro zone?

A. The percentage of exports and imports is roughly the same, between 50 and 60 per cent for both.

140. You mentioned various costs associated with trading between currencies. There is the currency risk and the transaction costs both for SMEs and for tourists changing money, if that is a different thing. I recall a figure produced two or three years ago which said that the European banks made a profit of something like £20 million from exchange transactions. Whether that figure is right or wrong, good or bad, does not matter. Is the argument really that if we join the euro zone all those costs would be therefore not incurred and therefore the SMEs would benefit? That is the plus side. But what about the minus side of their worries about accounting systems, handling cash, customer/employee relations and things like that? Is that a straight plus or minus or is there a fear of the change built in, rather like when we changed to decimal currency?

A. We have to look at the various costs which SMEs face and the various impacts on their bottom line. Clearly, if they are exporting to the euro zone and receiving funds in a currency other than sterling, they have a potential foreign exchange risk and a potential foreign exchange cost. Equally, we have to look at the changes that are taking place in the euro zone, particularly in terms of price transparency.

Many companies exporting to a number of different countries set their pricing as to what particular market will bear. They will set it in Deutschmarks, French francs, Spanish pesetas, but actually they have a different pricing policy across the euro zone. The question is: is that differential pricing policy sustainable in the longer term given that once you are quoting prices in euros it will be very easy to see the differences? I know there are differences in taxation rates, but those can always be factored out. I think they really have to look at what that means to their bottom line. In some industries it is probably sustainable; in others it will not be, and some companies I think will have a phased approach to ironing out that difference. Then there are the issues associated with impact on profit of price points. We are all very used to round price points. If you take something like 9.99 Deutschmarks, that actually converts to 5.04 euros which is not very customer friendly, so what is the company going to do? Is it going to stick with that odd amount and retain its profit margin, or is it going to round it up to say 5.25, which is an increase of about three per cent? Is it still competitive if it does? Or is it going to round it down, say, to 4.95, which is a reduction of more than 2.5 per cent, and what does that do to its bottom line? In the context of the various changes we need not get too hung up on any savings which may come from foreign exchange risk reductions. The other point you quite rightly raised is, what is the likely cost of having to convert all of their systems, train their employees, change all their marketing material, potentially for United Kingdom entry? You have two differences therefore. One is exporting to the euro zone and the costs associated with the changes in business there, and the other is, if the United Kingdom were to go in, what extra do they have to do and what is that going to cost and what is the bottom line impact on the business?

141. You mentioned quoting prices in euros, different prices for different countries. Are you suggesting that an exporter from the United Kingdom would have a different price in euros for his goods in Germany to Italy, to France and to Spain?

A. What I am saying is that at the moment he is probably exporting to Germany, France and Spain, and he is setting a price for Germany which reflects the German market in Deutschmarks, French francs likewise and Spanish pesetas. When you apply the fixed conversion rates to those legacy currencies you will find that those prices in euros are all different.

Lord Berkeley: It could be an interesting problem for DG IV, could it not?

Baroness O'Cathain: It could be a very interesting problem for the countries themselves.

Lord Howell of Guildford

142. I cannot understand the line you are taking on this because surely first of all anyone with a calculator can in a second see through price differentials and see the transparency or not in the situation now. Secondly, prices are different for all sorts of local reasons around Europe to do with taxation, local conditions, quite aside from what the market will bear. Those price differentials are going to remain, as are the tax differences, until we have totally harmonised taxes and local conditions,

Lord Howell of Guildford *contd.*]

whatever currency and whatever denomination you price in. I cannot see what the argument is.

A. It depends on the industry that you are in. It depends on your competitors. Certain things like taxation, you are quite right, remain, but it very easy to strip that out and see what is the underlying difference. Companies have been pricing very differently. I know we are talking about the SME market now but if we take the pharmaceutical industry, which is a classic example, they typically manufacture in a few locations, have national sales forces, and their prices at wholesale level are very different. They have had to say what happens going forward. You are starting to find this elsewhere. You are quite right, people can do it with a calculator now, but you have got differences in exchange rates, and now it is a single currency across a big area those differences are very apparent.

143. As you rightly said, this is all about changes in the market place and medium sized businesses trading into the euro zone. This is rather a crude question. Are they going to find that the bank still charges them for transferring the money even though they are not putting it through "exchanges"? I have heard it suggested that, hey presto, bank charges for moving money will increase. Secondly, the euro does not come by itself. It comes with all sorts of baggage of regulatory threats and dangers and benefits. How do you think SMEs or medium sized firms view all these other problems they may find in trading into the euro zone, of different tax rates, different regulations and so on? Do they weigh those up and find that the benefits of the single currency outweigh them or under-weigh them? Finally, what about medium sized businesses trading outside the euro zone, the other 50 per cent? Are they going to find disadvantages if we were part of the euro zone, or are they coming to you and saying, "We are quite happy. It does not make any difference"?

A. On your middle question about how the companies thought these things through, I have to say from my experience with medium sized companies that they have not yet thought these things through. They have not thought about the changes in the market. I was out in India in May, because as a group we have operations there, doing a euro roadshow, and I was very struck by the medium sized companies out there importing into the euro zone, particularly Germany but others as well, that had thought about the changes that this meant for their competitors in places like Portugal and had started to say, "They have now got an advantage so I have got to be even more competitive to compete against that". You go round the United Kingdom and you do not find United Kingdom companies have given it that amount of thought. To me that is the concerning point, not any action they decide to take or not to take, but they have not weighed it up and then thought about the real implications for their business.

144. What about the 50 per cent of trading we do outside the euro zone currencies? Do you get any feedback on that?

A. No. A lot of that is dollar denominated. A lot of it is with Asia. The view tends to be, "We do not expect that to change at this point in time". There is

the theory that says if you go forward long enough, far enough, you may see some of that being denominated in the euro, but we are a long way off that. As far as that is concerned, no, we do not see a change. What I do find as I go round the country talking to our medium sized businesses is that, whereas last year they could compete for business in the euro zone in sterling and win it, they are now finding that they are having to quote in the euro to win the business. To give you an example, exporting to Germany they are probably competing with a company from Italy and one from Spain, which are now quoting in euros, or legacy currency but with a euro rate, so United Kingdom companies are having to quote in euros or are having to be very competitive in sterling in order to win the business because their customers are saying, "We will not be taking the foreign exchange risk".

Baroness O'Cathain

145. Of course they cannot do that with the high value of sterling at the moment.

A. That is right.

146. Lord Howell has asked more or less the same question that I was prepared to ask, but I would say that not a lot of people actually go round with calculators comparing the prices. I would estimate that only about 10 per cent of the population is financially literate. I think, however, that when push comes to shove and everything is denominated in euros they could have a really serious problem. I am very concerned about your statement that our small and medium sized enterprises really have not even thought about it. My question was going to be regarding differential pricing, the impact on companies, and the viability of companies. First of all, they are going to have to experience huge increases in productivity to try to compensate, huge reductions in costs and huge expenditures on marketing budgets. How have you looked at that in terms of the impact not only on United Kingdom companies but on a lot of companies who have been hiding behind differential pricing since Adam was a boy?

A. We have put a lot of effort into going round working either with the Chambers of Commerce or the Business Links or in our own seminars, getting in groups of customers to go through the practical implications associated with the single currency, and encouraging them to think about the impact for their business. We have put a lot of time and effort into thinking about what euro products and services do they need to help them with this business. We have found that some of the ones who have thought about what it means for their business and maybe have been both exporting and importing, have done things like worked through their cash flows and said that, rather than convert this back to sterling with all of the costs of foreign exchange risks and costs associated with that, I will try to match my euro income with euro expenditure—either exports versus imports or, we have had a few who have said, "Because I have a reasonable level of sustainable euro income, I will switch some of my sterling borrowing to euro because I match my foreign exchange risk. I am not

Baroness O'Cathain *contd.*]

entering into unnecessary foreign exchange risk." As interest rates are currently, they have actually succeeded in reducing some of their funding costs. There is no one-size-fits-all answer to this, but we have been trying to encourage customers to go through those issues. One of the other phenomena which is often talked about (and it is talked about rather than being a reality from my perspective) is this issue of euro-creep, which is the use of the euro as a parallel currency for trade within the United Kingdom. Particularly if you speak to medium sized businesses, perhaps the automobile industry supply chain, where that is the one where there is the most talk about euro-creep happening, what we have said to customers is, "If you are approached by one of your major customers to consider the euro, do not reject it out of hand. It may be the right thing to do to reject it for your business, but think about it first of all, talk it through and say, 'Is there any advantage to my business in perhaps being able to offset some euro income and euro expenditure?'" They have started to think about price transparency and price points now. What they have not done is taken the price points issue and said, "What does that really mean in terms of repackaging my products or maybe redesigning my products?", which obviously for many companies takes quite a long lead time to implement. It is trying to get them to think one step ahead and to think it through. I think they are also slightly comforted at the moment by the fact that, if you look at medium sized companies in the in-countries, very few have actually yet moved from their own national currencies to the euro, unlike the major corporations who have made the change. The medium sized businesses have got three years to make the change. Human nature being what it is, we all tend to put off some of those things until nearer when we have to do it and focus our expenditure on other things at the moment. Also, they have got the millennium rapidly approaching so that is tending to be the focus of their energies, and so you have not actually seen very many of them make the change yet. But as they start, in my view in the middle of next year, to make that change in the last 18 months of the transition period, you will start to see more and more of our companies faced with some of these issues.

Chairman

147. Do you think that that dualism, if I could call it that, is causing particular problems for SMEs relative to large companies?
A. At the moment, no, because what I see is large companies saying, "We would like to talk about it". There has not, from what I have seen, been, for want of a better word, a big brother that says, "If you want to carry on trading with us that is the way it is going to work". It has been very much a case of, "We would like to talk about it". It is a bit like the major corporations in the in-countries dealing with their medium sized domestic suppliers. They are not saying to them, "You have to deal with us in euros". It is very much a partnership approach and an encouraging approach, and I think there is a realisation in many of the large sized companies' minds that for them to just say, "This is the way it is

going to be" will not work. That will give distortions in the supply chain—it needs a co-operative approach. How long that will continue is the question.

Baroness O'Cathain

148. The very first statement you made when you came in — and it has all been fascinating stuff — was about the differences that you saw and the advantages of big companies against SMEs. You made this very important point about no treasury function being available to SMEs. As soon as you said that I thought, "Gosh, yes, you are absolutely right". Have you thought this one through, whether the organisations, the system, governments, or even the Commission can actually devise some way where there will be available a treasury function to micro and small and medium companies? It is very important. The very point that you made about a managing director doing all of that summed it up. A managing director should not be bothered with something like that. A managing director should be out making sure that the products that they are making are what the market wants and doing the very things at the margin that you were talking about in your answer to the second question, about reformulating products and repackaging products. Have you thought this through? Do you think there is any merit in the suggestion that maybe something at a European or national level could highlight this issue to SMEs, for example, in the way we have highlighted the millennium bug problem to all companies and all organisations?
A. I have to say I have not thought it through. We very much encourage our customers to talk to our regional treasury centres around the country, because again there is no one-size-fits-all. I think that, particularly where you get medium sized companies who are faced with it for the very first time, you get a "Where do I go for help?" situation. I suspect that it is probably better led by national governments than the Commission because I think that will probably be viewed as being a bit too remote. Maybe there should be things that are done on an industry basis, so maybe it is also quite a lot of getting some of the industry bodies —

149. The trade associations?
A. — the trade associations, to assist with specifics relating to that industry.
Baroness O'Cathain: My experience with trade associations would not fill me with great hope that that will be achieved.

Chairman

150. It is a bit of a leading question, but I certainly have been impressed from what you said by the initiative that the HSBC is taking in this context. You have talked about going round the country with seminars and so forth. I am not quite sure how to phrase this without your saying, "But of course", but is your bank unique in this respect or are your rivals and friendly competitors doing the same things?
A. I would like to say that we are unique, and we have got one or two unique strands, but basically you

Chairman *contd.*]

will find that all of the major United Kingdom banks that have small and medium sized enterprise customers are doing things. We are all doing them slightly differently but we are all encouraging our customers to think through the impact on their business.

151. To what extent, and please do not answer this if it is privileged information, are you co-operating with other banking groups in this context? Do you put your heads together? Do you have joint seminars?
A. To my knowledge we have never had a joint seminar.

Baroness O'Cathain

152. Competition.
A. I think it is competition and the invitees to the seminars will be our customers and our target customers, and likewise theirs will be their customers and their target customers. There will be some duplication. There will be some overlap. Where you tend to address a wider range of customers is where we do things (and most of us to my knowledge do them) with local chambers of commerce or we do things with, say, the Engineering Employers Federation.
Chairman: It just occurred to me that I should have declared an interest as a customer of the HSBC.
Baroness O'Cathain: And a very satisfied shareholder.

Viscount Brookeborough

153. Historically, are the SMEs in the United Kingdom, as far as cross-border trade goes, working from a different base from SMEs in other European countries from the point of view that geographically we have got the sea between us and the remainder of Europe, and in Northern Ireland we have a land boundary? Are we working from a totally different basis as far as our SMEs' relationship with trade from outside their own boundaries is concerned and what can we do about it?
A. There is a psychological difference. I do not think it necessarily is the Channel that is separating us but the language issue...
Baroness O'Cathain: Culture?
A. It is culture, but it is also language.

154. But was the trade between our SMEs and businesses outside our own borders historically less than the trade within Europe between SMEs and outside their own borders?
A. No, because over the last 20 years the amount of trade we have done with the rest of the European Union has increased significantly. If you go back many years, the United States was our major trading partner but that was reversed quite a long time ago now. I do not think it is the distance. I think a lot of it is the language and the culture.

155. Many SMEs in Northern Ireland now have bases in the Republic in order to work from them.
A. That is right.

156. Have European institutions responsible for the introduction of the euro, the Commission and the European Central Bank, taken sufficient account of the changes and are they, as you are as a bank, promoting the trade?
A. The European Central Bank has tended to focus very much on financial markets. It has been the European Commission that has worked on the communications programme. What it has tended to do is to work with national governments in terms of communication programmes for the individual countries. I do not have any figures on how that programme has been split between what I call the man in the street and business people. Whilst there has been a European Commission budget to assist with that work, it has very much been down to individual countries. In some of the first wave countries, they have had a national changeover board which has had representatives of industry, banking, government and everybody on it, to say, "This is how it is going to operate in reality." In other countries they have not done that. There has been no common picture. What we are looking to do is very much to follow what they did do in the first wave countries and how it worked out in practice. Of course it is a little bit early to learn any real lessons from that.

Lord Brooke of Alverthorpe

157. I am with First Direct so I am part of your company. Have you a presence in Eire?
A. We have one of our personal financial services operations in Eire. One of the things the larger companies and the top end of the medium sized market very much needs to help them gain the most from the introduction of the single currency is a more efficient payments and cash management service, so we have what we call payments and cash management branches in a number of the EU countries. They are not retail branches for people to go in and out of. They are very much to serve the business customers. We are opening a payments and cash management branch in Eire later on this year.
Lord Brooke of Alverthorpe: So we would have the common language there between us?
Baroness O'Cathain: Sort of.

Lord Brooke of Alverthorpe

158. I can understand you.
A. But unlike, say, Natwest who have got Ulster Bank, we do not have a domestic banking operation in Eire.

Baroness O'Cathain

159. You used to and then you sold it.
A. Yes.

Lord Brooke of Alverthorpe

160. Are there lessons that you could draw from the assistance that has been given to SMEs in Eire by comparison with what we are doing or not doing?

Lord Brooke of Alverthorpe *contd.*]

A. We are as an industry, and this is an industry initiative rather than individual banks, looking very closely at what is happening in a number of the first wave countries, and Eire is one of them, because there are lots of similarities between us, to see what lessons we can learn. What is quite interesting is that the United Kingdom banks have for several years now been planning what the practical implications of this would be and have given quite a lot of thought to a number of the practical issues – so much so that from time to time we find ourselves being approached by banking associations in the first wave countries to say, "This is an issue. Have you thought about how you might tackle it?". We are watching very closely what happens.

161. Are there any preliminary findings?

A. I think one of the preliminary findings coming out of Ireland is that the major banks in Ireland, in terms of communicating with the man in the street, which obviously has an impact on businesses, all tended to do their own thing, which we think has probably led to a little bit of confusion. So, one of the areas we are discussing with the banking industry is, "What about some common language for some of these issues?" We will all want to put our own marketing message round it, but if we can identify some common language that not only we use but also people like the chambers of commerce use, then that will help going forward—you should not bring unnecessary confusion into the equation.

162. One of the pieces of baggage that might come with the euro is the possibility that there could be lower interest rates for capital for SMEs. Is that the experience in Ireland?

A. Yes. If you look at Ireland, towards the end of last year they had interest rates around the six per cent mark, and in a very short space of time they had effectively halved them. One of the things we should perhaps be careful about is making the assumption that if the United Kingdom did join, interest rates for the euro would be where they are now because that may or may not be the case.

163. But in your consultations with your customers has it been drawn to your attention that there is a possibility that this could be the case and are they aware of it? It may not be, as you say.

A. We find that customers who have thought it through tend to assume that, if we go in, then rates will be lower than they currently are for sterling – so they have tended not to take out interest rate hedging products. The point we make to them is that, if we do go in, depending on lots of things about where the economies are in the cycle, the rates may not be where they are now. If you are choosing not to take an interest rate hedging policy, do that deliberately rather than by default and be aware of the risks and opportunities that may or may not bring.

Chairman

164. We spoke earlier about the dualism, the move from national currencies into the euro. Ten countries are affected at the moment. If one or more of the remaining countries in the European Union elect to go in, what do you think is the optimal transitional period when national currency and the euro would operate together? Again I am always talking from the viewpoint of the SME.

A. In my opinion, it would be less than the three years that the first wave countries have. The primary reason for saying that is that, for any current out-country that does decide to go in – as there is a growing expectation that that country may go in, we will start to see the euro being used more and more anyway. Unlike the first wave countries where the euro did not exist, for anybody going in afterwards the euro will exist and so that will probably have a big impact on the rate of take-up. I think therefore it will be less than three years. However, you would still need to allow a very reasonable length of time because it is going to take an SME quite a long time to make the changes. They will not, quite reasonably, make that investment until they know for absolute certain that their particular country is going to join. It would have to be more than months in my mind. I think you would be talking in the order of 18 months, because one of the biggest issues they will face is the adjustment to their IT systems. Medium sized companies tend to be dependent on third-party suppliers. Very few of them develop their own programmes. That then raises the question: do their third-party suppliers have the financial and human resources required to change those programmes, how fast can they do it and what is the cost going to be associated with that? You have to allow a reasonable time, but if you allow too long it just drags it out. Let us say, for the sake of argument, it is Greece that goes in later on. They will have an issue of the euro notes and coins available circulating in the first wave countries. They will not have to be their legal tender, but will shops and hotels and restaurants accept them? You get that added complication, so you have to minimise the time frame whilst allowing SMEs the time required to make the change.

Lord Berkeley

165. Miss Soden, half an hour ago you mentioned the process of euro-creep, quite a nice word, where the big corporations are often working in euros already and therefore the SMEs and their potential suppliers may well be asked to quote in euros. Can you see that extending to countries outside the euro zone, in other words exporting by SMEs with or without a big company to outside the euro zone, so in fact over maybe a two or three year period some SMEs will probably be quoting and trading almost exclusively in euros both within the European Union and outside? Is that a problem?

A. I think it is very likely to happen. I think the timescale is the question. I do not think it is a problem because a number of those SMEs now are probably doing that export business in US dollars which, if you are a United Kingdom company, is still a foreign currency. So, if they do it in euros, they might actually have an opportunity to marry both the euro income and euro receipts because they may be importing from the euro zone, so they can try to do that and eliminate totally their foreign exchange risk. I do not believe it is a problem. It might suit the other party equally to do that.

Lord Berkeley *contd.*]

166. What happens to the British government's export guarantees if they still have them? Is that going to apply still to euro trading or is there going to be a potential uncertainty or loss there?

A. To be honest, I do not know the answer to that. My assumption would be that often with the export guarantees you are not actually covering primarily the foreign exchange risk. You are covering the credit risk of the buyer, so there would be no reason why that should change.

Lord Skelmersdale

167. Miss Soden, may I divorce you in this discussion from the euro? What else in requests do you get from small and medium sized enterprises? For example, there was a time when they were very jealous of Credit Agricole in France which had a lower interest rate for small and medium sized enterprises, particularly, but not uniquely, in the agricultural sector, was there not?

A. Yes. One of the things that small and medium sized businesses are always looking to us for is information on a whole host of issues, such as the millennium bug. They are always looking for information and to be kept up to date. Clearly issues of how they can get cheaper funding are also ones that they are continuing to look at, as you would expect. But often, for small and medium sized businesses, their first port of call for information tends to be their banks and their accountants. Research shows that that is where they go for information rather than to a chamber of commerce, for instance.

Chairman

168. Do you get asked, following up Lord Skelmersdale's question, about things that are really completely outside the banking sector: social legislation, employment legislation and so on?

A. From time to time. What we would seek to do there is to direct customers to an authoritative source for information. They do tend to come to us sometimes and we try to point them in the right direction.

Baroness O'Cathain: According to statistics that we have received, both on these little cards —

Chairman

169. Do you know what we are talking about when we refer to "these little cards"?

A. No.

Chairman: They are two interesting little bits of plastic from the Federation of Small Businesses. They are what I drew from when I mentioned a difference of definition.

Baroness O'Cathain

170. If you just take broad figures, these figures show that there are a hundred million people in the private sector workforce in the whole of the European Union. If you subtract the figures of employees who are in the large companies, which is 35 million, 65 per cent of the labour force in Europe is actually in small and medium sized enterprises. Looking at the ones in the United Kingdom, it is slightly less: large companies account for 36.3 per cent. We are talking in and around 65 per cent. I asked a question earlier about government institutions in Europe helping these enterprises in things like the treasury function so as to deal with the euro. But there is a bigger question here surely, that with the impact—and my mind is racing here—of increased competition, transparency, price integrity, all of that, there could be a huge fall-out in terms of employment. Do you think that there is any room for advice from European institutions or local governments about getting their act together, irrespective of the euro at the moment, but in order to make the single market work? The single market, as we all know, is not really the single market but it is inexorably getting there, and the euro will be part of it. Do you think that something should be done now because there are all sorts of local customs and mores, ways of doing business, which just will not survive? Is anybody looking at this because the implications for unemployment are really quite serious, particularly with recent problems in the Far East resulting in spare capacity which can be used to source products for the EU, nor forgetting that the values of their currencies have deflated to such great extent? I can see a scenario where most of the things we need in Europe can be supplied from the Far East and we will have this residual huge unemployment.

A. I agree with you. I think it is not just the Far East. It is the former Eastern Europe as well, which is the other area that is so closely aligned to the euro zone. I think there is a role, but what I am not sure is how you capture the imagination of the SMEs—

171. And say, "Look, you are up against it"?

A. Yes – to take it seriously. Given the way they are structured, the question is how can they be helped to think longer term, because they tend to be—not always but often—short-term focused. It is getting them to think longer term and giving them the prompt to do that. There ought to be a way of doing it. I do not know what it is but it has to be put in such a way that it grabs their attention.

Baroness O'Cathain: This is one of the features of our report. We are looking at ways where we can help SMEs.

Chairman: I want to come to a sweep-up general question at the end.

Lord Howell of Guildford: I want to come back to these figures and numbers because I am still a bit puzzled.

Lord Howell of Guildford

172. I think you said that those SMEs who were in the exporting business export about half their production to the euro zone, which is the same as for the whole economy. Did you say that?

A. No. It is about 50 to 60 per cent of United Kingdom exports that go to the euro zone, so it may not be of their actual production because the focus of a lot of SMEs is very much domestic based. The point about the single currency is that, for those countries that are in, that domestic base has gone from

Lord Howell of Guildford *contd.*]

however many there are in their individual country to a population of 290 million. For United Kingdom companies, if they are exporting some of their production, their competition has just changed and equally they have to think also about their own domestic market, because some of their competitors in those countries may be taking a view as to whether or not they believe the United Kingdom is going to go in and saying, "Do we position ourselves to tap into their domestic market?"

173. I will ask the question the other way round because this is not quite what I was getting at. For the country as a whole we have the figures, do we not, that something over 50 per cent of our exports of manufactured goods go to the euro zone, and that as a nation we export about 34 per cent of our total output, and half of 34 per cent is 17, so we are talking about 17 or 18 per cent of our production goes into the euro zone, 82 per cent does not. I am trying to get at whether that figure is roughly the same for the SMEs. If it is the same, it still raises questions, does it not, of to what extent we let that 18 or 17 per cent tail wag the whole dog, and whether SMEs feel it is really worth it. If it is actually a very much smaller percentage and SMEs do not export as much as the average of the whole United Kingdom economy, say 14 or 15 per cent, then it is an even smaller tail wagging an even bigger dog. I just wonder whether the SMEs come to you and say, "Is this not making adjustments for rather a small amount of our total output and production and sales and revenues that bring costs that we would rather not incur?" Or do they think that it is all inevitable for them and they are going to be engulfed in the euro system anyway, even though it is at present only a small part of their production?

A. Nobody has actually got figures for what you are talking about with any certainty. I do not think it is measured that way. The only way you could get at it would be to do some market research with a statistically sound sample. The SMEs do not all fit into one category. They vary because those who do export are either starting to think these things through or thinking they ought to but it is too difficult. Then you have others who think it is a foregone conclusion and they are going to get wrapped up in it. Then you have got a very large number of others who are either convinced it is not going to happen and it will not affect their business, or are completely apathetic. They all fall into very many different categories.

Baroness O'Cathain

174. But does it not still get back to this unemployment problem? If you take these figures again, 63.7 per cent of employment of firms is actually in this sector. In the United Kingdom small firms account for about 32 per cent of total business employment in this country. If they are apathetic, to use your word, we could find that the SMEs on the continent of Europe and Ireland who now operate in a home market of nearly 300 million people could gain economies of scale and impact seriously on our home market, which would have a huge impact on

the 32 per cent of our own population involved in business.
A. Yes.
Lord Methuen: I think we have a problem here because it is such a wide group. An awful lot of these SMEs are the small garages, the back street shops, who are not in the least bit interested in the common market *per se*. What we are talking about in this instance are the people who are a relatively small minority of this total group who are the ones who are actually concerned.
Baroness O'Cathain: The 12.5 per cent of the medium firms.
Lord Methuen: The five people who work part-time in the corner shop, which we have got in our locality. This is where the bulk are and this is where they are going to be unaffected by what we are talking about. There are a number of small firms, yes, who are interested – probably in the 10 to 20 area. I think this is the problem which we are talking about and these are the ones who are going to try to export to Spain and Portugal and where we might be susceptible.

Chairman

175. Is this the experience that you get from your roadshows, using your word, that when your customers come to you are they by and large those who are expansion minded, or do they include Lord Methuen's corner shop-cum-garage-cum-whatever?
A. We do not get many of the corner shop-cum-garage customers coming to our roadshows, only because they often think, "It does not affect my business." You tend to get a few more companies like that when you do things with some of the chambers of commerce because it may be that they regularly go to the chambers of commerce meetings because it helps them to network within their local community, so they would not by and large come to the sorts of events that we would run. They would say, "There are better things for me to do with my time than to attend that sort of event." There was a television programme on a few weeks ago which you may have seen which showed a gentleman who had a Renault car. He was French, but lived and worked in the United Kingdom. When he wanted his car serviced, he went over to France and had his car serviced, and had a meal whilst they were doing it. The programme compared the prices of having that car serviced in France versus over here which was really quite interesting. That is an extreme because, if you live in the north of England, you are certainly not going to go on a day trip to France to have your car serviced.
Viscount Brookeborough: But if you live in Northern Ireland, it happens the whole time. People come up to get their teeth done and you have this difference in the price. It is three times the price.

Lord Berkeley

176. Lady O'Cathain talked about the fear, and I think you have confirmed it, about competition from the Far East or wherever. We hear so much about how much the Member State governments have tried to help SMEs. There is more than a little evidence

Lord Berkeley *contd.*]

that, yes, they try to help, but they also bring in more and more legislation which actually makes it more and more difficult for SMEs to survive – not spend all their time bean counting when they should be going out and getting orders and managing things. Is this a serious problem and what are they going to do about it?

A. I think it is a serious problem because the small businesses often do not have the resources. Some of the legislation is not written in very user-friendly words, so it takes them quite a long time to read it through, work out what it means and then try to apply it to themselves. It needs explaining in words which the businessman can relate to without having to spend too much time working out what they mean. He then spends his time on, "How am I going to implement this in a way which minimises the bureaucracy for my business?" That is a key thing that was commented on earlier, that managing directors should be out there selling their goods, making sure they are watching the competition. It is those issues which are very important.

Chairman

177. You started to answer my final question, Miss Soden. That is going right back to the original question about what the Commission is doing, what it should be doing and what it should not be doing, and you have touched on a very important point. Are there any other main points that, in your opinion, would fit into the last two categories: what should they be doing and what should they not be doing?

A. Trade within Europe is very important to Europe, but we now live in a global economy. They need to be doing what they can to ensure that Europe is not hidebound by bureaucracy and is able to freely compete across the world. It is also attractive for inward investment and takes all of those things into consideration. I think that really is one of the things that the Commission needs to look at, because it all tends to be inward looking and we are a very active global economy.

Chairman: Thank you very much. I hope you did not find that too much of an ordeal. We are very grateful to you. Thank you.

THURSDAY 22 JULY 1999

Present:

Berkeley, L.
Brooke of Alverthorpe, L.
Brookeborough, V.
Geddes, L.
(Chairman)

Howell of Guildford, L.
Methuen, L.
Montague of Oxford, L.
O'Cathain, B.
Skelmersdale, L.

Memorandum by the Department of Trade and Industry (DTI)

INTRODUCTION

1. The challenges faced by European economies are very similar: the need for sustainable growth and the need to create lasting employment. There is increasing recognition by the Commission and by Member States that only businesses can create the wealth and opportunity that in turn create employment. The role of governments is to establish the conditions in which ideas can be created and exploited and in which enterprise, and particularly small enterprises can flourish in both the European and global market place.

EUROPEAN SINGLE MARKET

2. The Single Market, with its 380 million customers, has already created 900,000 new jobs in Europe and added up to 1.5 per cent to GDP. Competitiveness has been sharpened and Community-wide acceptance of product standards has led to manufacturing efficiencies. Public procurement (15 per cent of EU GDP) has opened up new opportunities; customs forms, formalities and fiscal checks have been abolished. Eleven Member States now have a single currency. The UK's exports to the EU have grown dramatically—58 per cent of all our visible exports go to the EU, with exports to Germany alone now equal to those to Japan and the USA combined.

3. In the EU 15, there are around 18.3 million Small and Medium-sized businesses (SMEs)[1], 99 per cent of which have fewer than 50 employees. SMEs account for 66 per cent of employment and 55 per cent of turnover. (1996 figures, excluding agriculture and fishing). They now operate, whether or not they are exporters, within the Single Market and all of the opportunities it offers. But they face challenges too; the introduction of the Euro, rapid technological change and growth, the need for flexible forms of financing and the ability to deal with often complex and copious domestic and European regulation.

ENTERPRISE AND SME POLICY IN THE EU

4. There is widespread recognition amongst the EU 15 (and the candidate countries) as well as within the Commission of the importance of SMEs in providing economic growth and jobs. Increasingly, development of SME policy has recognised the need to take account, not only of existing businesses, but of the wider context of entrepreneurship and the promotion of a more enterprising, competitive and innovative culture. Examples of this include:

— the UK Presidency "Enterprising Europe Conference" (April 1998);

— publication of *Fostering Entrepreneurship* (COM(98)222final) (April 1998);

— the inclusion in the EU Employment Pacts (statements by EU Member States of what they are doing to create the conditions for employment growth) of an "entrepreneurship pillar" (introduced 1998; annual); and

— the setting up (1997) of the Business Environment Task Force (BEST), which reported in 1998 and on which basis the Commission has produced (April 1999) an Action Plan to take forward recommendations at both EU and Member State level.

Further evidence of a more cohesive approach to enterprise and SME issues was the announcement on 9 July of a new Directorate General, bringing together innovation, competitiveness, the information society and SME policy responsibilities.[2]

---

[1] SMEs are defined by the Commission as having fewer than 250 employees, with an annual turnover of less than 40 million euros or a balance sheet total of less than 27 million euros and not more than 25 per cent owned by a "large" firm. "Small" businesses are further defined as having fewer than 50 employees; "micro" businesses are those with fewer than 10.

[2] The Commissioner designate is Errki Likaanen of Finland. Proposals have yet to be ratified by the European Parliament.

THE MULTI-ANNUAL PROGRAMME FOR SMEs (MAP)

5. The 3rd MAP is the main Commission instrument designed specifically for the support of SMEs. It is a small budget programme (128 million euros over four years) which aims to encourage administrative simplification, improve access to finance, increase participation of SMEs in other Commission programmes, provide support for the EU information and co-operation networks, and to encourage the sharing of good practice.

6. The MAPs have had some success in championing the cause of SMEs. However, the UK and others have consistently urged a more targeted approach, less duplication of either Member States' own activities or those of other DGs, fewer indiscriminate "pilot" projects and greater account taken of Programme evaluation. (Deloitte and Touche have just completed an evaluation of the 3rd MAP). Discussions for the next MAP (2001–06) are currently underway and the UK is very encouraged to note that these concerns are being addressed fully, and will continue to work with the Commission, through the MAP's Article 4 Committee, to ensure that rhetoric is translated into reality.

THE BEST REPORT

7. Most encouraging is the Commission's proposal that the MAP should take full account of the recommendations of the BEST report. This was a wide-ranging report from a taskforce of EU entrepreneurs and officials (chaired by Dr Chris Evans, UK) which addressed not only the "simplification of existing and new legal and administrative regulations in order to improve the quality of community legislation and reduce the administrative burden on European business" (as originally proposed by the Commission) but the wider issues which affect the capacity of SMEs to compete and to create jobs (as proposed by the UK).

8. The Commission has produced an Action Plan for following up the BEST recommendations and is now working with Member States to ensure that tangible and practical results ensue.

9. Amongst the 19 main recommendations, however, was the proposal that a central Better Regulation Unit under the direct responsibility of the President of the EU be established. This met with a negative response from the Commission. The UK will be reopening debate with the new Commission on this issue later in the year.

ACCESS TO FINANCE

10. Access to finance is a key issue for SMEs in the UK and across the EU. The Commission has introduced a number of measures to address market weaknesses. Recent initiatives include:

— the European Technology Facility Start-up to provide, through intermediary funds, venture and equity capital for projects for small businesses;

— the SME Loan Guarantee Facility, managed by the EIF;

— the Joint European Venture, to support the establishment of trans-national joint ventures within the EU; and

— an Action Plan to stimulate the provision of risk capital across the EU.

11. The UK welcomes the Commission's activities to increase the forms and sources of finance for SMEs in Europe, particularly so in the field of equity finance. We are anxious however that there should be a measure of coherence between the various measures and that they should complement work being undertaken in the UK.

THE FIFTH FRAMEWORK PROGRAMME FOR RESEARCH AND TECHNOLOGICAL DEVELOPMENT (FP5)

12. The Commission and indeed all Member States recognise the importance for all businesses, and especially SMEs, to get help with research and development through the sharing of costs and risks. The EU FP5 is designed to forge links between Member States and between industry and academia through collaborative and strategic projects. The participation of SMEs in the 4th FP was 66 per cent, double that of the previous programme. The Commission has set up a special Entry Point for SMEs to make it easier for them to apply for funding and to get rapid feedback on applications.

UK SME POLICY

13. The key principles of the Government's approach to SMEs revolve around:

— identifying and removing barriers to growth (particularly in respect of regulation);

— providing high quality business support for firms at all stages of development;

— providing and maintaining a supportive economic environment; and

— fostering a culture in which entrepreneurs and risk takers are acclaimed and rewarded and in which genuine business failure does not attract stigma.

14. Last year's Competitiveness White Paper set out the role Government and business needed to play in improving the UK's competitiveness. It outlined the importance of enterprise and entrepreneurship, of the knowledge driven economy, and of innovation. Following the White Paper, the DTI has announced proposals to establish an "Enterprise Fund" to support the financing needs of SMEs with growth potential.

THE SMALL BUSINESS SERVICE

15. The announcement earlier this year of a Small Business Service for England (Scotland, Wales and Northern Ireland have their own arrangements) also reflects Government commitment to SMEs. The consultation paper reflects that small firms find it harder:

— to access information and finance;

— to absorb the costs and risks of investment and R&D;

— to draw on appropriate skills and experience;

— to deal with regulation; and

— to influence Government thinking.

It also makes clear that the SBS will need to:

— act as a voice for small business at the heart of Government;

— simplify and improve the coherence of Government support for small businesses; and

— help small fims deal with regulation and ensure small firms' interests are properly considered in future regulation.

16. The SBS is to be set up as an Agency from April 2000. A Chief Executive is to be appointed this Autumn. An Advisory Council, independent of Government and composed of representatives of small firms and individuals with experience as entrepreneurs, will be set up to advise the Chief Executive.

17. The SBS will embrace all existing and future activities on behalf of SMEs. It will contract with local providers of business support services (probably around 50) to provide local support to SMEs. Existing Business Link partnerships will be able to put together a proposal to be the initial franchisee. Many Departments have an interest and involvement in enterprise issues and, to ensure "joined-up-thinking", the SBS will work closely with Government departments, the Regulatory Impact Unit, Better Regulation Taskforce, and also with the range of European institutions.

RELATIONS WITH OTHER MEMBER STATES

18. As part of its efforts to promote the cause both of SMEs and entrepreneurship, the UK has actively engaged, on a bilateral basis, with a number of other Member States, The Franco-British Taskforce, under Lord Simon and Christian Pierret of France, has been identifying and taking forward initiatives such as:

— training for entrepreneurs;

— business support;

— better regulation;

— access to finance; and

— electronic commerce.

The UK and Germany have been co-operating on innovation and enterprise issues. Two conferences have been planned on these issues, one in London in September, another in Germany in 2000.

19. The recent (4–5 July) Oxford based UK/Spanish conference on employment focused on the importance of flexible working practices, and there are plans for a group to be set up on economic reform. There is to be an Anglo-Italian seminar later this month and the idea of an Anglo-Dutch seminar on innovation and entrepreneurship is being investigated.

20. The EU applicant countries need to be involved in this process. A useful dialogue on competitiveness and enterprise issues has been started with Poland following Lord Simon's visit to Warsaw and DTI's involvement in a conference on SMEs and restructuring in Kracow.

INTERNATIONAL COMPARISONS

21. The EU needs to deal effectively with competition on a global scale and has a good deal to learn from other countries, notably the USA. Statistics on job creation speak for themselves: between 1970 and 1995, the EU added 8.5 million jobs, or 6 per cent of its workforce. In the same period the US increased its workforce by 46 million, or 65 per cent. In 1996, small businesses in the US created another 1.6 million new jobs.

22. The US/UK Conference on 2 July this year represented an opportunity to exchange ideas, and for the UK to learn about the US culture and way of doing things. The US is perceived to have a number of major advantages over Europe. These include:

— a more developed venture capital industry—one that is more ready to support high-tech, high risk businesses than the UK industry which, whilst ahead of the game in Europe, concentrates overwhelmingly on management buy-out activity. (The Enterprise Fund is being developed to address this issue in the UK; the Commission, too, has produced an Action Plan on risk capital);

— attitudes to enterprise and entrepreneurship are more favourable in the USA[3]; and

— there is more of a stigma attached to bankruptcy and business failure in Europe. In the USA business failure is regarded as a valuable learning experience.

CONCLUSIONS

23. The major issue for the EU remains competitiveness, which must be improved still further within the Union and globally if economic growth and job creation are to keep pace. Small businesses are the main vehicle of growth and job creation, and more concrete solutions need to be found to remove the barriers that impede their set up and growth.

24. Remaining barriers to trade in the EU impact particularly on SMEs. It is a Government priority to make the Single Market work better and a clear strategy with targets and regular monitoring is needed. The UK is pressing the Finnish Government and the Commission for a follow up to the effective Single Market Action plan which ran for 18 months until 1999.

25. The Commission's Dialogue with Citizens and Businesses is a welcome development, providing better access for business, and SMEs in particular, to information on opportunities in the Single Market and how to exploit them. This needs to be developed further and brought to the attention of all SMEs.

26. Mention has been made earlier of Commission initiatives on accessing finance which the UK broadly welcomes.

27. The Social Chapter clearly states that directives shall avoid imposing administrative, financial and legal constraints in a way that will hold back the creation and development of SMEs. This is not a perception of social legislation that the majority of UK SMEs share. Further work needs to be done to educate SMEs about the commercial benefits of minimum standards of fair treatment at work, whilst reducing as far as possible the costs for SMEs in time and other resources of implementing regulation.

28. The new round of European Structural Funds programmes (including the Social Fund) are currently under preparation for the period 2000–06. It is vital that the new programmes support the regional economic strategies and development plans of the Regional Development Agencies. If they are to have maximum impact on the eligible areas, it is essential that best use is made of the synergy between ESF programmes and other programmes and policies which impact on business competitiveness and development. The Small Business Service must work closely with RDAs and Government Offices in England to ensure that this happens.

29. The European Commission is now pursuing an agenda that accords strongly with the UK's own priorities for enterprise. The devil, however, often lies in the detail and the UK will continue to work closely with the Commission (seeking early opportunity to establish good relationships within the new Directorate General for Enterprise and the Information Society) and with other EU Member States.

Examination of Witnesses

MR MICHAEL WILLS, a Member of the House of Commons, Parliamentary Under-Secretary of State for Small Firms, MR NEIL MCMILLAN, Director of EU Internal Trade Policy and Europe, and MS MARIA KENYON, Director of SME General Policy, Department of Trade and Industry, called in and examined.

Chairman

178. Minister, you are very welcome, as indeed are your colleagues. May I just say two things initially? Firstly, it is now mandatory that we declare individual interests on these occasions. When it comes to SMEs, I think it is fair to say that every member of this Committee directly or indirectly has some connection with one or more SMEs. We have a list of our declared interests which I hope you have seen otherwise we will spend our entire session going through them. Secondly, I must emphasise that this enquiry is perforce a short one. We are calling it a paving enquiry. We are trying to look into what the EU is doing for SMEs and what, in our opinion, it should be doing and what it should not be doing. Our

---

[3] The Global Entrepreneurship Monitor, produced jointly by London Business School and Babson College in the US, showed that entrepreneurial activity was high (around 6.9 per cent) in the US, Canada and Israel, medium (3.4 per cent) in Italy and the UK and low (1.8 per cent) in Denmark, Finland, France, Germany and Japan. Furthermore, when asked "do you think starting a new business is a respected occupation in your community?", 91 per cent answered "yes" in the US, compared with only 38 per cent in the UK.

Chairman *contd.*]

successor committee might then pick this up as a major subject and get stuck into it. So, this is only a paving enquiry. Our objective is more to find the questions that our successor body should ask rather than find the answers now. After those two preliminary remarks, please be kind enough to introduce your colleagues—you do not have to introduce yourself because we know who you are. I should say, of course, that we have received the DTI memorandum for which we are most grateful. Undoubtedly our questions will home back on that to an extent but the floor is now yours.

(*Mr Wills*) Thank you very much. Before I introduce my two colleagues from the DTI, can I just say how much I welcome this enquiry. I think it is enormously important. Obviously I am biased as the Minister for Small Firms but these issues are incredibly important for the health of our economy. These questions have to be addressed in the European dimension as well so I think it is extremely welcome and I hope we shall be able to help you with your enquiry today. I should start with a note of apology. I am the Minister for Small Firms but for historic reasons, which predate my arrival there, within the DTI the European dimensions are dealt with by Lord Simon. My own detailed knowledge on these areas is therefore somewhat limited. I shall do my best to help, and I have brought two very able colleagues from the DTI to whom, if it is all right with you, I may turn for some of the more detailed information. Obviously, if any of us are unable to answer any specific questions we shall be delighted to write to you with more detailed answers. On my left is Maria Kenyon from small firms policy and on my right is Neil McMillan who deals more with the European dimension of small firm policy. I hope between us here we have got enough expertise to answer most if not all of your questions.

Chairman: Thank you very much. It was suggested that Lord Simon should come to give evidence to us but, at the very short notice, he simply was not able to come.

Baroness O'Cathain

179. Minister, on the point you have just raised, it seems to me incredible that, within the DTI, you should have one department dealing with small and medium sized enterprises and one dealing with the European dimension of small and medium sized enterprises. Surely this leads to confusion? Can I ask you a frank question: do you think it is the right way to go about it?

(*Mr Wills*) I should make it clear that actually the European department deals with the whole of Europe and all European issues as they affect DTI territory so it is not that. Inevitably, all government departments grow up geologically. We do not start with a blank sheet of paper at the start of each year. There has got to be a managerial issue all the time. These things are being constantly looked at within the DTI. So far, I have to say we have not found any divisions that arise out of this issue. Lord Simon and I talk about these issues all the time. We have set up mechanisms within the Department to make sure that separate sets of officials liaise together and work

closely together on these issues where—on the competitiveness agenda the officials who work to me and the officials who work to Lord Simon are now working jointly on how we can push that forward particularly under the forthcoming Portuguese Presidency. So I do not see any real issues. All I was saying was that, in some of these areas, Lord Simon is more involved day-to-day. I am sorry if I gave the impression that there was some great fire wall between us because there is not.

180. I did not think that at all because you said you brought along officials who actually deal with that side and that is fine. But it is a perception issue, surely. If I were a managing director of a small or medium sized enterprise and I heard what you said, that you deal with small and medium sized enterprises and the European dimension is done conjointly but not necessarily focused...? The reason I am asking this is because we had some very good evidence from the Hong Kong and Shanghai Bank earlier this week where we were talking about the need for small and medium sized enterprises to get out and export and be aware of the large European market. Euro-land is now embracing all those small and medium size enterprises and they, of course, now have a huge home market of nearly 300 million. Small and medium sized enterprises which, by their nature, tend to concentrate more on the domestic and national market would be caught out in the cold.

(*Mr Wills*) I absolutely agree with that. To round off the point, all Ministers have to do a large amount of representational work as well as policy work. Physically, no single individual could go to all the European councils and do all that sort of liaison with our European partners. Lord Simon has been involved in an horrendous list of bilaterals with all our European partners—if you are interested I can let you have more details. In the same way, I have to liaise with the small firm community. There are 3.7 million small firms and I am doing my best to touch some of them if not most of them. Organisationally, there is always going to have to be more than one Minister. I am a relatively new Minister still and, as far as I can tell coming in with a fresh pair of eyes, there are no big institutional issues. On the contrary, it seems to work particularly well on an official level and there is very close liaison on this. I feel awful that I have given you the wrong impression because I think it is the wrong impression.

Chairman

181. We will not pursue that too hard but Lady O'Cathain raised a very interesting example that I wanted to ask you about and that was exports. What help does the DTI give to British SMEs regarding exporting particularly to the rest of the EU?

(*Mr Wills*) I think perhaps if I could look forward rather than back because we are now just about to start a new stage in the way that we address this particular issue in both areas, as it were. In terms of the business support services that we offer small firms, we are now in the middle of the consultation period on the setting up of the Small Business Service. This is to bring together, streamline and make more coherent the delivery of business support

Chairman *contd.*]

services for small and medium sized companies. At the same time British Trade International has been set up as a joint DTI/FCO agency to promote British exports. We are now looking—and I have just had last week a meeting with Sir David Wright of BTI—at how we can make sure the Small Business Service and BTI absolutely dovetail in this area. Of course, Europe is going to be the key target area for us. As the Single Market develops and deepens, as it progresses, it is going to be critically important that our small companies—and the smaller the company almost the more important it is—are aware of the fact that we have a home market there with which we already do over 50 per cent of our trade and which is critical to their success. I can go on at some length about that but perhaps you will come back to that in a moment. We are deeply aware of the need to co-ordinate this. The Small Business Service will be charged with sign-posting the small firms towards the services operated by BTI. We are now exploring ways in which we can cement that relationship and make sure those two agencies work very closely together to do just the job that you referred to.

Lord Howell of Guildford

182. Minister, your memorandum begins with the words: "The challenges faced by European economies are very similar". That is true and not true. It is true at a very general level but, at the more specific level for SMEs, we seem this side of the Channel to be making rather a better fist of employment creation than Spain, Italy, France or Germany and doing rather better on deregulation and enterprise promotion than they are. I wonder whether that impression is borne out by the facts? Are we creating more start-up businesses and, if we are, what messages are we sending to Brussels about changing their ways rather than us adjusting to them?
(*Mr Wills*) I think it is accepted by everybody that small firms are critical to the health and economy and that they will be more critical in future. They have the flexibility and speed and adaptability that is needed in new global markets. As you rightly say, in this country we have a very vigorous commitment to competition, to minimal regulation, and to driving the spirit of enterprise throughout our economy and indeed throughout our society. The Government is taking a very wide range of measures to promote this. We think it is absolutely critical that our European partners sign up to the same agenda because we have no doubt that this is the way we are going to become competitive. If we do not sign up to this agenda and deliver it we will not do very well in the future. So I think we have a job to do. I think just as we still have more to do in this area so does Europe and I think we have to be very careful and very energetic in making sure that this agenda is delivered in Europe.

Chairman

183. Almost to follow up on that, do you think that there is a case for an EU agency in the context of SMEs?
(*Mr Wills*) Just to row back from that particular question for a moment, I think we have to be very

careful what the EU does as the EU and what Member States do. By and large, my own feeling is that the principles of subsidiarity have got to apply here. Although everybody signs up, as Lord Howell has just said, to the overall principles, there is a difference in how vigorously the principles are implemented. There are, of course, great cultural, social and economic differences within each Member State so every Member State has slightly different problems to tackle in tearing down the barriers to growth. Therefore, to think of an overarching agency, a European Small Business Service if you like, I think would not be a good idea. Nevertheless, I think it is very important that some initiatives are taken on a European level and there are forums in which we can drive forward the sort of agenda that we have been talking about. In terms of a European Small Business Service, the short answer is no.

Lord Brooke of Alverthorpe

184. Can we have a look at the other side of the coin on that? There is a general complaint that the EU does too much and there are too many regulations for SMEs. One of the recommendations from the BEST Committee[4] was that there should be a Better Regulation Unit established in Brussels and the Commission of course rejected that. In your evidence to us you are saying that you are intending to try to get that back on the agenda and seek to get it implemented. What will you be doing, how many allies have you got and what are the chances of getting the goods?
(*Mr Wills*) This is something that I have talked about briefly with Lord Simon to whom it will actually fall, so what I am going to do is hand over in a moment to Neil McMillan who will tell you in a little bit more detail about the day-to-day negotiations in Brussels on this. All I can say is that we think this is very important. The political gloss from a politician is that this is very important indeed. There is a central role for the Better Regulation Unit and Better Regulation Task Force here. The Prime Minister in all the efforts we have taken about modernising government has made it clear that he personally attaches great importance to this. Within the DTI, the Secretary of State attaches great importance to lightening the burden of regulations. We have already had two red tape summits and there are going to be more. We have launched a large number of initiatives already on how we are going to deal with this not only in removing regulation but making it more accessible and making it as minimal as possible. One of the fundamental remits of the Small Business Service is to help small firms cope with regulation. We know that regulation impacts particularly heavily on small firms. It is very important to our domestic agenda and Brussels cannot be immune from this in our view. A lot of regulations come out of there that affect us—many of them very, very helpful indeed. But we have to make sure that small firms are not disadvantaged in this. We think it is going to be crucial in ensuring that. I

[4] *Report of the Business Environment Simplification Task force (BEST),* European Commission 1998, ISBN 92–828–3418–2

Lord Brooke of Alverthorpe *contd.*]

will hand over to Neil now to talk a little bit more about the details.

(*Mr McMillan*) To add to what the Minister has said, the point that we very much supported out of the report on BEST was in particular to try to strengthen the voice of better regulation and taking more care on the regulatory impact of measures from Europe particularly on SMEs. We already have a system of regulation impact fiches which are attached to most legislation but I think most people accept that has not really worked in the way it should have done. Having a European Better Regulation Unit is an idea we very much support. We are also pushing forward under the economic reform agenda a very strong argument for better regulation throughout Europe both from the EU but also among individual Member States and looking at the burdens of business to try to create more employment through removing some of the barriers to people coming in or starting up new businesses.

185. Have we any allies lined up?

(*Mr McMillan*) Strangely enough, it is something which we have been remarkably successful in getting a lot of people to at least sign up in the first instance to the language. Our experience is if you get people saying the same things they start accepting the concrete measures a little bit later. Particularly since the British Presidency last year we have been remarkably successful in getting that assistance.

Chairman

186. Just picking up the dreaded word "subsidiarity", surely it is only worthwhile having any form of Directive or legislation from Brussels if that in itself is going to make the overall whole better otherwise the answer is no we do not want it. What is it that Brussels is doing or should do in that context? What is it that from a European point of view will make a lot of the SMEs better than a national initiative?

(*Mr Wills*) There is an overall answer to that question and there is a detailed SME answer. It is in every small firm's interest in this country that the Single Market works as a Single Market. It is not there yet and more needs to be done. So, clearly, anything that Brussels does to further that process will in the end be in our interest and in the interest of our small firms. Quite specifically, in relation to small firms, if I can just deal with the slightly negative implication in your question, we have to be careful (and it is not always the case that we avoid this) that European initiatives in this area are complementary to national initiatives. That is what I take to be the fundamental point. It is not always easy and that is something we have got to be aware of both as politicians and officials—that we are genuinely adding value. If we can now look at the positive side, what is clear is that the sharing of best practice, the undertaking of studies, research work and, as it were, the promotion of best practice among European partners is very valuable. There are things that can only really be done at a European level because the Single Market is so important to us as an economy. That includes small firms many of whom do not trade, although interestingly 45 per cent of SMEs

have some trading link with Europe so even the very smallest SME—the very small micro businesses—are increasingly going to be affected by what happens in those European markets. It seems to me that it is very important that there is a forum within which their interests are promoted and explored and they can learn from what European SMEs are doing and vice versa. It is in everyone's interests that this market works as well as possible. At that level, I think the European dimension is important and can add value, but subject to the caveat I said at the beginning, as long as it is complementary and does not displace or replace work that is more properly done at a national level.

Lord Skelmersdale

187. Minister, you said in your opening words that SMEs are incredibly important. During the course of this micro enquiry we have established that only four per cent want to grow. I must say I was rather surprised particularly given the figure you gave us just now that 45 per cent of small enterprises have exports.

(*Mr Wills*) Some trading link.

188. That is imports and exports so it is not just exports?

(*Mr Wills*) Some trading link are the words we use.

189. I half understood. However, you and the Department are putting an enormous amount of effort not to say quite a lot of money into small and medium sized enterprises. What are the returns you are getting? What do you expect? Will the Small Business Service do better than up to now—without you I might add?

(*Mr Wills*) If I may, I will take some time to answer the question because you have raised a lot of very important issues. I think the first thing to say is that I inherited a very good portfolio—a very well-managed portfolio. I am not sure I would accept the fact that we have been doing badly up until now. I think we have been doing well but I think the fundamental lesson that I take from all this is that we can always improve. We expect businesses always to keep improving, never to be complacent and government must be the same in what we do for small businesses. The whole purpose behind the Small Business Service is not to say we have reached this point with this constitutional mechanism and that is it—it works or it does not work. The whole mechanism is designed to be ratcheting up the performance. We have put in place in the consultation various measures which are designed to keep Government and the Small Business Service up to the mark. I will give you one example of that. We are setting up, no one asked us to do this, this is something I did particularly for this reason, what we are calling the Enterprise Council. This will be a users' council completely independent of government but tasked with reporting on the work of the Small Business Service regularly to the Secretary of State, with the assumption that that report will be used as the basis for an annual report in the House. This is a rod for our backs if we do not deliver—at our backs, politicians' backs and at the back of the Small Business Service. We will always have this

Lord Skelmersdale *contd.*]

Enterprise Council on which will sit representatives of small businesses, I hope some small businesses themselves, people who own and run them if they can spare the time, employees of small businesses and other expert and interested parties. That is a very powerful prod for us to keep our game up to the mark. What I am hoping we will see is a constant ratcheting up of our performance. There are other measures as well that we are exploring now and, at the end of the consultation, we shall see what comes out of all this. I am certainly determined to make sure that at such time as I move on (it might be next week, who knows) I will have left behind a mechanism that is going to be driving up performance constantly. You quoted this figure of four per cent—it is not a figure I am familiar with myself, although I am certainly familiar with the idea as I go around the country that many small firms say, "You keep talking about growth but we are perfectly happy; we just do not want problems". And I understand that and, frankly, as long as businesses are doing well and making profits, not every one of them is going to be a Microsoft that is going to dominate the world. What we want is a vibrant sector where people can grow if they want. That is the crucial thing. We are about putting in place, if you like, permissive structures. This is not interference or intrusion. We are not forcing things down people's throats. We are not demanding that they grow, but a lot of small businesses do want to grow and I think it is important to recognise that the growth can be taking on one new employee a year. If ten per cent of SMEs took on one extra person we would have an infinitely more dynamic labour market than we have got. It is pretty good as it is, but we can do even better. When people talk about high growth there is a very important sector of small firms which is high growth, often driven by technology and which we want to encourage and that is part of the remit. There is a whole raft, the majority of other firms that need help in other ways. We need to make sure that regulation impacts in the right way on small business. A lot of regulations do not have any impact at all. Food safety regulations for most small businesses are irrelevant. Some of them are very helpful in opening up competition. We have made 20-odd regulations to open up the telecoms market to more competition. That is a good thing for small companies. It opens up more possibilities for small and medium sized companies there. The compliance burden is disproportionately greater for small firms. The job for the Government and the Small Business Service is to ensure that that is lightened. That is something we will do for all small firms whether or not they want to grow. Small firms may start out deciding they do not want to grow at all. It is what we refer to in the Department as a lifestyle business, the freedom to be able to organise their own lives, and that is great too. We want to give people opportunities and choices. That is the over-arching mission of the Government in every area that we do. Helping people set up a small business even if they are never going to employ more than one or two people. That is part of the Government's job: to help them at the start, not to subsidise them. If they get it wrong, if they identify the market wrong, if they do not put in the work that is needed, that is their lookout. We are not there to

bail them out but we are there to say, "If you want to do it, here is some basic guidance on how you run a small business. Here is a map through the process of setting it up". We are pretty good in this country. In Austria, I was told it costs something like £30,000 to £50,000 to set up a small business. 99 per cent of our businesses could not afford that, you need to really think about £50,000 if you are starting up from nothing, but we can do better in this country too. When you look at that figure of four per cent we need to be there for them but we also need to be there for all those other businesses as well because they change over time and their aspirations change over time. I came across a company—you did start me off so I will carry on if I may.

Chairman

190. Not at too great a length. There are a lot of other points.
(*Mr Wills*) One last example, if I may though, because this is very important. I came across a company that had been going for twenty years the other day, a man and his brother selling what was called non-lethal riot control equipment.

Baroness O'Cathain

191. Coshes.
(*Mr Wills*) I did not enquire in huge detail into what this was but what they told me was that, for nearly twenty years, they had trundled along perfectly happily employing three or four people and nothing had really changed. They had come across the Internet through a DTI local support centre and thought this was a good thing and got on to it and to cut a long story short they had realised that their whole business could be transformed by this. They are now growing at an exponential rate. They now supply the US Army with virtually all their non-lethal riot control equipment and requirements. They are exporting to Zambia and all over the world now. That is an example of a company that has been changed through a government mechanism. They went along to a local support centre and the business has changed and grown in a way they could not have foreseen even five years ago.

Lord Berkeley

192. Minister, I have been interested in your DTI brief, paragraphs 5 and 6, because it does appear to me that the European Commission is actually doing virtually nothing for SMEs. If you take 128 million euros over four years it is something like £20 million a year spread across every European Member State. It is not very much and, if it has been successful, I would suggest it must already have a targeted approach because it could not do anything else. One minute you have talked about subsidiarity as being a good thing and you have then produced this new Cabinet Office Guide to European Regulations[5] that some of us were sent yesterday which is a very glossy, shiny thing telling you Ministers how to do your job

---

[5] *The Guide to Better European Regulation,* Cabinet Office 1999.

Lord Berkeley *contd.*]

and suggested it should apply Europe-wide. When it comes to SME help, I think the line of your argument was it should be left to each Member State. I put it to you that the Commission could be quite useful with the Small Business Unit in checking on legislation that comes forward through the Commission and making sure that it does not adversely affect the SMEs but also probably more importantly checking that other Member States are implementing the policy. You mentioned Austria and £30,000 to £50,000 to set up a business and I think other Member States may be the same. Is it because we think it is best to leave it the way it is because Britain has an advantage because it can do what it likes and we have not got setting up costs like that and you do not want the Commission to have a greater role in these things?

(*Mr Wills*) The short answer to that is no. Where this can be devolved to a national level, it should be. A lot in my answer to Lord Skelmersdale are things that can only be done at a national level and often at a sub-national level where, appropriately, they look particularly to us for delivery at the regional and sub-regional level, and I think that is proper. There are things the Commission can do, which I referred to earlier, promotion of best practice and so on and that is something that can properly be done on a European-wide basis. I also think I referred earlier in my answer to Lord Howell to the fact that it is very important that everybody in the Community recognises how important these issues are for their own countries and their own SMEs. That is an agenda we are driving forward in Europe. We do think the Commission will benefit from having a Better Regulation Unit and that is why my colleague was saying we want to push for that. We think we are making some progress there. There is no question of us wanting to keep our competitive advantage to ourselves. Our competitive advantage in the end has to be a global one and that can only be built on a properly functioning Single Market where everything is open to enterprise, flexibility and all those issues around competitiveness that you and I have been referring to.

193. Surely the Commission needs a bit more budget to do this than £20 million a year spread over all the Member States?

(*Mr Wills*) Money has to follow function. Let's get the agreement on the function first and then worry about the money.

Viscount Brookeborough

194. Minister, you stressed that the Small Business Service and the DTI/Foreign Office policy will go very far in helping these companies but you have also said that businesses can come to you and you must make it more accessible. How are you going to give businesses information when they are not necessarily looking for it because they are frightened by the European regulations? Secondly, you have already mentioned DTI local support services, the business links which may disappear and our chambers of commerce and so on and people simply do not have time for that. How are you going to put it in a way that is fully translated from Europe and is freely available to them?

(*Mr Wills*) I wish I could give you a 100 per cent guarantee that it is all going to be fine in the future because it clearly has not been in the past—and I cannot. This is the thing that I am most concerned about in all this. How do we reach that great mass of firms who can benefit from all this but are too busy, have got their heads down all the time and cannot raise their sights up? It is very hard running a small business.

195. This is where the high proportion of growth or exports would come.

(*Mr Wills*) Absolutely right. To be honest, any ideas anyone has got on this would be welcome. I have lots of ideas. I do not know if they are going to work. I am going to keep trying is all I can say. We know the current Business Links reach only a very small proportion of the people they should be reaching and also by definition they are reaching the wrong people. Once you know enough about your business to know that you are going to need support you are actually half way there. What we need is people who do not know that they need this advice and support to become more competitive and know what they have got to do. That is the problem. Let me give a couple of examples of the sorts of things we would like to see. We have got in the Department very good brochures, things I inherited, I claim no credit for this at all, very clear, simple brochures but we have to find ways of getting them out to people and opening their eyes. I want to look at the ways in which we use the existing mailing mechanisms to small firms, perhaps working with banks—most small firms do bank, they do get regular statements—to try to see if we can persuade the clearing banks to help us promulgate things. The Inland Revenue and Customs and Excise also have contact with small firms. They may not be the best cultural vehicle for delivering supportive information in the world but we know that large numbers of them are reached. I am looking at ways in which we can make things accessible—not just to give worthy documents out. One example—I will not dwell on this for much longer unless you want me to—is to try to send out through various mechanisms anecdotal case histories, to try to persuade prominent business leaders, Richard Branson if he has the time, to give us a case history, a little anecdote from their own business past, which will exemplify some bit of business wisdom, managerial wisdom that all small firms need to know but with a signposting at the end if they want more of this—"Here is the Business Link number to call". We are trying to reach them in more sophisticated marketing sense than we have up until now. At the moment I am worried that although we do our best, in a sense we are saying, "Here it is, come and get it if you want it", and not enough people know that they need to want it.

196. How do you prioritise your objectives? Is number one new employment, people taken off the dole, start-ups or what? Secondly, you quoted Austria as being £30,000 to £50,000 per business start-up which is not totally valid because it depends on the value of the business. How much does it cost per job created in this country?

Viscount Brookeborough *contd.*]

(*Mr Wills*) That is a very difficult question to answer. I am not sure I have the information here. We will find out for you and let you know. We will write to you. I suspect methodologically it is going to be quite difficult to come to a very precise answer on that.

197. Priorities?

(*Mr Wills*) In terms of priorities there are three priorities for the Small Business Service that we have put in the consultation document which are: a strong voice within Whitehall, help with regulation, and streamlining, and more coherence of delivery at sub-regional and local level. Those are the overall priorities. We have various priorities set out in the White Paper about helping potential high growth businesses. We have specific sums of money targeted at them. There will be other tasks given to the Small Business Service about helping, for example, self-employment in deprived areas and so on, but in a sense what we are trying to do is not to say this kind of small firm is more valuable than that kind of small firm but we see our role as much more to support small firms at every stage of what we call the ladder of opportunity. We know that small firms do not grow in a straight line. They grow very jaggedly if they grow. At every stage of growth there is a barrier and whether you move from unemployment to employment to self-employment that is a big step. If you move to self-employment and take on your first employee it does not sound much to anyone who has never run a small business but actually taking on responsibility for somebody else's mortgage as well as your own is a huge cultural shift. The time that their own manager decides that they need new equity in the business and to have to give some of it away, that is a huge cultural step. At every stage of that we think there is a role for government to be a support, not to insist, not to impose, but to support. In a sense, that is what our priority is—to be there when we are needed and not otherwise.

Chairman

198. Not surprisingly we have already ascertained in evidence that on the subject of regulation the problem is as much time as inclination to read. We have a situation, not taking any party sides on this, where the United Kingdom opt-out of the Social Chapter has come to an end. Could you comment please on the impact of European social legislation on SMEs? Does that legislation contain sufficient safeguards and exemptions?

(*Mr Wills*) I think just a note about the Social Chapter. It does state that measures that would constrain small firms should be avoided so I think we should start with that. Of course, that is not the perception of the Social Chapter, I have to say. I think there is a great deal of worry among small firms that European legislation is going to hobble them.

199. How are these constraints going to be avoided? Wonderful words, but how is it going to happen?

(*Mr Wills*) This is a process that we are embarked upon. We have to make sure that it does not happen. Our priorities have to be to ensure that any new legislation promotes labour market flexibility, it promotes more employment and it actually develops competitiveness. We have got to make sure that it does not place excessive burdens on United Kingdom businesses. We have to make sure from the outset that they are developed with the needs of small businesses to the fore. In Europe just as much as in this country we have to think differently about small firms. Too often in the past—this is true of Britain just as much as Europe—small firms were being ignored. Regulations have been put in place for perfectly good, valuable reasons and we would not want to remove the regulations without thinking through the consequences for small firms. We have a remit for the Small Business Service of think small first. We have got to make sure that happens in Europe too.

200. Will you succeed?

(*Mr Wills*) We have got to succeed. This is not a static problem. The problem is changing all the time. Twenty or thirty years ago the importance of small firms in the economy was quite different for reasons that I think are probably familiar to everyone on the Committee. Small firms are more and more important and this will grow in importance to a dynamic and successful economy.

Lord Berkeley

201. Could you give some examples of where new regulations have been drafted where small firms have been excluded for reasons like that?

(*Mr Wills*) Neil?

(*Mr McMillan*) On the whole I do not think you have very many examples of where small firms have been specifically excluded. In some cases where there is a regulatory burden there are measures that perhaps have slightly different approaches to larger and smaller firms. If one takes some of the Directives under the Social Chapter and indeed the things that preceded the Social Chapter some of them do not apply to companies under a certain size.

Chairman

202. If you could find such examples would you be kind enough to write to us? I am still conscious of the time and five more members of the Committee want to ask you questions.

(*Mr Wills*) If I can give one example. The Packaging Waste Directive exempts small firms with a turnover below £1 million and it has just been increased to £2 million. If I may make one quick comment on this. It is not just exemptions that help small firms. They can be valuable but they can also be a barrier to growth. If you have an exemption at a certain level, there is evidence to suggest firms do not like going above it because they see it as a barrier. What often is more important is making sure that the systems are in place and the regulations are easy to comply with for the very smallest firms and there is real assistance to do so. That is the sort of thing we are putting in place, things like the automated payroll service, and we have also got to make sure that the way regulations are implemented is sympathetic to small firms, which is one of the reasons behind the changes we have made to the

Chairman *contd.*]

Working Time Directive. We are looking at regulations to make them simpler to apply.

Lord Montague of Oxford

203. Minister, we know you are getting out and about and meeting lots of small companies. That is one of your roles, to be on a continual fishing expedition. I want to get a little bit nearer to what it is you are hearing. I am sure you are trying to find out what their concerns are in relation to Europe. Can you give some indication of what you have personally been hearing from some of these small companies?
(*Mr Wills*) Inevitably it varies.

204. Some of the things you have heard?
(*Mr Wills*) Let me give you an example. In my own constituency which is North Swindon, which is not necessarily representative of every constituency in the country, in many ways it has got very special circumstances, many firms are very hungry to get into Europe. They see it as a great opportunity and they want us to be pushing the kind of reform agenda that we are pushing.

205. I cannot imagine a small firm coming up and saying, "Minister, how lovely to meet you. I hope you are pushing this." What are they actually saying, the nuts and bolts?
(*Mr Wills*) "We want to get into Europe. How do we do it? How do we exploit the opportunities? What are you doing to make sure these barriers come down? We want to get in there." That is what they are saying.

Chairman

206. What do you do, send them more bits of paper?
(*Mr Wills*) I do whatever they want me to do. That is what I am there to do. If action is needed, I try to think how we do it and if they need information I give it to them.

Lord Montague of Oxford

207. Some examples of what they actually say?
(*Mr Wills*) Let me give you the other side of the coin as well because that is not all I hear. That is my constituency and that is a very strongly held view among many small businesses in my constituency. In other areas of the country there is undoubtedly amongst small firms a worry about Europe. It is often among those small firms who have least contact with Europe, I have to say, that there is the great worry that Europe is out there waiting to be a problem for them. They see Europe as something to be resisted and fought and there is huge anxiety that Brussels, which they see as some sort of monster, is going to spew this horrible torrent of regulation which is going to get in their way and interfere with their lives.

208. You have not heard a range of things about which businessmen are saying, "This is affecting my business adversely"?
(*Mr Wills*) Interestingly, what they say often in this case is, "We are very, very worried about things." You say, "What are you worried about?", then they say, for example I have had this a lot, "We are very, very worried about the impact of the Working Families Tax Credit", which is not a European regulation but this is something that was particularly driven home to them and I think the general point of principle often applies to European regulations also. I said, "What worries you?" and they said, "The Working Families Tax Credit is really affecting us". I said, "You do realise this is not going to have any impact on your business even if you have workers who are going to be affected by it until next April?" and they suddenly realise this is something they are picking up around them. It is not affecting their business at all. I ran a small business for 14 years before I became a Member of Parliament and I am therefore, I hope, particularly sensitive and empathetic to their concerns. I know from my own experience, and I speak only personally, that when I worked I worked all the time, seven days a week, worried about every bit of business I had in to make sure I was doing it right and what I was going to get in next time. Anything that impinged on me I did not have time to find out about it but I did not want anything to get in the way of that. I had too much else to worry about. I think that is often the attitude among small firms who are most worried about Europe. As I say, it is often those who have least contact with it. I do not wish to sound complacent about what needs to happen in Europe because I am not. There need to be real changes. We are not sufficiently competitive as a country in a global context and neither is Europe and we need to drive that agenda through here and in Europe. I do not want there to be any doubt about that. I think a lot of the anxiety I pick up on is based on a misperception of what Europe is about. It focuses always on what are media myths about Brussels. I am not saying there does not need to be change, there does. There are too many myths promulgated about how the system works and too little on the real opportunities there are for our small companies in Europe. The Single Market is a fantastic opportunity for our small companies and many of them need to raise their sights, see what is there and take advantage of this—and we are there to help them. Inevitably it depends on the company.

Lord Methuen

209. I would like to raise the question of mutual acceptance of standards. You state in your paper that Community-wide acceptance of product standards has led to manufacturing efficiency, but we had an earlier witness who complained bitterly that although he had BSI certification of his product it was totally unacceptable for the German market

Lord Methuen *contd.*]

because it was not acceptable to the German standards authority and hence he could not export to Germany. He had other problems elsewhere in Europe. What are you doing about that?

(*Mr Wills*) There are a number of issues around harmonisation of standards. This is not an issue I deal with personally so it may be helpful if Neil could take you through the various actions we have taken.

Chairman

210. In the interests of time if you have an answer on that could you write to us? This is a very important issue and it is not just one witness who brought it up. We are very anxious to know what the answer is. There seems to be a mismatch on standardisation and acceptance.

(*Mr Wills*) We would be delighted to write to you. Can I just say it would be very helpful to us if we can get access to what you have heard.

211. The relevant extracts we have had on that?

(*Mr Wills*) Not only the general points but also the specific points and if necessary we will see what we can do to help individuals because there may be specific things we can do to help.

Lord Howell of Guildford

212. We have not mentioned taxation which is, in fact, the most important issue of all to business. What are you getting in the way of complaints and what have you been doing about them for improving the VAT system and not being too driven by the requirements of the EU, which are very strong? Secondly, most micro businesses are currently in uproar at the moment over the renewed attempts of the Inland Revenue to turn consultants and people providing a service to a firm regularly into employees, allegedly under pressure from the EU. Is that right and what are you doing about it?

(*Mr Wills*) You are referring to the IR35 issue in relation to that?

213. Yes.

(*Mr Wills*) On that particular issue it is a simple measure. I should say first and foremost that this is a matter for the Treasury. I have to say that. Let me give you an answer as far as I understand it—I would hate to be thought by the Treasury to be pre-empting their territory. My understanding of this is that it is a measure designed to deal with tax avoidance. It is the Revenue's job to close loopholes. I think we would all agree with that, but we have to do it sensitively in line with what the situation is on the ground. We must be aware of unintended consequences in dealing with avoidance. I know for a fact that there has been extensive consultation on this particular measure over the last few weeks. As far as I am aware, the Treasury and the Inland Revenue are now considering what response they are going to make to all the consultations. I have written from the DTI to the Treasury about this issue and obviously we will continue to take a keen interest in it.

Lord Montague of Oxford

214. Could I draw the attention of the Minister to the exchange that took place in this House the night before last on this issue? He will find it very revealing[6].

(*Mr Wills*) Thank you. On the question of the overall tax burden, of course all businesses and particularly small businesses are worried about the tax burden. They always have been. It is always with us. Very interestingly, I saw some research two days ago from the Manchester Business School[7] which shows that the burden of taxation on small firms has fallen steadily and this takes in all the aspects of it, all the payments out including UBR, VAT, corporation tax but also compliance costs as well. It shows a very marked fall for very small businesses and also for slightly larger SMEs as well. I would commend this to the attention of this Committee because it is extremely interesting work.

Lord Brooke of Alverthorpe

215. A very quick question, going back to your previous engagement as a small businessman. We have got TV programmes about doing up the car, doing up the home, when are we going to have some TV programmes about starting up your own business?

(*Mr Wills*) I absolutely agree with that. I must declare a personal interest because when I ran a television production company—that was my small business—I made programmes about business which I found fascinating. These did pretty well in terms of audiences, and did fantastically well in terms of advertising. It was mainly in the late 1980s when there was a huge amount of interest and a great entrepreneurial buzz. Unfortunately, this is quite clear, there was a bitter recession which knocked the entrepreneurial spirit out of hundreds of thousands of people. People lost their houses, and television just backed off it at that point. That, incidentally, without wishing to dwell on this point, is why this Government is so committed to stability and the Chancellor says at every turn that we must avoid that situation ever happening again. Television lost interest.

216. We have a public service channel.

(*Mr Wills*) We have the BBC and I would hope the BBC is going to do this. They have begun to show some interest in this. It is wonderful television. I speak as a former television producer. It is full of drama. It is incredibly important to the enterprise culture in this country. Everybody could see through television—which is their living room friend—how rewarding a career in business can be.

---

[6] During Committee Stage consideration of the Welfare Reform and Pensions Bill, House of Lords Official Report (Hansard) 20 July 1999, col 921 et seq.

[7] *The Impact of the 1999 Budget on Small Firms in the Economy,* Manchester Business School, The University of Manchester.

Baroness O'Cathain

217. I was going to make an observation. We talk about small and medium sized enterprises and the problem is we are trying to impose upon enterprises a non-entrepreneurial spirit in terms of far too much regulation. I was horrified when I heard about the Enterprise Council because to me it is a type of National Audit Office. Can we try to relax some rules because they stifle all this entrepreneurial spirit?

(*Mr Wills*) I seem to have made a habit of misleading you this morning. It is absolutely not a National Audit Office. It is going to consist of people who are doing the job and people who represent them.

218. That is taking them away from doing the job. It takes more time.

(*Mr Wills*) But we have to know what they think. They have to tell us. How are we ever going to get it right unless they tell us?

Chairman

219. Are you not getting it from the Federation of Small Businesses? Are you not getting it from the CBI?

(*Mr Wills*) Yes. They have got lots of jobs to do in relation to government and this is a specific task for them. If they are too busy to take part, that is a matter for them. We want the forum to be kept up to the mark and surely you must want that too. We need to be kept up to the mark and they will do it for us.

220. On that note I think we must stop, sadly, because I think we could go on for at least another hour without any problem at all.

(*Mr Wills*) I certainly could.

Chairman: We are very grateful to you and your colleagues and also for the fact that you will be kind enough to write to us on a couple of points we have raised.

Baroness O'Cathain: And anything else that strikes you.

Chairman: We have not got enough time.

Supplementary memorandum by the Department of Trade and Industry (DTI)

Public Expenditure Per Job Created Through Establishment or Growth of SMEs

There is no overall figure for public expenditure targeted specifically at SMEs. You may find this a little surprising but it stems from the fact that much of the support we provide is open to firms of all sizes. Furthermore some of the ways in which we are helping SMEs—for example getting the regulatory environment right and creating stable economic conditions—cannot easily be costed.

Of course the DTI takes great care to evaluate regularly the effectiveness of individual programmes. For example a recent evaluation of the Small Firms Loan Guarantee Scheme (SFLGS) estimated that the cost per job was somewhere between £9,500 and £16,600. This range reflects the problems of estimating which jobs would have been created anyway, and the extent to which new jobs created displace existing ones.

The aim of programmes such as the SFLGS is to help SMEs become more competitive, by removing barriers to finance and encouraging innovation and growth, and in the long run creating sustainable employment. In this respect a simple "cost per job" calculation does not do it full justice.

Examples of Regulations Tailored to Meet the Needs of Small Firms

The examples given below are all either legislation introduced or commitments given by this department over the last two years.

The examples can probably be split into three broad categories. The first is regulation intended specifically to address problems faced by small businesses. Probably the best example of this is the Late Payment of Commercial Debts (Interest) Act 1998 which entitles small business to the interest on their debtors' late payment.

The second category is where special provision has been made for small businesses, most commonly through exemptions. Examples include:

— businesses with 20 or fewer employees will be exempt from the statutory union recognition provisions of the Employment Relations Act 1999;

— the Competition Act 1998, which was in itself broadly deregulatory as it replaced the bureaucratic restrictive trade practices legislation, provides for immunity from penalties for SMEs. It recognises that it would be inappropriate and burdensome to apply the maximum 10 per cent of UK turnover for infringement to small undertakings. The Department will consult on orders setting turnover limits for this purpose;

— the Department has recently consulted on proposals to raise the threshold beneath which companies can file abbreviated accounts with Companies House, and is committed to consulting on proposals to increase the threshold above which accounts need to be audited; and

— in the Consumer White Paper (Cm 4410) published last week we gave a commitment to exempt smaller shops from the requirement to unit price pre-packaged quantity-marked products where it would be an excessive burden.

In the longer term, one of the key issues for the Company Law Review, which is due to be completed in 2001, is the range of legal forms available for business. In the consultation document *Modern Company Law For a Competitive Economy: The Strategic Framework*, published in February this year, the Company Law Review Steering Group said that they were inclined to favour radical restructuring of the legislation, treating the small company as the basic entity and adding on the relevant requirements for exceptional, larger and more sophisticated entities in further discrete layers.

The final category is harder to define, but would include regulations that, while they do not distinguish between small and large businesses in terms of requirements being placed on them, are implemented or amended in such a way that the benefit will be felt particularly by small businesses.

In this category we would include the amendments made to the draft National Minimum Wage regulations in response to business concerns, which reduced the record-keeping requirements. We would also include measures such as the Patents (Fees) Rules 1998, which reduced patent fees by approximately £9 million in a full year. Major reductions were made to renewal fees, weighted in favour of the early years when patent holders, especially SMEs, are harder pressed. Abolition of the patent filing fee had the effect of increasing access to the patent system for all, but particularly SMEs.

DIFFICULTIES CAUSED BY THE LACK OF MUTUAL RECOGNITION OF STANDARDS

Mutual recognition of standards where harmonised standards do not exist is a cornerstone of the Single Market which allows for increased market integration and greater variety of products on offer whilst cutting business costs. It facilitates the free movement of goods within the Community and can only be waived by Member State governments under strict conditions involving overriding requirements of general public importance such as public health, consumer or environmental protection. Any such waiver must, however, be both necessary and proportionate: the importing Member State must show a product poses, for example, a risk to health and any ban eliminating that risk must have the least effect on intra-Community trade consistent with achieving that aim. The Department has a special unit—Action Single Market—which assists businesses facing unjustified legal barriers in other Member States to resolve. For products covered by harmonised legislation—such as those which require CE marking—it is unlawful for Member States to require other local standards to be met and Action Single Market can also help in such cases (although it is unable to help if the requirement is nothing more than customer preference, ie not a legal requirement in the Member State).

However, there is clearly room for improvement and a recent European Commission business survey highlighted problems with mutual recognition as a key barrier to trade in the eyes of business.

Following a request from the Internal Market Council last year, the Commission has recently submitted a Communication analysing difficulties faced in connection with the application of the principle of mutual recognition[8]. The suggestions include better monitoring and improvements by national authorities of the application of mutual recognition, improved case management by the Commission and increasing awareness among citizens and economic operators of the principle.

In some cases preference for local standards may stem from lack of awareness of the principle of mutual recognition which is why raising that awareness is so important. We are treating the follow-up to the Communication as a matter of priority within the Internal Market Council and, more specifically, within the context of the Commission's new Single Market strategy which should be agreed by the end of the year.

Memorandum by Mr Lorimer Mackenzie, EC Director for Enterprise Policy and SMEs

1. 99.8 per cent of all enterprises within the European Union fall within the definition of a small or medium sized enterprise as used and recommended by the Commission. Currently, our statistics suggest that only 35,000 out of more than 18 million enterprises are outside the definition. Consequently, any policy which seeks to address the needs and interests of small and medium sized enterprises, by definition, must address the problems of enterprise as a whole. For this reason the Commission has, over the last two years, not only adopted a clearer horizontal enterprise policy within which the specific requirements of certain sectors and size groups are dealt with, but it has also strengthened the services concerned by twice reinforcing the Directorate-General for Enterprise Policy and by creating a group of Commissioners chaired by the Commissioner responsible for enterprise policy to co-ordinate the delivery of the objectives of enterprise policy by other Directorates-General. The grouping together of the services responsible for enterprise policy,

---

[8] Communication from the Commission to the Council and the European Parliament—Mutual Recognition in the Context of the follow-up to the Action Plan for the Single Market (COM(99)299 Final). An Explanatory Memorandum (9430/99) was submitted by the Department of Trade and Industry on 19 July 1999.

industrial policy and innovation into one portfolio on enterprise policy under the new Commission appears to be a logical extension of this trend.

2. Enterprise policy must be a comprehensive policy for all enterprises, regardless of size, legal form, sector and location, but with particular emphasis on Small and Medium-sized Enterprises (SMEs). While their (small) size is often a weakness, they have the advantage of being flexible, innovative and able to adapt rapidly to changing circumstances. Indeed, almost all enterprises in the European Union are SMEs and account for 66 per cent of the total employment and more than half of the turnover.

3. The focus of enterprise policy is not on direct financial support for companies but rather on the improvement of the environment, in all its aspects, in which businesses operate. As a consequence, enterprise policy is essentially a horizontal policy where co-ordination is critical, covering every level of public action— Community, national and local—and every policy which impacts on enterprises.

4. Given the great diversity of enterprises, the overall objective of enterprise policy can only be realised through carefully targeted goals. These objectives are currently the improvement of the business environment, access to finance, the provision of a number of information and co-operation networks as support services, pilot actions addressing specific problems faced by SMEs and co-ordination with other policies as well as with Member States.

5. These objectives are implemented through instruments such as concerted actions with Member States (the aim of which is to promote mutual consultation and exchange of best practices), through Community policies either specific to SMEs (such as those contained in the current Third Multiannual Programme) or through more general policies such as the Structural Funds or the 5th Framework Programme for RT&D.

6. Although these objectives remain valid, enterprise policy has to take into account new challenges arising from the current economic context and be an integral part of a dynamic process tackling current issues and identifying those which help to anticipate enterprises' needs. This implies looking at new areas of action such as the link between innovation and competitiveness, the introduction of new forms of technology and forms of organisation, the increasing globalisation of markets (including the special issues of consolidation of the internal market through EMU and the challenges of enlargement, new and expanding markets based on new demands), and the further liberalisation of trading and services regimes. These will provide opportunities and challenges to all enterprises and entrepreneurs.

7. Concerning the tools used to implement enterprise policy, new instruments will have to be developed, such as best practice adoption and benchmarking, in the systematic improvement of the business environment. Existing successful instruments such as the Euro Info Centres Network, the Round Table of Bankers, will also have to be further developed. Following the example of the Business Dialogue 'One Stop Information Shop' (ie the Commission's new website), new feedback mechanisms, such as Internet discussion groups, will permit individual businesses and business organisations to engage in dialogue on policy development and implementation.

8. Targeted objectives for future enterprise policy are:

— To continue actions that encourage the development of a business environment in which enterprises and entrepreneurship can flourish.

— To promote entrepreneurship as a valuable and productive life skill, identifying barriers which impede entrepreneurship, proposing remedies and encouraging business skills at all levels of European society, and in the education systems of the Member States.

— To offer valuable and efficient support services to enterprises through a range of instruments such as information networks and electronic networks, to be used by enterprises and entrepreneurs.

— To prepare enterprises for the challenges brought by the next enlargement of the European Union, so that businesses and entrepreneurs both from the Member States and the pre-accession states can be smoothly integrated in an enlarged competitive environment.

9. Particular attention will be paid to small enterprises employing less than 50 people, which account for 52 per cent of all employees in the enterprises of the EU, and craft enterprises, the majority of which are small enterprises (small and craft enterprises are, as a whole, less vulnerable to business cycle fluctuations). Statistics show very clearly that new jobs in Europe are created mainly in the smallest enterprises.

10. Finally, the diversity of our actions is such that we have to be closely involved in the work of our colleagues in other Commission services. For example, new management techniques and the evolution of working practices have a direct impact on the competitiveness of SMEs. Therefore policies relating to working conditions and employment guidelines require close attention. So too do RT&D policies, where the successful transfer of RT&D results into the productive process is essential for improving competitiveness. Similarly, regional policies, through the application of the structural funds, also have an impact.

Examination of Witness

Mr Lorimer Mackenzie, EC Director for Enterprise Policy and SMEs, called in and examined.

Chairman

221. Mr Mackenzie, you are very welcome. I am getting concerned about the size of that suitcase and whether it is full of material. Are you going to blind us with science and keep us away from our job? Thank you very much for taking the time to come and give evidence to us. I do not think you were here at the beginning of the Minister's evidence so, if I may, I will repeat two points. First, we have an obligation nowadays to declare our interests. You have, I hope, been given a sheet of paper where we have written down our interests because inevitably on the subject of SMEs to a greater or lesser extent all members of this Committee have a direct or indirect association with one or more SMEs. The second point is that this is a paving enquiry to try to tease out more questions than answers on what it is that the European Union is presently doing for SMEs, what should it be doing and, equally relevant, what it should not be doing. It is a short enquiry. It is not, sadly, one of considerable depth. My first question, if I may, is the same as the one I asked of the Minister, using that awful word "subsidiarity". What is it that the European Union can do for SMEs in Member States that the Member States cannot themselves do?

(*Mr Mackenzie*) A rather vast question, although a simple question, my Lord Chairman. May I first of all reassure you that although this case is full of documents, I have no intention of reading them out or referring to them all. I thought it might be useful for the Committee to have access to these documents for any research that you may wish.

222. Thank you, that is very helpful.
A. I would like some time to situate the policy framework of what our policy is, if you will permit me five minutes. On your first question, the most important thing we believe is that we should not be undertaking any actions which do not provide added value at the European level. Indeed, the multiannual programme, to which we will no doubt make reference, specifically says that the funds which are allocated to the multiannual programme may not be used, it puts it in a positive rather than a negative aspect, for activities which can be carried out by other European policies, for example Structural Funds, the Research and Development Fund, nor which can be better carried out by the Member States. This is something which we wish to adhere to. To put it bluntly, the small business voice is difficult enough to hear anyway for people in central authority, whatever the central authority is, to understand the problems and to deliver results. The last person in the world who could impose a solution on a small business is a bureaucrat sitting in Brussels. That is the attitude that we would like to begin with and I hope we can deliver on that.

223. You said you would like to set the scene, if you could do so as briefly as possible, I think you heard the problems we have on time.
A. I will try. As I say, I will send a typed copy of this if I speak too quickly for the shorthand writer.

224. With respect, if you have a typed copy can we take that as read[9] and get into the question and answer session? We find that immensely helpful.
A. May I just make one point, because you have raised it in your question? 99.8 per cent of all enterprises in the European Union come within the definition of the small and medium sized enterprises.

225. 99.8 per cent?
A. 99.8 per cent. We have more than 18 million enterprises and according to our latest statistics only 35,000 of these are not SMEs.

226. We have heard similar figures before.
A. In these circumstances an SME policy is by definition an enterprise policy. You cannot have an SME policy which looks at just this particular group of SMEs or that particular group of SMEs, it has to be an enterprise policy across the board and within that enterprise policy you have to identify the specific problems of specific groups, like the micro enterprises, the high tech group, the high growth, young entrepreneurs, etc, etc. You will see in my statement that the development of the last two years of the Commission policy has been to have an enterprise policy with targeting rather than trying to target everything that everybody is interested in and somehow by the back door arrive at a coherent policy.

227. If I understand you, that is targeting by section on SMEs, by micro, small and medium. Is that what you mean?
A. Targeting by need. The very small enterprises have specific needs; the high growth companies have specific needs; high tech companies have specific needs; women entrepreneurs and young entrepreneurs who are still discriminated against in some areas, they have special needs. We have to look at what the problem is, but we need to have a coherent platform upon which we can launch specific policies. Simplification should apply to all the business community. The fact that it helps a smaller business more than a larger business is part of the gain, but the larger business should not have unnecessary burdens imposed on it any more than a small business should.

Lord Methuen

228. I would like to raise the question of harmonisation of standards which is something that you may have heard me mention with the Minister. We had this example given to us of a person who had BSI certification and yet Germany would not accept his product because he had not been certified by German standards. What are you doing about that? This is critical.
A. We are doing quite a lot. First of all, you have pinpointed exactly the reason for the Community being involved in standards at all and harmonisation of standards. There is no particular virtue in harmonising standards if it does not help competition and indeed overcome restrictions on

---

[9] This memorandum is reproduced on pp 55 and 55 above.

Lord Methuen *contd.*]

competition which are established in national markets. You quoted a very good example. We have been trying to establish standards in areas where that is obvious. We do it by consulting with the industry. We do it with expert committees on which industrial companies put experts and we try to come to some agreed standard which can apply across the board. A lot of the internal market legislation in the industrial sector is specifically directed to try to overcome these problems. The greater problem now is that this is not just a Single Market issue, it is a global issue because there is a global market in many areas. Therefore, we have to be in a position to make sure that European industry does not only respond to its own demand but to global demand. We are not content just in saying "here is a standard, stick to it", but we involve businesses – and, increasingly, small businesses – in discussing what the standards should be and how they should be set up. We are also giving a priority, and this will be an increasing priority in the next year and in future years, to the whole question of the management of the supply chain from the final industrial user to the small business that produces components, inputs services, etc. There is a real problem here of the evolution which is taking place in purchasing. Some years ago a purchaser, a big company, let us say Ford motor company, would say "we want cogs of such and such a size and of such and such a tensile strength, that is it, can you supply them?" That is less and less the case now. What is happening is that the big companies are saying "this is the kind of product that we want, what can you produce for us?" and they are putting the responsibility on the smaller business to do the research, the technological innovation and produce the standards. That is one big change for the smaller business world. We have to be involved in helping them to adjust. We have a programme inside the multiannual programme called, for historical reasons, subcontracting. We will produce a Communication this year on the problems of subcontracting and what we are going to do about it. You will find that, in my case here, there is a report of the last forum we had on the problems of subcontracting[10]. We are also doing studies on benchmarking, both in industrial sectors and in service sectors. We have just received a consultant's report—I have not yet read it—on benchmarking the tool-making industry. Why the tool-making industry? We import 70 per cent of our machine tools.

229. When you say "we" do you mean the EU or the United Kingdom?
A. The EU. I am used to putting it at a European level. We are importing 70 per cent. We need to benchmark to make sure that we are globally competitive. There is a lot of work at different levels going on.

Chairman

230. That is not answering Lord Methuen's question. What is the EU doing about mutual recognition of national standards? That is the complaint that we have got from witnesses.

A. There are two things. One is if you have a clear case of a national Member State not respecting mutual recognition then the Commission can take action against the Member State.
Chairman: How long would that take, as an example, from the first complaint to the resolution of the problem?

Baroness O'Cathain

231. And what would it cost?
A. It depends very much on the kind of complaint and the level of interference with the market.

Chairman

232. I am sorry, that is ducking the question. It is a fair answer but it is still ducking the issue. You have a small, maybe a micro business—let us call it a small business because micros are less likely to be in this position—that gets into the position of which we were given a specific example. Basically that individual, as a generalisation, cannot afford either the time or the money to go pursuing this case. What is it that the EU ought to be doing to achieve this mutual recognition of national standards?
A. What we have done is we have legislation and, where there is no legislation, mutual recognition applies. That is the law as it stands. In all situations where a problem arises because of non-conformity with the law then you have to make the complaint so that the law can be implemented. How that is done is through the Member States' professional associations, the industrial associations, particularly the sectors, Members of the European Parliament, and writing direct to our Single Market Directorate General in Brussels or the Competition Directorate General in Brussels. There are various ways of approaching this. We have a business website now which is available through our information centres in the United Kingdom, as in all other Member States. It is an on line site where you can get information on any Single Market legislation and you can feed back into the website with questions about your particular business[11].
Chairman: That is interesting. Thank you.

Lord Berkeley

233. Continuing on this vein, I am first of all surprised that this multiannual programme has got such a small budget. It cannot do a great deal for the equivalent of something like £20 million a year spread throughout the Member States. In particular, does it see its role as not only resisting legislation, be it European legislation or Member States' implementation of legislation which would adversely affect small business, but actually looking at the more positive side of additional legislation like late payment—because there is a big problem with late payment of small business—and the protection of intellectual property? It seems to me that there is a positive and a negative side. My second question is

---

[10] *Proceedings of the Second European Forum on Subcontracting*, Graz, 5–6 October 1998.

[11] One Stop Internet Shop, http://europa.eu.int/business/en/index.html

Lord Berkeley *contd.*]

we have heard from the previous witness, the Minister, about the Better Regulation document[12] which some of us have just had a copy of and I quote one thing in here, my Lord Chairman. It says that Ministers talk to small firms and take their views into account, which is good. You were saying that there is some resistance in Brussels, among other Member States, to having a similar Better Regulation Unit in Brussels. Is that so? Would you be prepared to name the ones which are resisting or shall we guess?
A. All of them.

234. Except Britain?
A. Except Britain, Denmark and maybe the Netherlands.

235. The usual.
A. We have introduced a Directive on late payment and a version has been agreed by the Council of Ministers. It will be referred to the new European Parliament in September for decision and with a bit of luck we will have a Directive by the end of this year or the beginning of next year. It will have to be translated into United Kingdom legislation but since we were in close contact with the United Kingdom Government before we drafted ours and they drafted theirs, there will not be too much adjustment in the United Kingdom legislation I am glad to say.

Baroness O'Cathain

236. Is that a promise?
A. I am not responsible for the United Kingdom Government but it is the best that I can say at the moment.

Lord Berkeley

237. Not bad.
A. For the other legislation, we are trying to work on intellectual property and there shall be more Communications coming out on that area. That is an area that we recognise. As far as business organisations are concerned, I am not terribly happy about formalising our relationships with these business organisations. We meet the European level business organisations which include UNICE, which is the CBI equivalent, EUAPME, which is a small business grouping, with Chambers of Commerce, Euro Commerce, which represents the distributive trades. We meet them about once every six weeks and we do not just say "this is what we are doing, now you are informed", we bring around people dealing with the Structural Funds, environment legislation, social legislation, and explain to them what is happening so that they can go back to their members and say "this is what the Commission is considering, what do you want me to tell them?" and then they come back and tell us what their problems are. On the Better Regulation Unit, first of all we have contacts with the Better Regulation Unit in the Cabinet Office. The question is at what stage do you say in a legislative process "this Better Regulation Unit refuses to permit you to pass this legislation"? The only

organisation I know which has that power is the Advocate for Small Businesses which depends on the White House, where the President is allowed to veto legislation which has too great an impact on business on the advice of his Special Advocate attached administratively to the Small Business Administration but actually politically attached directly to the White House. I cannot see any way of avoiding the fact that, if Parliament passes legislation, changes legislation, does things which maybe the administration does not want, we can say after, "you have made it far more complicated than it was originally and it does not work any more". We believe that the way to do it is to start with simplicity at the beginning. The guidelines for the Commission's Business Impact Assessment System, which has been much criticised, starts off by re-stating that legislation must take account of subsidiarity, it must be proportional and you must look at the impact on the economic and social structure of the environment. Why do we do that? Because it is at the stage of creating the legislation that you can have the biggest impact, not at the stage of monitoring it when it is already drafted, because there is a vested interest amongst all managers in defending their own brief. So if nothing arrives at the Better Regulation Unit until whatever department of state has already drafted its legislation it is already too late.

Lord Howell of Guildford

238. Does the European Union see itself as having a role in promoting and facilitating e-commerce or is that something that is best left to national governments?
A. Different levels, different interests. At some stage or another we will almost certainly have to consider what kind of ground rules we are going to put into the Single Market for using e-commerce. We believe in promoting it because we believe that not only does it give greater opportunity within the Single Market but it obviously gives greater opportunity in the global market. We believe that small businesses can overcome some of their obstacles of having only local markets through the Internet, through e-commerce. The basic problems are three-fold. One is training and making people aware of the opportunities. The second one is confidence because everybody buys books from Amazon but, if I were to put "L Mackenzie, Brussels" on the Internet and say I would send them books when they send me the cheque, I do not think many people would want to purchase from me. You have to have a name—you have to have a brand image. We are trying to consider how we can bring SME organisations together to provide confidence for the business. Then, of course, there is the whole question of legislation. I hate the word legislation in this context because it suggests we are going to impose another huge bulk of legislation and that is not the case—but there are certain ground rules that have to be worked out so that you do not have differences of opinion or differences of law in France, Germany, Britain, etc. The other problem, and it is a major problem, is cost. Telecommunication prices in

---

[12] *See* Q 192.

Lord Howell of Guildford *contd.*]

the European Union in many countries are far too high.

239. You mentioned the fact that this is a global issue, as indeed was the issue of standards raised by Lord Methuen. Is it not a bit of a worry that more and more of these things are global issues and/or national government issues and it is getting very hard to see what added value the EU has to contribute to this global structure rapidly emerging?

A. Precisely because it is a global issue, e-commerce and the rules surrounding e-commerce are very much part of the continuing dialogue with the United States and Japan. The White House, again, has got a special ambassador who deals with nothing but e-commerce, which gives you an idea of the importance that the United States puts on this issue. In Europe as a whole we have to give it a similar importance, we cannot do it with 15 Member States running to the White House asking what legislation they should introduce. Europe must stand together and produce legislation which gives all industry an opportunity to compete on a worldwide basis.

Lord Skelmersdale

240. Mr Mackenzie, you have been talking about yourself and your organisation in the context of the Commission as a whole being pro-active. To what extent are you and your organisation reactive, for example in terms of the last VAT Directive? Did you make representations on behalf of small and medium sized enterprises from your perspective, a legislative perspective?

A. I am not sure if we did in that particular one.

241. Or social legislation?

A. Social legislation, yes. I see almost all the comments coming out of my department to other Directorates General on legislation and I suspect something between 30 and 40 per cent of the consultations involve us saying "we would like you to adjust it in this or that particular way to take account of business needs or certain aspects". You will find scattered throughout the legislation, environmental legislation for example, where the environmental thresholds are at a level which effectively, although it does not mention small business, eliminates small businesses from application. You will find exemptions for size of business. The Accountancy Directive, for example, exempts small firms but not on the basis of the European definition, on the basis of different levels of turnover and profit.

242. Is that not an inhibition on growth of SMEs which the Minister suggested to us only a few minutes ago?

A. I do not think so. I think there are levels at which you have to recognise that the burden is proportionately too great in relation to the good and that is what we are trying to do. At a certain stage the burden becomes too great in relation to the good so you try to reduce the burden but you will never eliminate it entirely.

243. So you are saying that the Minister was wrong when he made that comment?

A. I did not hear him make that comment so I would hate to contradict the Minister but I would be very willing to enter into a discussion with him or with his representatives in Brussels.

Lord Montague of Oxford

244. Mr Mackenzie, you are in a unique position to see all the Member States at work furthering their small businesses. I am wondering how—Britain apart—you rate other countries in terms of their activity in the small business area. Do you think this is particularly effective? What prompts you to identify whoever you may be identifying?

A. That is scarcely a fair question to ask somebody who is responsible for 15 countries. Let me tell you the good countries, if you like. Let me tell you the ones where you will be able to look and find examples here or there of how they organise things which are beneficial for a small business. The Irish Government in the last two or three years has introduced so many measures for simplifying the environment and improving the environment for small businesses that small businesses are booming. I think that is a good example to look at. The Netherlands have been looking at legislation and helping in the taxation field. The Danes, for example, have a social security system where they do not distinguish between paying social security payments and normal tax commitments. It is all wrapped up in the same tax, which you may think is far away from the interests of small business until you realise that a large part of small businesses' time is taken up with filing social security returns as well as tax returns. So, in Denmark, it is much more simplified. There are little pockets like that you can find around the EU. The training in Germany is superb for businesses except it is totally untransferable to the rest of Europe because it is a very German system and it is based on restrictions on participating in certain trades. But, if you want to be trained as a master plumber who can run a plumber's enterprise well with good quality workmanship and all the rest of it, the best place to be trained is in Germany.

245. It is rather restrictive because, if you have not got their certification, you cannot trade as a plumber.

A. Exactly, that is why I say it is totally untransferable to the rest of the EU.

Chairman

246. Mr Mackenzie, I would like to come back to a point I made earlier on. Why does the EU produce any legislation at all? It can only be if it is for the greater good over and above that which Member States can do. For good and proper, or very obvious, reasons one of the main messages we have been getting is that particularly micro businesses do not have time to read the reams and reams of legislation. You have just given a very good practical example of how Ireland is trying to simplify this. My question is why should any small or micro business read any EU Directive at all? Why do they not just wait to read it nationally?

A. If they are just looking at the final effect on themselves, there is probably no reason whatsoever. If they are looking at it from the point of view of what is likely to happen when they hear that this is

Chairman *contd.*]

becoming an issue it is different. For example if they hear, let us say, that we have to legislate in the field of e-commerce for data protection, if we have to do something on data protection, anybody in the e-commerce line who is running a data bank with customers may want to know what might be proposed before it actually comes through. They can then make representations to the Commission before the legislation is actually proposed. We consult the business community through their organisations. We try to find out from them what is worrying them before we make the proposals, not try to tell them what is happening afterwards. That is an essential part of our procedure. That is what permits me to say to some of my colleagues on things that I know nothing about, like VAT or what have you, "you have got it wrong, the business community is telling me the following" and when we look at it we feel that the business community are right and we are wrong. That is where the Directives come in. That means not so much that somebody sitting in his garage somewhere in England wondering what the Directive on pollutants is going to mean for him has to read the Directive, what he needs to do is to make sure that his industrial organisation, or his Chamber of Commerce or whoever, has found out or made sure that they are hearing from the people who represent them in Brussels – because most businesses have got representatives in Brussels one way or another – that they are on the ball and saying "what is this Directive all about?". They only do things through intermediaries. I speak to very few small businesses, I speak to an awful lot of intermediaries.

247. Do you favour an EU agency for small businesses?
A. No.

248. Why not?
A. Because you would have exactly the same situation with an awful lot more bureaucrats.
Chairman: Thank you. I like the reply.

Viscount Brookeborough

249. Mr Mackenzie, the umbrella of SMEs is vast, 99.8 per cent of all businesses, but it also covers a host of entirely different kinds of businesses. Multinational companies with thousands of people are entirely different from large SMEs who have different problems and there are different problems in medium and micro. Their problems are entirely different from people who do not yet have a business but need to start up. Yet SMEs is a term being used by the EU, and therefore by the national governments, covering such a vast myriad. When we have had other witnesses in I have felt that a lot of their responses have been very vague—they want to start up more businesses, they want to help them into Europe, they want to ease the burden of bureaucracy. Do you think that categorising so many things as SMEs causes a problem for national governments in trying to focus on issues involved with each of them? For instance, I am a micro business. I would not necessarily go to my local Chamber of Commerce because I know that the people who are involved are bigger businesses with 30 or 40 people but they probably talk about issues that involve me. This is

exactly the problem because, for micro businesses and people who want to start up, there is not somebody to look after them. I know if you divide them all up you are going to end up with so many agencies that it is not possible, but perhaps we have got the categorisation of SMEs wrong?
A. If you will permit me, when I arrived in 1996 in my present job one of the first things that struck me was that too much of the policy was, "add the phrase 'particularly SMEs' on to the end of everything and you have solved the problem". I then started speaking to the organisations themselves and saying "this is just like ten years ago when anything came up and we said 'and women' because of the problem of discrimination against women, so as long as you said 'and women' the problem was solved". The result has been that, by simply ignoring that there was a problem, ten years later you have to pay three times more to solve the original problem than you would have done if you had tackled it in the first place.

250. We are paying 128 million.
A. Yes, indeed, but as I say we are horizontal, we work through intermediaries, we do not give money to these businesses. The result of that is when you make the analysis, make the precise analysis, if they are all SMEs why have we got an SME policy? We need an enterprise policy. You will find that the language has changed. We need to encourage the spirit of enterprise, we need a culture of enterprise. We need to talk about enterprises and we need to talk about the environment of enterprises. We need to train people in the idea that entrepreneurship is a professional skill in itself.

Baroness O'Cathain

251. Exactly right.
A. It is even going on in the United Kingdom. Since 1992 north of the border in my native territory there has been a scheme run by Scottish Enterprise in primary schools to teach children of five or six years old what entrepreneurship is about—where they get them to start their own businesses with their own ideas and their own products. The commitment is there in this Member State and in other Member States. The problem is trying to bring it together and to see who does what and where the real problems are: access to finance, venture capital and all the rest of it. The small garage does not need venture capital, does not need an equity loan. But if an IT company that wants to develop parts has not got venture capital or equity, it is dead very quickly. These are the sorts of things where we have to say "let us provide the environment, let us make sure that we are doing things where businesses feel comfortable". We cannot do it from Brussels, we have to do it with the Member States. We are doing it through a process called Concerted Actions where we sit down with Member States and identify best practices. We sit down with Member States and we examine certain things, start-ups, the transmission of businesses, support services for businesses, try to identify best practices, try to benchmark so that Member States are learning from each other and developing different techniques for delivering services themselves to their small businesses. That is the kind of work we are

Baroness O'Cathain *contd.*]

doing targeted on specific problems but always in the context that if you have got the environment wrong to begin with the rest of it is just playing on the fringes. That is why I do not think it is any accident that we set about two years ago under President Santer and Mr Papoutsis, the Commissioner in charge of enterprise policy who was made the Chairman of a group of Commissioners, to co-ordinate all the enterprise policy objectives across the board in research, social policy, financial policy, regional policy, etc. As I say, it is no accident to me that Mr Prodi has proposed putting all of the industrial sector, the innovation sector and the enterprise sector into one portfolio. Now we have arrived at the stage of an enterprise policy with particular reference to SMEs, not SMEs with particular reference to whatever else is going on.

252. You mentioned access to finance. Is it really a big problem for SMEs in the European Union? If it is, what pressure can you put on financial institutions to make it easier and make them more aware of what you call the enterprise culture, or else is there another way which is to give subsidies? If you do that then you cause a distortion. Are they given and do they cause a distortion?
A. There is a general reluctance to consider subsidies in the EU but we know that. There are special rules. There is an ECOFIN decision on taxation incentives which came out this year simply to void this question of distortion of competition. We are trying to address different problems at the different levels, encouraging equity holdings, setting up a network of business angels, trying to encourage venture capital. Venture capital is one of these strange things. The United Kingdom, Netherlands and Sweden actually have a higher venture capital ratio per capita than the United States—but Germany, France and Italy have a particularly low one in comparison. It is a European problem if you take it at a European level but, individually, it is not such a problem. Venture capital is terribly valuable for certain areas but not for everybody. Seed capital is vital. The Prince's Youth Business Trust will set up an enterprise but will not give them any more than £3,000 for example. That is a very small price to pay if you could get that enterprise set up and running. They do most of their work using mentors, business managers from industry, retired people who help youngsters or handicapped people or ethnic minorities to develop their business and get them through the start up stage. It is another variant of doing the same job. We are interested in that and we have pilot projects in this area to see how we can encourage it. Credit unions or mutual guarantee societies are other ways of ensuring that you can provide capital which the banks will not provide to very small businesses. In addition to that, we have what is called the Round Table of Bankers and SMEs. That brings together banks, accountants, mutual guarantee societies and representatives of the small business community to discuss the problems at a European level as to why certain things are not happening.

253. Does anything happen after that talking shop?

A. Yes. I think things have gradually eased. To some extent we have realised, and this may not be surprising, that there is no one solution right across the board, that some sectors are more sexy than other sectors as far as bankers are concerned, that risk aversion is a standard practice in all banks particularly at the moment when they are subject to mergers, takeovers and consolidation. We cannot affect that level of the economic climate, but we can identify where risk aversion is perhaps not justified and then the banks can adjust. We are also finding that financial institutions are as interested as we are in diversifying the availability of different forms of financial support. I was very surprised when I was called by a British bank to ask about studies on social credit unions, "it is a commercial bank, what is it interested in social credit unions for?". They wanted to become involved in social credit unions. The banking community itself is open to knowing how it can resolve this problem.

Chairman

254. How do public procurement rules fit into that particular mesh?
A. Unlike the Minister I will not say I am not responsible for public procurement, although it is true. What I can say to you is that on public procurement there are problems. We published a White Paper[13] in March 1998 and we will publish a Communication on public procurement in SMEs later on this year. I am afraid I cannot tell you exactly what it will contain.

255. I am not looking for privileged information but, in your opinion, are SMEs disadvantaged at the moment in that context?
A. I do not think they are disadvantaged by the way the market works but by their own organisation. Other than locally—locally it is a different matter—SMEs tend not to look at big public contracts because (a) they are not big enough, (b) they do not have the experience and very often they have to have three years of experience of contracts of this size or whatever. They have another characteristic, which is something that we will have to help them to get over, which is that they do not like co-operating with anybody else.

256. They do not like what?
A. Co-operating with anybody else. Public procurement is an area where even the big public procurement companies co-operate with small companies, they have their own not necessarily subsidiaries but sub-contractors who they use regularly. So there is a question of organisation. There are certain other problems too which we have come across in other countries which the countries themselves have been dealing with. How do you get over this? From what I understand at the moment, and here I am speaking without the full knowledge of the recent research on public procurement, I do not think it is a question so much of the legislation which governs public procurement or the openness of public procurement, although that might be a

[13] *Public Procurement in the European Union,* European Commission, COM(1998)143.

Chairman *contd.*]

problem in particular instances, I think it is really a question of small businesses saying "it is too complicated, it is too much bother" or "it is too big for me". It is getting over these two attitudes which we have to address. If they are just attitudes, although we are not psychologists, we can put into place systems which help them to overcome these attitudes, make it easier for them to overcome these attitudes, and that should be done.

Lord Montague of Oxford

257. You stated that you tend to rely on consultation with Chambers of Commerce and with trade associations, I think that was what you said.
A. Amongst others, yes.

258. Do you think that British companies are as well represented in Chambers of Commerce and trade associations as other Member States? I know, for example, that in Germany it is mandatory to be a member of the local Chamber of Commerce but we do not have anything like that. Do you think that puts us at a disadvantage? I am not suggesting that we should make it mandatory—I am not fishing for that answer—but are we actually disadvantaged because we do not encourage a sufficient number to be members of trade associations and Chambers of Commerce?
A. No. I have a personal prejudice in favour of the British system of Chambers of Commerce. When I go down to speak to a Chamber of Commerce in France I could just as easily be speaking to an official of the DTI—in fact, it probably is an official of the DTI. That system does have disadvantages on the question of representation. Britain does have one problem. We are well represented at Chambers of Commerce level. The previous Chairman of the Euro Federation of the Chambers of Commerce, Euro Chambers, was British. We are well represented in UNICE, which is effectively a European run CBI. We are well represented in sectoral areas, trade areas like industrial areas, the production and manufacturing sectors, the electricity industry, distributive trade, etc. Where Britain is not badly represented but is under-represented at the European level is on small business organisations. We do not have quite clear organisations which represent small businesses particularly. We have two which are very active, both of them at the European level I may say, but with two completely different outlooks and with completely different partnerships and alliances at the European level which of course has a consequence. The British voice is very often two voices.

259. Which is the European state that you regard as best in that particular role?
A. I could not point to any of them. I understand that some of the Scandinavian countries have formalised consultation. They have the same sort of voluntary membership as the United Kingdom of these organisations but they formalise their discussions to a higher level. I am not sure that formalising these discussions necessarily helps. From my point of view it is far better for me to go and have lunch with the Secretary General of one of these associations and ask him to react to a problem which we have, or to say "do you really agree with what the

Commission is doing, what do your members say?" and he can say "I will come back to you in a week". That seems to me to be as good a way of getting information out of somebody as sitting down at a committee meeting where everybody sticks to a script because they dare not speak otherwise.

Lord Berkeley

260. You mentioned UNICE and the CBI. Does the CBI actually claim to represent SMEs within the definition in a big way? I did not understand that, but maybe I am wrong.
A. Yes, they do.

261. Do they?
A. Yes. They do not claim to represent them exclusively but they do claim to represent SMEs. It is probably correct, given the definition, that they represent as many, if not more, SMEs as any other organisation.

262. That is why there is a difference of opinion between the two groups. It must be very difficult.
A. The two groups I was thinking of are the Forum of Private Business and the Federation of Small Businesses. Neither of them are linked to the CBI and both of them say different things.
Lord Berkeley: Thank you.

Chairman

263. Mr Mackenzie, you have been very tolerant with us and we are extremely grateful, but I have a last wrap up question. All the evidence that we have had in this enquiry, and indeed in others, has emphasised the importance of the Single Market. You rightly started off your evidence with the huge percentage of business within the European Union that falls within the SMEs. What is it that really needs to be done to encourage SMEs, if one could take them as a block, and we are already querying that, we doubt if that is a homogenous block but leave that to one side, what can be done to encourage SMEs to take advantage of the Single Market? Dare I say it as the last question, to what extent is the euro important in that?
A. The answer to your last question is that it will become increasingly important. In fact, it is already important. If you have tried to transfer money or buy any foreign currency in Europe all the transactions are now carried out in euros, so the euro is already beginning to have an impact even on the consumer. It will be vitally important in tourism, and increasingly important in tourism, both incoming and outgoing. The currency exists so, inevitably, it will become more and more important. What can we do to encourage the SMEs to be interested in the Single Market? Part of it is simply a perception problem. I started by saying "we" referring to the EU and then replying to Lord Montague I started saying "we" meaning the United Kingdom. It is a perception problem that there is this market here and the Single Market over there. There is not a Single Market over there, this is the Single Market. Unless that perception is constantly projected to British business, they are always going to think that wisdom and

Chairman *contd.*]

economic sagacity stops at Birmingham or Glasgow or Manchester; they will not get out of the idea that the market which their company is supplying is in fact potentially 350 million people. The second thing—we do a little of this, we do not do a huge amount because we have got a small budget—is we do have specific events called Partenariat Events. We also run INTERPRISE events which is a partnership at international level. We also run what we call *Salons Renversés* which are really fairs but instead of people coming to market their goods we bring together purchasers who are looking for goods saying "this is what I want" and we send the suppliers in to look and see if they can supply any of the goods.

264. How long have you been doing that?
A. At least five years, I think.

265. Have they been growing in success?
A. The *Partenariat, Interprise* and the *Salons Renversés* are regarded as very successful actions. It is a colleague of mine who runs them. They identify a sector and they say "we want to get European companies who are active in this sector to come together and see if they can set up partnerships". To avoid this business of setting up a subsidiary or an agency outlet in other countries, they go and say "here is a firm which is doing precisely what I need to be done in this country, so I will make my introduction and then we will market each other's products in our countries". These have been quite

successful, *Partenariat, Interprise,* where we link them with neighbouring countries, and *Salons Renversés.*"[14]

Lord Montague of Oxford

266. Do we have them here?
A. Yes, they are held here. They have been held here. I do not know when the last United Kingdom one was. I think in 1997 there was a Partenariat event in Glasgow but I do not know if there have been any since then.

Chairman

267. Mr Mackenzie, thank you very much indeed. I am sorry that I shut you off in your opening remarks but we have had virtually an hour of questions and answers, and that is the real benefit we get in these sessions. We will read your opening comments later, with great interest.
A. And the other documents, my Lord Chairman.
Chairman: Of course, and the other documents. Thank you very much indeed, Mr Mackenzie.

[14] The witness subsequently added:
The programmes Europartenariat, INTERPRISE (initiative to encourage partnership between industries and services in Europe) and IBEX (International Buyers Exhibition—*salons renversés*) are designed to stimulate and facilitate international co-operation between SMEs and between SMEs and large enterprises. In the framework of these programmes events are organised that bring together heads of enterprises for face-to-face meetings at pre-arranged business gatherings with a view to negotiating partnership agreements.
For example in a Europartenariat event about 2,000 enterprises on average from 60 counties will participate. These events cover different sectors. In INTERPRISE the average number of enterprises is between 100 and 150 from at least three Member States of the EU. These events are targeted on one or two sectors. IBEX or *salons renversés* target one particular sector or a special category of enterprise which are linked through the supply chain.
All these programmes are available to candidate countries.

TUESDAY 27 JULY 1999

Present:

Berkeley, L	Howell of Guildford, L.
Brooke of Alverthorpe, L.	Methuen, L.
Brookeborough, V.	O'Cathain, B.
Geddes, L.	Skelmersdale, L.
(Chairman)	

Examination of Witness

HERR HANS-HERMAN JÜRGENSMANN of Deutscher Industrie- und Handelstag (DIHT), called in and examined.

Chairman

268. Herr Jürgensmann, you are most welcome, as I have had the pleasure of saying to you before: for the record, I now say it again. We are particularly grateful as I understand you have made a specific effort to come just for today—courtesy of British Midland Airways. Are you returning, incidentally, by British Midland at all?

(*Herr Jürgensmann*) No, by British Airways. It is all British.

Chairman: I advise you that Lady O'Cathain is a director of British Airways. So any problems you have, please address them to Lady O'Cathain.

Baroness O'Cathain: Please forget that dig.

Chairman

269. You are most welcome. You are aware of the enquiry we are just towards the end of, in fact. We are doing a paving enquiry into SMEs in the European Union, as to what the EU is doing for SMEs, what it should be doing and what it should not be doing, with a view to our successor Committee (that is the Committee that will be in existence from November onwards) if they wish, to pick up the subject again and do a full enquiry. Could I ask, first, a very simple question? We have the definition of SMEs as described by the European Union, which deals, as I am sure you know, with the number of employees, from micro, small, medium and then large. Is your definition within the Federal Republic the same?

A. My Lord Chairman, first of all, I would like to thank all of you for the kind invitation. It is a great honour for me to be here and I hope to be able to answer all the questions you have. To start with the first one, the DIHT does not have a definition of what small and medium sized enterprises cover. It just uses a working definition because there is no legal or official definition, just a working definition which you need for some state programmes. This definition has two criteria: the first one being the turnover and the second one being the number of people employed. According to those two definitions all enterprises fall into the category of being small and medium sized if they have a turnover of 100 million per year—

270. One hundred million what?

A. Deutschmarks.

271. I wondered whether you had gone into euro yet.

A. Not yet; later we will transfer it to pounds or to euro. In addition, up to exactly 499 people employed. That is our working definition. However, what is much more important for the DIHT as criteria is not a quantitative number but it is the quality. According to this, enterprises count as being small and medium sized if the entrepreneur takes his own money and puts it into the company he runs, and if he acts independent from the state and if he acts on the market in heavy competition. This qualitative criteria differentiates between an entrepreneur and a manager of a big concern. This is what really counts. So, even if a company has only up to 500 employed and a turnover not exceeding 100 million, then it can be small and medium sized if the owner takes his own money and runs the company and if he does it completely independent from the state. So what I would like to get over is that not quantitative criteria count but qualitative criteria. The EC, as you know, has a different notion and a different understanding. They have the criteria you mentioned, and this does have some severe effect on the German economy and small and medium enterprises. For example, the criteria of 250 people means, for German companies belonging to the branch of industry, that 3,000 German industrial companies may not apply for a programme of the EEC that is for subsidising development and research—the Fifth Framework programme for development and research.

272. I think you are saying that 3,000 are between the 250 and the 499.

A. Yes, they may not apply for this programme because they do not fulfil the criteria of just having up to 250 employees. This is, maybe, the real effect if you apply such strong and merely quantitative criteria.

273. Let me ask you two questions related to that. As I understand it, the DIHT do not try at all to break down below the 499 employees and 100 million Deutschmark ceiling. You do not try to define micro, small or medium — you just have one block.

A. That is right. We call it "*mittelstand*" but there is no translation that means "small and medium sized". But we do not break down into middle sized, smaller, smallest and so forth. We do not do this.

Chairman *contd.*]

274. Second question: what percentage of German industry falls within your criterion?

A. When we apply our working definition, then more than 98 per cent of all companies fall into the category of being small and medium sized. They account for approximately 80 per cent of all places for apprenticeship (that is very important because we have a dual system of vocational training) and they account for approximately 70 per cent of all working places. They give approximately 55 per cent of Gross National Product and 45 per cent of all investment. This is the quantitative meaning of small and medium sized enterprises.

275. If you—which you do not—were to use the EU definition and you came down to 499 to 249 employees, what percentage within German industry would be covered? You said over 98 per cent, but what would that drop to? Have you any idea?

A. No, we have not made this calculation.

Baroness O'Cathain

276. That is extremely interesting, but it does beg the question, Herr Jürgensmann, of what are you doing about it if you feel disadvantaged in terms of not getting the grants etc for research or whatever? My first question is, what would you do about it? Secondly, in view of your position with the DIHT, and you obviously have links with other European Union members, is what you have described to us applicable in any other EU Member State, or is it just a German phenomenon?

A. Your first question is "What would you do?". I would ask "What have we done?" — we have tried to bring our understanding of larger criteria to the EC, but we did not succeed.

Baroness O'Cathain: Were you on your own?

Chairman

277. Were any other countries supporting you?

A. No, we were on our own. This was the first time we tried it. Your second question was whether this phenomenon holds true only for Germany. I do not think so. In other countries which have a similar structure to Germany, they use other criteria — even, for instance, Austria. We tried to bring across the idea of not having such a quantitative restriction, working together with other associations in Germany and in Austria, especially.

278. What criteria do Austria use?

A. Austria also applies qualitative criteria, differentiating between entrepreneur and mere manager.

Baroness O'Cathain

279. Ownership, etc?

A. Ownership. Taking risk. Being independent from the state. Having no great amount of shareholders. Having the equity quite alone.

280. The point strikes me, in listening to this, that there must be situations in other Member States that actually have this sizeable number of companies between 250 and 499 who are also disadvantaged because they do not fall within the general criteria that you have mentioned. In the situation which we are in, where we are trying to have a Single Market, do you not think it right that, if the other Member States are penalised, then Germany should not be looking for special treatment?

A. The border going through Europe is north and south. The higher criteria would apply mainly for the countries in the northern part of Europe and the other would hold true for the southern countries. I think, if you think of progress, when the European Community tries to bring forward start-up and sustainability of small and medium sized enterprises, and you have those criteria of the EC, then you do not reach the really important companies that are small and medium sized. If you think of technological development, then you cannot just apply to the smallest, you have to keep within the range of 250 to 499, and even higher, because they really bring about technical progress. The others are too small, if you just concentrate on the smallest, up to ten employed. We think this would be the wrong approach, and, therefore, we were very disappointed when this cut-off criteria of 250 was introduced. In former times the EC had up to 500, but they reduced it.

Lord Skelmersdale

281. What was the Commission's reason given to you for rejecting your plea, or request?

A. They said that the typical small and medium sized company, looking all over the 15 countries of Europe, would fall more into the category of being below 250, and that our criteria would only apply to a few countries in Europe. Most countries have this category of being below 250.

Lord Berkeley

282. I am very interested by your comments about the breakdown of size. The impression I am getting is that you do not think that the smallest—the micros—companies of up to 10 employees, or something, are in particular need of support. Maybe there are not that many in Germany, but the impression we have had from other witnesses is that certainly in this country they are a very important source of new development technology, and they need special help because they find it more difficult to do all the administration and fill in the forms, which the bigger companies may be able to do. Are there a very large number of micro companies in Germany, or is it different, certainly compared with this country?

A. It depends what branch you are looking at. If you take handicraft, for example, the average employment is, even in Germany, nine employed. This is the average size of companies in handicraft. If you look at industry, of course, you have a much higher number. If you look at the service sector, then you have smaller numbers. So it depends on what branch you are looking. Therefore, I think it is always a question "What does the EU try to achieve when it wants to bring about more start-ups and more sustainable growth and sustainability of small and medium sized companies?". The first question

Lord Berkeley *contd.*]

for us is always "should the European Community engage in this field, or is it more for the national level or even the local level?". Our opinion is very clear: we think that taking care of small and medium sized enterprises and of start-ups is, in the first place, a matter and a concern at the local level—at the Länder level. Therefore, each of the 16 Länder in Germany has a special law for the establishment and development of small and medium sized companies. In the second place, taking care would be at the national level—the *Bundesländer*, probably, in this case—and only in the third place comes the European Community, because we think that the local authorities and local government are closer to small and medium sized companies. When starting, small and medium-sized companies act locally as a rule. Only if they try to grow and try to conquer markets outside their home region and foreign markets do they expand.

283. Can I follow that up? I think that is very interesting, and I do not think anybody would disagree with you about the need for local delivery. Are you suggesting that the European Commission, however, should not have a role in setting policy throughout Europe? Otherwise one risks the problem of each region, in this country, for example, implementing policies which would set them in direct competition with next-door ones. Should there not be a framework policy, and then implementation and delivery at the local level?
A. That is exactly our opinion. It should be the task of the European Community only to set the framework and to take care of not having parallel framework legislation and regulation. Our opinion is that all the programmes which the Commission has tried to offer for small and medium sized companies should be transparent. That is a very important point, because if you ask small and medium sized companies what the European Commission is really doing, as a rule they do not know, because it is not transparent. The second point is it is not consistent – consistent means consistent with programmes at the national or local level. Nor is it efficient, because the European Commission does not have the local means to transform their programmes to the local authorities.

Chairman

284. Do you find there is any disagreement between the 16 Länder on how they interpret the guidelines?
A. No, not at all. If you look at the 16 different legal frameworks, they are similar even word-by-word, and I think it would be sufficient if you were to have only one legal framework for all 16 Länder. There is no big differentiation. They have the same points; they concentrate on start-ups and on small and medium sized companies. Then they see the weakness of small and medium sized companies in the same fields. They need information, advice, with problems as far as financing is concerned and problems of going abroad into foreign markets. Training is also a weak point, and this is all the same in all the 16 Länder.

Lord Brooke of Alverthorpe

285. Would it be possible for you to give an analysis of the number of firms that you have in different categories within the three million members in your organisation? Say, the number with up to 10 employees and the number with from 10 to 50 employees?
A. Yes, we have this statistic but I do not know it by heart. I can give it to you[1].

Chairman

286. If you could send it to us?
A. I would be glad to.

Lord Brooke of Alverthorpe

287. What is the nature of the relationship you have with the Commission? Is it a good relationship, leaving aside the argument you had about raising the figure to 500?
A. As far as small and medium sized companies are concerned and the policy for those companies, it is very good—not to say it is excellent. We try to keep in contact with the responsible DG XXIII, which will not exist any more—it will shift over to DG III, in combination—and we do not know what the effect will be. We are always asking for a reliable partner we can keep in contact with. So far, this DG XXIII was such a reliable partner, but not a strong partner. It was reliable, but the effect in relation to other DGs was very weak—its own position was weak. For example, if you think of programmes for the development of research, or if you think of going into foreign markets or enlargement towards eastern countries, then DG I is much more important, even for small and medium sized companies, than DG XXIII. Or, if you are thinking of the small and medium sized companies in the new *Bundesländer*, the former DDR, DG XV and XVI, being responsible for the Structural Funds, is much more important to small and medium sized enterprises. So our argument always was that DG XXIII should try to keep in contact with all the other DGs and to make a combined effort for small and medium sized enterprises and to be consistent in their aims and instruments.

288. Finally, what do you see as being the main achievements which are coming out from the EU, which do not duplicate the activities at Länder and at Federal levels?
A. Related to small and medium companies?

289. Yes.

---

[1] The witness subsequently supplied the following breakdown of firms in membership of DIHT in 1998.

Number of Employees		Number of Firms
up to 10		2,477,000
10–49		496,000
50–250		93,000
250–500		29,000
	Total	3,095,000

Lord Brooke of Alverthorpe *contd.*]

A. I think the best instrument, but it is not very effective so far, would be what we call *fiche d'impact*. That means, every regulation, every law that is put forward should be screened as far as it affects, especially, the small and medium sized enterprises. To bring the answer to a point: what would be the biggest achievement? The biggest achievement would be if the state and, especially, the European Commission would leave the small and medium sized enterprise—entrepreneur—quite alone. That is what we are always told. The typical entrepreneur says—and this holds true for the local government or at what level whatsoever—"The best policy would be if the state leaves me alone: I care for my own business and the state should just look after fair competition, it should look after lower taxation, and, especially, it should take care to get rid of red tape and bureaucracy, and give my enterprise more freedom and more room to move". So the common notion is to get rid of the state, but this is not possible, of course. Therefore, the first task would be for the European Commission to look after good framework policy to make this transparent and clear, and to keep it stable. In addition, as far as legislation and regulation is concerned, it should be screened, because legislation and regulation is always adapted and applied for bigger companies. They always have the picture of a big company, and for them it is no problem to cope with those regulations, but what does it mean for small and medium sized enterprises? Therefore, it is very important that the instrument of *fiche d'impact* becomes reality: at present, it is just a paper tiger.

Baroness O'Cathain

290. That is right.

A. Before any legislation is passed, it must be clear that it is really necessary, and when it is necessary whether another legislation from former times could be reduced, or be got rid of, and what the effect would be on small and medium sized enterprises.

Chairman: You are not the first witness to make that point.

Lord Skelmersdale

291. Herr Jürgensmann, can I take you up on the "leave us alone" philosophy that you have just enunciated? The European Commission has gone a long way to completing the Single Market. Have your members taken advantage of this? That is point one. Point two: other than the restriction of the development subsidy, which you talked about earlier, have you any other complaints about SME policy from the Commission or, on the other hand, have you areas of praise for the Commission and their policies for SMEs?

A. If I may start with the last question, with the complaints, because it is most topical. The multi annual framework for small and medium sized companies is now being constructed for the new period, 2000 to 2004. However, this will be a wrong approach because the Commission tries to interfere in different branches, even in the whole range of small and medium enterprises. For example, they try to

subsidise special start-ups for women or so-called social services, whatever this means. They try this by financing all these branches and programmes. We think that the European Commission should not invent new financing instruments, especially not for small and medium sized companies, but should be restricted to framework policy. That is our complaint. But a part one could praise, and where the European Commission achieved a lot, is in the field of cross-border co-operation and activities for small and medium sized companies. They have instruments such as Europartenariat. That means co-operation exchange, where entrepreneurs themselves are brought together and can have contacts, and be together for two days actually doing business. This is without financing, without money. It is just bringing together partners. These are good instruments and have worked well. This has been taken advantage of by many German small and medium sized companies and is a positive effect of the European Single Market.

Chairman

292. Are they brought together by the Commission? Who organises these?

A. The programme is organised by national co-ordinators.

293. Like yourselves.

A. Yes. For example, a company belonging to the DIHT is doing this for Germany, and in Italy there are other co-ordinators. How is this done? The Commission sponsors this catalogue, having all the features of each company looking for a partner and for co-operation, on one page: telling the size, what branch and so forth. Then the getting together is organised for two days. Before this there are seminars for all people interested in the different conditions of the country where one tries to go and be active.

294. It is a form of marriage bureau?

A. Yes. There are two other different instruments we are not very fond of. This is B C Net. It is a *bureau de rapprochement*. This is done electronically. You can give your offer and then the European Commission tries to match this. But this does not work. We think that real co-operation only works if people really meet and see each other, look each other in the eyes, and can speak to each other. It does not work just on the electronic basis.

Chairman: We want to come back to electronics in a minute.

Lord Skelmersdale

295. I had another question, which is about the Single Market. How successful have your companies, the SMEs in Germany, been at using this to further their businesses?

A. I am sorry?

Chairman

296. Could I add half a question to that? What effect do you think the enlargement of the EU, assuming that the Single Market also is enlarged, what effect will that have on German SMEs?

A. We know that the Single Market had a great effect as far as the booming of foreign trade was concerned. This holds especially true, for example, in Germany and the Netherlands, where the traditional co-operation is good. I think small and medium sized enterprises get a lot of profit from the Single Market and that they recognise this. This will also hold true for the enlargement, as far as eastern countries are concerned. You are thinking of the next six candidates, especially seen from a German viewpoint—Poland, Hungary, the Czech Republic, the eastern lands—where they are already taking action now cross-border, even trying to install twinning local authorities, having the same policy as far as infrastructure is concerned. This will be done over the next four or five years when this enlargement will happen. This is a good perspective if you think, as far as infrastructure is concerned, to small and medium sized companies in the construction sector, being close to the frontier of Poland, the Czech Republic, and Hungary. You have the same effect of restructuring and rebuilding of Kosovo and the Balkans. Our chambers, for instance, have installed what we call a "pool of companies". There is one chamber situated in Dortmund in Northern Westphalia, and they made this "pool for firms" that are interested in helping to rebuild and restructure Kosovo. This pool has, by now, more than 370 firms interested and sponsoring office representation in the Kosovo area and taking care of them. This is a new instrument and is working very well. This instrument is what we call a "pool for firms".

Chairman: Very interesting.

Viscount Brookeborough

297. To what extent does the lack of harmonised technical standards affect the cross-border trade of German SMEs? How do you think it should be taken on by the EU?

A. As far as we know, there is not much complaint, especially by small and medium sized companies, as far as harmonisation of norms of technical standards is concerned. This is because they leave it to the big companies. However, this depends in the pyramid of assembly on what step they are: whether they deliver components or whether they are in the third role, just a common supplier. So this is more a question of big companies. In the relationship of sub-contracting, small and medium sized companies leave the question of norms and technical standards more to their big competitors. They are not engaged. For the exception of small and medium sized companies being really specialist in some field, then they try to work in the different authorities that are responsible for technical norms and harmonisation.

298. So what you are saying is that the majority of your SMEs are involved in the production of components?

A. That is right.

299. Will this be a problem or will it become more of a problem with the six new states; or importing products from them in order to assemble in Germany?

A. I do not think so because during the period of preparation, before they are allowed to enter, there is a certain harmonisation of technical norms and standards they have to apply to, those other countries. This will not bring about the real problem. The real problem will be more in the wage agreements and lower wage levels in those countries. This will bother the small and medium sized companies more than technical standards.

300. So you really do not see many inhibiting factors for your SMEs trading cross-border?

A. No, not in this area, no, except handicrafts where this is notified as a hindrance—but this is a special branch, a specialist area in Germany.

Baroness O'Cathain

301. A follow-up on that one. When you consider the situation of the SMEs in Germany with these new countries on your border, which will be part of the Single Market, surely there are going to be problems regarding wage rates and the competitiveness between them? They may be very small, they may be literally across the road, but you will have companies which could go under once the tariff barriers are removed. Have you grappled with that one? How is that going to level out?

A. We have some experience but not good experience. It could work or not work the same way as it does now with the so-called—I do not know the English expression—*Entsendegesetz*. It is a law saying that in the construction area no foreign worker or sub-contractor is allowed to work to a lower wage than the lowest level in Germany. But this causes, especially in the United Kingdom, some concern, as far as the construction sector is concerned. You have here—I do not know what this paper is called—a form stating that the one who holds it is self-employed.

Lord Brooke of Alverthorpe: Oh yes, it is the Inland Revenue.

Chairman

302. It is a tax form.

A. But it is very easy to get this paper.

Chairman: Well—

Lord Brooke of Alverthorpe

303. It should not be—but it is.

A. This is a complaint that we often hear. This paper—whatever it is called—is presented to the German authorities. A lot of people in the construction sector would not, after our notion, be self-employed. They work as sub-contractors, not applying to this *Entsendegesetz*, thereby being able to offer their jobs, their work, at a lower wage level.

304. The employer does not pay up tax or insurance.

A. That is right.

Chairman

305. Could I go back to Lord Brookeborough's question on standards? We had evidence earlier in this enquiry from a British representative of an SME who said that the recognised British standard, the ISO, was not recognised in Germany. He was unable to sell in Germany, even though he satisfied the ISO British standard, which was itself recognised in Brussels. Please comment.

A. I think that should not be possible because you have the liberal movement of goods and the same standard. In this special case, I would suggest that he complains and goes through the whole procedure. I cannot imagine how this is possible. We had a similar case with the president of our association—we have a special association in charge of small and medium sized companies—and his firm is the third biggest European producer of pipes. He had his own standards but he had no problems with the European standard in this field.

Chairman: I do not want to dwell on it. When you receive a copy of our report you will also receive the verbatim evidence. You might like to read that particular piece but we do not want to dwell on it.

Lord Methuen

306. What impact do you see electronic commerce and internet trading having on Germany?

A. A very great effect. Electronic commerce has a big effect for all countries. This is one area where the European Commission should engage (and does not) — not with programmes giving money, but with rendering what we call best practice. We would like to know how e-commerce is used and applied by small and medium sized companies — with what success and failure — in other countries. How do other countries work on this? This best practice: that could be gathered by the European Commission and then should be published and spread. That would be a good task providing what is always needed for European programmes, the so-called added value. This would be by giving examples of best practice.

Baroness O'Cathain

307. I am thinking now of small businesses and what their problems are *vis à vis* the large companies. In evidence last week, we heard that the people who are involved in small and medium sized enterprises—and we like to emphasise the "e" for enterprise, so that it has the entrepreneurial feel about it—those are the people who get very bogged down by Treasury functions and all the other things. The managing director should really be out getting orders, or making things and inventing things, or something. Now, in Germany, do your small enterprises have significant problems caused by late payments and that type of financial situation? Organisations will always pay up with big companies because they know they can be taken to court, but sometimes they will not do so with small companies. I am just wondering if there is still a problem with the small enterprises and, if so, is there anything the EU should be doing about it in terms of late payment?

A. Yes, it is a problem, but not a problem covering all sectors of small and medium sized companies. It is concentrated in the construction sector.

308. Again.

A. There it really is a problem. It is a problem, not in the relationship between private enterprises, but as far as state orders and state payment is concerned. There is evidence—and we have exact statistics—that the state is the worst payer. It uses all the time it has for late payment and even goes beyond that. Therefore, we will have a new law where the interest rate will be higher. It is no longer necessary to ask your partner to pay if the payment period is over. We call it *Mahnwesen*. I do not know—if you ask somebody and say, You have to pay me," and I remind you, and I set you a new period. I give you a new period and say, "If you do not pay, so—" If the payment period is over, then a higher interest rate starts right at the beginning and you do not need this reminder any more.

Chairman

309. It is automatic.

A. The first reminder, the second reminder, the third reminder. After that the court would come in and do something.

Viscount Brookeborough

310. But that is only within Germany.

A. Yes, that will be in Germany.

Baroness O'Cathain

311. Do you think that there should be representation to the European Union on behalf of all SMEs to try to get that similar law installed in our countries? We are getting a bit better on that, are we not?

Lord Brooke of Alverthorpe: Getting very slowly better.

A. If the problem is all over and holds true for all the European countries, then this would be a good idea, or at least one should think it over.

Baroness O'Cathain

311. Similarly, thinking in terms of the financial implications for small and medium sized enterprises, and the impact of financial bureaucracy on this, how do you think they are coping with the introduction of the euro and the fact that it comes in, in the year 2001, with the notes and coins? Are they experiencing difficulties in the transition, or at least in the change-over?

A. First of all, as far as this transition is concerned and coping with the installation of the euro, it was a task and a matter for big companies. They took care of this right away and they invested a lot of money: bank, insurance companies, the automobile sector, and so forth. Small and medium sized companies up to now were and are reluctant to care for this problem, but by now they know they have to do it—and they do it. They do not complain as far as the instalment of the euro is concerned, but they do complain because this is a burden as far as financing

Baroness O'Cathain contd.]

is concerned. But there is no big resistance any more as far as the euro is concerned. One big concern, however, is how stable the euro will be. This is a big concern. It is not the technical installation of the euro. That is okay because it can be done with a little bit of financing, but what happens if the German economy and the small and medium sized companies lose Deutschmarks or some of their reputation, and if the euro was weak for a longer period of time? This is of great concern.

313. May I give you some words of comfort on that? Mr de Silguy in London made his last public utterance as a commissioner and said there is absolutely no problem. The euro will be more stable than anything else.

Chairman: He said!

A. But I do not think it is as easy in life as that.

Baroness O'Cathain: Nor do I.

Lord Howell of Guildford

312. That last point. You are talking about stability there, meaning the internal currency value. They are frightened of currency depreciation, which is a traditional German fear.

A. Yes.

313. But most of them would not worry about the external exchange rate of the euro rate against the dollar at all.

A. That is not a bigger concern. On the contrary, when we had a strong dollar, it was in favour of our export industry. If you look at the four sectors—machinery equipment, cars, chemistry and electronics—those four make 60 per cent of our exports. They were satisfied.

314. I wanted to ask a slightly different question. There were reports, a year ago, that smaller French service companies were finding the regulations of taxation and other requirements so onerous that some of them were relocating and re-registering in the United Kingdom. There was a famous example of the hairdresser from Valence who relocated in Cardiff, while she continued to do work in Valence. I wondered if you had any similar experience in Germany.

A. No.

315. Nothing like that?

A. No. Indeed, we have to do research on this but I just do not know. I have never heard of this.

Lord Berkeley

316. A completely new question. If I wanted to start up a business in Germany—and it would be a small business obviously—what do I have to do before I can start trading?

A. It depends on what you want to do. In principle we have freedom of entrepreneurship, that is to say you could start up in whatever business you like in theory; in practice it depends where you start. In general you just have to announce your business at the local office, what we call Gewerbeaumeldung and this announcement is passed on to the local chamber of industry or handicraft and to the financial institutions and if you employ people it is passed on

to the social security system, that is all. But if, for example, you want to engage in the field of transport whether persons, material or whatever, or in different service sectors, then you have to take several steps. You have to get permission or a concession. You must be personally reliable. You must get special training facilities and so forth. So, as I said before, it depends. For the normal start-up I do not think there is too much bureaucracy but in certain fields especially in the sector of transport it is highly regulated and there are so many obstacles or if you start up in the field of industry you have to deal with pollution and with noise and then you have the environmental protection. If you come into the field of environmental protection then it starts to get complicated with long periods to get an allowance and so forth.

317. If you ignore transport and ignore environmental pollution what is the cost of setting up very roughly? Is there a cost? Do you have to be a member of a chamber of commerce and things like that?

A. You know that our chamber system is different from the one you have here. Membership in Germany is compulsory for every start-up and every small and medium sized and big company, no matter what. We have 3.2 million enterprises and payers and they have to pay to their local chambers of which we have 82 in Germany and it is up to their ability to pay. That means the smallest and not so self-sufficient company pays as a rule 150 Deutschmarks per year, annual contributions, that is all. That is one side. On the other side you have big companies which are big contributors. If you take the credit sector, for example Deutschebank, or the energy sector, for example, VEBA or REW and so on, their annual contribution is at the rate of double digit millions so—

Baroness O'Cathain: Quite right too!

Chairman

318. Herr Jürgensmann, you have been very tolerant with us and extremely knowledgeable. I should have said right at the beginning of our evidence session that we are obliged by modern practice to declare any interests that members of the Committee may have and I apologise for not doing so. I think you already have a sheet of our interests because one way or another all of this Committee, every member, is involved directly or indirectly with an SME. That is for the record. Equally relevant for the record we are enormously grateful for the trouble you have taken to come and give evidence to us and for the way that you have given that evidence to us. My only sadness is that we are not able to repay a little of that kindness by way of hospitality. Thank you very much indeed. Now, I am trying to read a note here. You are going to send us a paper with some information?

A. Yes, breaking down the records.

Chairman: The note asks if you could include some—

Lord Skelmersdale

319.—Some indication of the growth of new start-ups over the last five or ten years? Would that be possible? We want to see whether these policies of yourselves, the German Länder and the German Government, and the EU are working for Germany.

A. If you take the average of the last five years then you have real start-ups year per year at 350,000. This is what we found out because we do not have an official and exact statistic for start-ups.

Chairman

320. Do you also have statistics of failures?
A. Yes.

321. If you could give us both of those.[2]
A. At the same time, year by year, you have failures in the range of 300,000. This is the record for the last five years as an average.

---

[2] The witness subsequently supplied the following analysis of SME start-ups and failures:

Year	Start-ups	Closures	Net Increase
1991	391,000	297,000	94,000
1992	398,000	288,000	110,000
1993	407,000	298,000	109,000
1994	419,000	328,000	91,000
1995	452,000	358,000	94,000

322. So you are always 50,000 ahead, net?
A. Yes, 50,000 more enterprises.

Viscount Brookeborough

323. Is that evenly distributed between the area that was Eastern Germany and what was Western Germany because you have unique circumstances?

A. Yes, the actual figure now is that you have zero difference for East Germany. Start-ups and failures are at the same level and after reunification it was quite different, start-ups were exceeding failures tremendously, but this shows that the problem now in East Germany is not having more start-ups but caring for the existing companies to make them sustainable. This is very important for policy and in West Germany the tendency is that failures are slowing down and start-ups are going up more and more.

Chairman: Thank you again very much indeed. We must let you go and catch your plane.

WRITTEN EVIDENCE

Memorandum by Professor Robert Blackburn, The Business School, Kingston University

1. EU policies for Small and Medium-Sized Enterprises (SMEs) cover a wide range of areas and derive from a variety of objectives. EU policies for SMEs are relatively new compared with nation states policies. The evolution of EU SME policies and the plethora of initiatives and programmes can be gleaned from EU DG XXIII documentation (eg EU, 1999a). Suffice to state that an SME is currently defined as encompassing: micro (less than 10 employees); small (10–49) and medium (50–249) sized enterprises. Operationally, however, there are various definitions according to specific policy contexts.

2. Most analysts attempt to classify parts of SME policy and although these tend to be at a high level of abstraction, they do give some guidance to the complexity of policy. A strategy from the EU, forming the basis of the Third Multiannual Programme for SMEs and the Craft sector for 1997–2000, covered the following areas: reduction of red tape; better involvement of SME organisations in the decision making process; help with finance; reduce market distortions and inefficiencies; action to promote research, innovation and training; and enhance competitiveness and internationalisation (EU, 1999b). UK governments have grouped policy into similar areas for ease of understanding and delivery.

3. A major consideration of any policy which seeks to promote SMEs must be the attitude of business owners to government. Good policy needs to be people focused and derive from bottom-up data and knowledge. Research tends to show that UK business owners are sceptical of government initiatives. Business owners are very busy individuals, are reluctant networkers, avoid seeking outside advice and often prefer to stand on their own two feet rather than receive government support. When coupled with the government as a regulator and "taxer" of their activities, it is not an exaggeration to state that government policy, however well thought out, will receive a cool reception from the SME. Reaching business owners with policy is far from easy but they must be in the foreground of any SME initiative.

4. In reality, in Britain, there is a perception amongst businesses that EU SME policy tends to be invisible. This is partly because of the low eligibility of businesses, for example in relation to regional policy support, compared with less developed EU economies. The sheer number of businesses (over 3.7 million) relative to the numbers taking up initiatives must be proportionately low. Also, in practice, EU policy is dependent on state or local institutional provision. The latter means that some businesses on EU funded initiatives may not make the link with the EU. Further, it is also no secret that, in the past, British governments have not readily taken-up and promoted respective EU policies. For example, a most recent round of ADAPT funding has been made available to the UK because of the low take-up of its allocation in previous rounds compared with other Member States. Improvements in the institutional framework should therefore facilitate a much stronger connection with EU initiatives.

5. Any review of SME policy at a national and EU level must also be put in context. Most SMEs are not touched by SME initiatives but are almost always effected by wider fiscal, monetary and regulatory policies. This means that when policies are being introduced they must be formulated with the SME in mind. In some cases, the benefit from a specific SME initiative can be eliminated by a change in macro government policy such as a rise in interest rates or taxation.

6. The case for SME policy rests, *inter alia,* on the notions of: market failure; their relatively high fixed and compliance costs; their contribution to innovation and competition; and their job generation capabilities. Recognition of the contribution of SMEs to the economy and society has tended to turn them into a panacea for the cure of the ills in the economy and society. This is despite their high death, as well as start-up, rates and disappointing job generation capabilities in some sectors and relatively low export orientation. However, the sheer heterogeneity of the SME population, their different requirements according to business sector, location, age, size and owner-managers' characteristics render universal SME policies problematic.

7. Developing a policy agenda for SME policy is not as easy as it sounds. Although there appears a great deal of activity at the EU and UK government levels regarding policy for SMEs, the agenda is contested terrain and the priorities not clear cut. This is a result of the different if sometimes conflicting needs of SMEs and ignorance over the real world of the small business owner. For example, whilst some businesses complain of a lack of finance for expansion, the bulk of SMEs do not. Yet an emphasis on overcoming the barriers to securing finance has been the thrust of many SME initiatives. Similarly, in an attempt to raise the overall level of management and employee performance, many training initiatives have been qualifications driven (eg NVQs) despite the absence of a market for qualifications driven training in SMEs. Similarly, whilst Investors in People has been taken on by many public sector organisations and corporate sector businesses, it was recognised that it becomes increasingly difficult to encourage take-up the smaller the enterprise. As a result, in some instances policies have been driven by the exception rather than the rule or have been driven by another agenda. This may be based on the legitimate case that a particular group or type of firms require special attention, such as high-technology based firms, or less so merely because of a strong media focus on a specific issue or type of business.

8. There have been a number of false dawns or hyped problems for SMEs. These are often predicated on the notion of an ignorant or less informed business owner. Most recent examples include the hyping of the problems to be faced by SMEs over the introduction of the Minimum Wage and the Euro. Our evidence both in quantitative and qualitative studies shows that business owners are well informed and have been able to adjust to such macro changes (SBRC/HCW, 1999). There is a need for more research on the SME in order to assist in the setting of appropriate and realistic policy targets and raising its overall efficacy.

9. A recent assessment of SME policy in the UK (MTI, 1999) reported that it has been made up of a series of initiatives, aiming for instant solutions, rather than a careful appraisal and fine-tuning of existing strategies. Pressure on politicians and civil servants into "being seen to do something" was viewed as one of the reasons for this stream of initiatives. However, the difficulty in communicating adequately with SMEs meant that any new policy has no better chance at success than older policies. Paradoxically, this poor level of performance puts further pressure on policy makers to produce new policies quickly. This phenomenon has been termed "initiativitis", whereby initiative after initiative is introduced in an attempt to make a "big bang". Each policy change brings with it its own rhetoric and language. The latest round of this "ritual of policy change" appears to be emphasising "competitiveness" and "entrepreneurship" (Trade and Industry Committee, Sixth Report, 1998).

10. A major weakness in UK and EU SME policy is in the evaluation process, which is considered underdeveloped, if not crude. Policy evaluations, often undertaken by professional accountancy practices and consultancies, tend to focus on number counting using simple methodologies. This usually involves measuring displacement and deadweight of SME policies, leading to some assessment of additionality. Sometimes these evaluations never surface into the wider public arena, or are not acted upon. Estimating the number of businesses that have been involved in a public policy initiative would be a Herculean task. However, it is important that evaluations are factored into government policies and are taken into consideration in new policies. Unfortunately, evidence of accumulated learning in the design of new policies and related incremental improvements are absent in many initiatives.

11. There are examples of successful initiatives in the UK. A survey of academics and practitioners in the UK for the Finish Government (MTI, 1999) found that the most commonly cited successful intervention in the 1990s was the Loan Guarantee Scheme (LGS). Other more successful interventions cited included: Small Firm Merit Award for Research (SMART); DTI Enterprise Initiative (now expired); Management extension programme (now expired); and Late Payment Legislation (The Late Payment of Commercial Debt (Interest) Act 1998).

12. What is significant about the discussion of the most successful policies was the range and different vintages of policies. Hence, new policies are not necessarily improvements on the old. Successful policies tended to be those which had: been running for a relatively long period of time; benefited from evaluations and incremental refinements; and had become well known and had a perceived impact.

13. Successful policies require equally good structures to deliver them. The delivery structures of SME policies in the UK are undergoing major changes. It is crucial that the view from the ground rather than a top down "imported" model is adopted. The last major change in the institutional framework was the introduction of Business Links. However, these have had a mixed success and some respondents in the MTI research cited it as amongst the least successful intervention. As forced partnerships, the Business Link's network provides poorer services, is expensive and has displaced already established and successful institutions. The fluctuation in policies from the enterprise agencies and TECs and switches in their sources of funding (for example, from central, local and regional authorities to Single Regeneration Budget and City Challenge competitions) experienced over the past decade was widely condemned. A minority of pariticipants cited the then Rural Development Commission (now the Countryside Agency) as having a model of successful advisory intervention.

14. In contrast, the Business Expansion Scheme was most commonly cited as the least successful intervention. Some experts also viewed job creation ideas related to small firms' policies, mainly in the form of the Enterprise Allowance Scheme (EAS), as unsuccessful. The perceived weakness of these interventions was the public subsidy of businesses in low entry costs sectors, creating displacements of already existing enterprises and their activities.

15. There are currently a number of gaps in SME policy which may be assisted by EU initiatives. Our research for the MTI found a number of perceived deficiencies in policy design, targeting, communications and delivery. These could be improved by setting more specific objectives and by conducting more rigorous research on existing policies. The main aim for government policy improvements should be to produce a smaller number of better quality services. In addition to the better organisation of government interventions, three specific policy gaps were identified as entrepreneurship education; assistance with business exit and entrepreneurial recycling; and support for middle layer businesses.

16. Underlying many of the discussions we have conducted with business owners and other academics and advisers was disaffection with the public policy making process. Although reaching the small business is difficult, it is important that the view and experiences of business owners are put to the forefront of the policy making process. Combined with the experiences of practitioners, small business lobby groups and the results

of independent research they can provide a powerful force in appropriate policy delivery. The efficiency and relevance of the UK institutional partners will determine the successful take-up of EU SME initiatives by UK small and medium sized enterprises.

REFERENCES

MTI (1999) *A Critical Evaluation of Industry Support Policies in the United Kingdom and the Republic of Ireland: Stage Two Report,* Ministry of Trade and Industry, Helsinki, Finland.

EU (1999a) *Definition of Small and Medium-sized Enterprises,* DG XXIII, Unit A.1, European Commission, Brussels.

EU (1999b) *Third Multiannual Programmes for SMEs,* DG XXIII, Unit A.1, European Commission, Brussels.

More information can be ascertained from the above on: http//europa.eu.int/en/comm/dg23/guide—en/

SBRC/HCW (1999) *Dialogue with Small Business Owners, Biannual Research into their Motivations, Experiences and Views,* Small Business Research Centre, Kingston University/Horwath Clark Whitehill, July.

Memorandum by the British Standards Institution (BSI)

Standards set at the national, European or international (global) levels are established to create agreed specifications and criteria for the benefit of manufacturers, buyers and end consumers. Today most standards (over 95 per cent) are set at the European and international level. When established they can effectively become treaties for trade, setting the base criteria for any company wishing to participate in the market. It is therefore important that all those companies with an interest in that market play some role in setting the standards for it.

BSI is committed to securing the effective representation of SME interests in the widest possible number of standards writing committees. Our strategic policy in standards setting is guided by a series of sector policy committees. One of these committees, OC/18, is geared solely towards the interests of smaller businesses. I attach a copy of the current terms of reference for your information. A review of these terms of reference is currently underway with the SME sector to ensure that the committee meets the needs of this sector.

We have also been discussing with SME representatives the possibility of developing a new generic product specification standard which could be used by SME's in those areas where there is no published standard.

In response to the two specific questions you have asked, BSI would make the following comments.

1. *Any distinctive or especially acute problems SMEs encounter in adapting their products and services to technical standards which are harmonised at European level:*

Harmonised standards at the national, European and international level actually help SMEs win business by creating an agreed level playing field for technical specifications.

However, where products need to be tested against the criteria set in a standard, SMEs can suffer if the results of an accredited test body, for instance BSI in the UK, are not accepted in other countries. This can place an unnecessary burden on manufacturers having to pay for the same tests to be repeated in different countries.

Another problem that SMEs encounter relates to the understanding of what European Directives entail and what is necessary to ensure compliance with regard to their product or service sales into Europe.

Many SMEs may be unaware of the legal onus that European Directives place upon them, with particular regard to the application of the CE mark. BSI and other Notified Bodies, as well as Business Link and local Chambers of Commerce, can provide the guidance to SMEs of how these European Directives, such as Marine, Pressure Equipment and Construction Products, will impact their businesses.

SMEs may also be unaware of the direct links between Directives and standards, whereby conformity with a Directive may be achieved by the application of one or more standards.

Increasing the awareness of the timescales and requirements of impending Directives, as well as highlighting where help can be obtained, will increase SMEs' ability to meet these requirements within the European Market.

2. *Whether standardisation takes adequate account of the interests of SMEs:*

SMEs have historically been under-represented within the standard-setting process for a number of reasons:

— as small businesses they do not have the spare capacity to allow a member of staff to participate in standards setting meetings;

— they are unable to fund the costs of participation in the process;

— it is often difficult to communicate effectively with SMEs, particularly if they are not members of trade associations; and

— SMEs often operate in niche market areas without formally agreed standards (in the national, European or international sense) in place.

BSI has sought to address these issues in the following ways:

— by trying to establish a "trigger system" for our committee chairmen highlighting a number of issues affecting the interests of SMEs in their committee's work. Although not as successful as had been hoped, the debate around the proposal has served to raise the visibility of SME concerns;

— by establishing an electronic document delivery system for standards committee members, thereby greatly reducing the time commitment needed to participate in the standards setting process;

— BSI has established Projectline, which is an on-line system that allows interested parties to keep track of the progress of a draft standard. This is available on our web site and access is currently free of charge; and

— by actively promoting draft standards which will affect SMEs during the consultation period in the trade and technical press for that sector.

However, we recognise the limitations of these current activities and are discussing with representatives of the SME sector how we can more effectively involve them in the crucial areas of influencing the international standards which might in due course have a profound effect on their business.

29 July 1999

POLICY COMMITTEE FOR SMALL BUSINESSES—TERMS OF REFERENCE

To provide a central focus in BSI for promoting the interests of small businesses through standardisation and the encouragement of quality management systems, product certification and other related activities, and specifically:

— to convey to the Standards Board of BSI and to the BSI Executive the interests of small businesses in all areas of BSI activity;

— to further effective two-way communication between OC/18 and BSI and to advise BSI Sector Boards and other parts of the BSI structure on matters relating to small businesses;

— to ensure that small businesses are kept fully informed on the work of BSI and the services available to them;

— to contribute on behalf of small businesses to the work of BSI nationally, in Western Europe and at international level in the fields of standardisation, testing and quality assurance; and

— to establish such sub-committees and panels as may seem appropriate at any time.

As a matter of definition, the Committee should be concerned particularly, but not exclusively, with firms that are owner managed and not dominant in the market place. Such businesses are typified by their "different" or "special" management with minimum delegation and little or no management structure.

These terms of reference could be paraphrased to read:

"to help BSI to provide standards, information, testing, capability assessment and product certification services that will best meet the needs of small business and to help small businesses to make best use of those services".

Memorandum by CEN, the European Committee for Standardisation

PRELIMINARY REMARKS

CEN is not part of the Commission, nor national governments nor their agencies.

It is an independent organization dedicated to drafting voluntary, harmonized European Standards, through the network of our Members, the national standards organizations (the UK member being BSI).

It is not in our remit to promote SMEs and we have no opinion on what should be done and by whom.

However, since invited, we can offer some comments about SMEs and standardisation.

VIEW

Both manufacturers and service providers are affected by Union policies in respect of product standards, health and safety, and horizontal issues such as legislative requirements for the environment.

We have heard of concerns relating to difficulty in keeping up with Directives and/or the voluntary standards that support Directives. EN ISO 9000 for quality systems has been seen by some as a burden, by others as a benefit to exploit claims for quality. EN ISO 14001, for environmental auditing, has a similar image.

CEN has no evidence that standards discriminate in favour of large industries.

On the other hand, standards provide:

— a common passport throughout Europe, including Central and Eastern countries;

— interoperability;

— a state-of-the-art defence in product liability; and

— non prescriptive methods of achieving conformity with Directives through performance specification, thus allowing innovative solutions.

Standards are likely to become more prominent as the Union actively tries to de-regulate.

EN ISO 9000 is a widely recognised standard and we believe it has provided added value for many enterprises, especially services. Next year a radically revised edition will be adopted by ISO.

In general, standards are drawn up by consensus, and this participation is guaranteed through the national standards bodies, Members of CEN.

NORMAPME, the European Office of Crafts, Trades and Small and Medium-sized Enterprises for Standardisation, based in Brussels and an umbrella for national organizations, is an Associate of CEN.

More than 300 European Trade federations, which include in turn numerous SMEs at national level, participate in standards drafting and help diffuse knowledge.

The Central Secretariat in Brussels has co-operated actively with the European Commission's programme for Euro-Infocentres for more than 10 years and works particularly closely with the "specialised" EICs in standardisation, quality and certification.

A corporate brochure, *CEN—Responding to changing needs,* is available.

13 July 1999

Memorandum by the Department of Economic Development for Northern Ireland

INTRODUCTION

1. Northern Ireland has already contributed to the DTI Memorandum of Evidence submitted to Sub-Committee B on 22 July (see page 41), and many of the policies which are outlined in that document will also apply in Northern Ireland. However, small firms have a particular prominence in economic development in Northern Ireland. This memorandum therefore seeks to reflect some of the differences in NI in this policy area.

BACKGROUND

2. Government in Northern Ireland has recognised the importance of the small firms[1] sector to economic development, mainly through its resourcing of the Local Enterprise Development Unit (LEDU) since the early 1970s. Emphasis on small firms as a focus for policy stemmed from the firm notion that small firms could face particular problems because of their size (eg access to finance) that warranted particular assistance, and that they would be important contributors to economic growth and employment generation.

3. The most recent Corporate Plan from LEDU (June 1998) notes that:

"In NI, the small firms sector is a vital component of the economy, and is a major source of employment. Employment in small firms accounts for about 56 per cent of total employment in the private sectors of the NI economy. This is much higher than the overall UK proportion of 48 per cent. Small manufacturing firms in NI constitute over 90 per cent of all manufacturing units and account for 28 per cent of all manufacturing employment. Compared to the position in the early 1970s, when small firms provided only 10 per cent of manufacturing employment, there has clearly been a massive increase in the contribution made by this sector of the economy".

4. However, small firms are important not only in numerical terms. There is some evidence that small firms are the seedbed for the larger indigenous firms of the future, and that small firms give rise to new firms in manufacturing, since founders of new companies tend to come disproportionately from existing firms.

DATA ON SMALL FIRMS IN NORTHERN IRELAND

5. Taking the definition of small firms to be those employing 50 employees or fewer, small firms in NI make up some 99 per cent of companies and employ around 61 per cent of relevant employees. Comparable figures for the UK as a whole indicate a similar proportion of small firms in the total, but less reliance on small firms in employment terms (45 per cent).

---

[1] Small firms are defined as those employing 50 or fewer employees.

6. In the private sector the important sectors in terms of the share of all small firms are wholesale and retail (31 per cent), real estate, renting and business activities (13 per cent); construction (12 per cent); and manufacturing (10 per cent). A broadly similar pattern is evident in the UK figures, albeit with a significantly higher proportion of small firms operating in the real estate, renting and business activities sector (27 per cent).

7. Small firms are an increasingly important source of job creation in Northern Ireland. Between 1989 and 1993 small indigenous firms in manufacturing increased employment by 3,713 or 12.4 per cent, with most of this increase coming from employment in new firms created during the period. In contrast employment among large indigenous companies declined marginally (down 1.1 per cent), while employment among externally-owned firms fell by 13 per cent. Employment created by new indigenous small manufacturing firms was three times greater than that created through new inward investment during the period.

8. Employment in small firms now accounts for just under one-third of manufacturing employment compared to around one-eighth in 1973. NI's share of manufacturing employment accounted for by small firms is now higher than in the Republic of Ireland.

9. The importance of small firms to the manufacturing sector in NI can also be gauged by looking at the proportion of manufacturing output (Gross Value Added) generated by manufacturing units employing less than 50 employees. Such units generate over 28 per cent of output compared to 25 per cent in the UK as a whole.

10. However, Northern Ireland has historically lagged behind the UK (and the ROI) in levels of new firm formation as measured by VAT registrations as a percentage of the stock of businesses. In 1997, the new firm formation rate in Northern Ireland was 7.2 per cent compared to 11.4 per cent in the UK.

11. On the other hand business death rates are consistently lower in Northern Ireland than in the UK. In 1996 death rates (as measured by VAT deregistrations as a percentage of the stock of businesses) were 5.4 per cent in NI compared to 9.8 per cent in the UK. Similarly, the survival rate of businesses is much greater in NI than in the UK. For example, 74.8 per cent of NI new businesses registered in 1994 were in existence three years later, the corresponding percentage for the UK was 59.2 per cent.

THE ROLE OF LEDU

12. In Northern Ireland, Government support to small businesses is provided mainly through the Local Enterprise Development Unit (LEDU). This operates directly and through an extensive network of some 100 Economic Development Partnerships, which include Councils, Peace and Reconciliation Partnerships and Local Enterprise Agencies.

13. LEDU, which has an annual programme budget of £21 million, assists small manufacturing firms through a wide range of schemes and initiatives. The Unit aims to improve competitiveness and stimulate increased sales, particularly export sales. LEDU, in liaison with the District Councils and Local Enterprise Agency network, also provides support to individuals wishing to become self-employed and to start up new businesses.

14. LEDU has a range of core programmes designed to cater for each stage of business development within the small firms sector.

— Pre-start activities include training, workshops, target programmes etc. They are supported through LEDU's Economic Development Partnerships and are delivered primarily through Local Enterprise Agencies;

— Start-up support is offered through a partnership between LEDU and the Local District Councils. This support includes business advice, training, ongoing counselling and financial support; and

— Growth support is provided to businesses that already sell or that have the potential to sell their products/services outside Northern Ireland. They will also be capable of, and committed to, significantly expanding their activities in export markets as a vehicle for future profitable growth.

LEDU 1998/1999 PERFORMANCE

15. The key headlines were as follows:

— Full-time employment amongst LEDU clients increased by a net 2,616 during the year;

— 99 export focused start-ups were established during the year;

— Almost 40 per cent of jobs created by new LEDU clients were located in disadvantaged areas;

— Employment in LEDU clients increased by 8 per cent;

— The volume of sales generated by these clients increased by 5 per cent; and

— The amount of sales made to markets outside Northern Ireland increased by 12.5 per cent.

NI SMEs IN THE EU CONTEXT

16. Within the European Community there is wide recognition of the important role that SMEs play in promoting economic prosperity.

17.   The DTI memorandum to the Sub-Committee sets out the broad outline of EU policies and initiatives to promote the development of small and medium size businesses. These include:

— the UK Presidency "Enterprising Europe Conference" (April 1998);

— publication of *Fostering Entrepreneurship* (COM(95) 222 final) (April 1998);

— the inclusion in the EU Employment Pacts of an "entrepreneurship pillar";

— the setting up (1997) of the Business Environment Task Force (BEST) and subsequent production of an action plan;

— the recent announcement to set up a new Directorate General, bringing together innovation, competitiveness, the information society and SME policy responsibilities;

— the Multi-Annual Programmes for SMEs (MAP);

— The Fifth Framework Programme for Research and Development and the UK National Employment Action Plan also recognise the importance of expanding the SME sector as the chief driver of wealth and job creation. Financial support for SMEs is also provided via the European Investment Bank and the European Investment Fund.

18.   In Northern Ireland SMEs benefit from the European Structural Funds under the NI Single Programme in areas such as sectoral studies, marketing, seed and venture capital, local enterprise programmes and a mentoring scheme. Northern Ireland also benefits from Community Initiatives such as Konver, Retex and SMEs which are specifically designed to assist the development of small firms in NI.

19. Access to finance is also a key issue for SMEs in Northern Ireland, as it is in the UK and across the EU. The DTI memorandum lists a number of measures introduced by the Commission to address market weaknesses in this sector. In Northern Ireland two specific initiatives are being introduced to improve access to private sector sources of finance by SMEs:

— the establishment of a new £10 million venture capital fund to provide "mezzanine" finance to companies (particularly in the high technology/IT sectors) seeking investment of between £50K and £250K. The European Investment Bank (EIB) has indicated a willingness in principle to participate in the new Fund; and

— a £3 million Research and Development Challenge Fund which will address the recognised funding gap faced by innovative spin-out/spin-on companies throughout Northern Ireland.

Both funds will become operational later this year.

CONCLUSION

20. The Northern Ireland authorities recognise and welcome the Commission's activities to increase the capacity of SMEs to compete and to create jobs. The next round of EU Structural Funds (2000–2006) will provide a further opportunity to develop EU support for the small firms sector in Northern Ireland, particularly in the area of electronic commerce. Given the existing importance of the SME sector in NI, and its contribution to the economic well-being of the region, every effort will be made to construct a range of policy instruments to enhance even further the growth potential of this sector.

August 1999

Memorandum by the Environment Agency on the Opportunities and Challenges for Small and Medium-sized Enterprises (SMEs) within EU Structures

1. BACKGROUND

1.1 All companies whatever their size are expected to comply with the law. Over the last two decades the amount of environmental protection legislation has been steadily increasing, both in terms of number of laws and their complexity. This trend is not expected to change. Although some environmental legislation is very specific to particular industrial sectors, often there is no cut-off with respect to the size of the companies to which it applies.

1.2 A primary means of applying environmental legislation in the UK is through the granting of a permit. Examples of such permits include consents to discharge to water, waste disposal licences and the duty of care transfer notes. The Agency issues such permits and has a routine inspection programme to ensure the conditions of the permit are met (including the holding of a permit where needed). The permitting and inspection regime is targeted at those activities that pose the greatest risk to the environment (within legislative constraints). Hence larger companies may be visited by Agency staff on a routine basis, whereas SMEs are visited less frequently, if at all.

1.3 Some legislation is, however, all encompassing. For example, it is illegal for anyone to make a polluting discharge to a watercourse. All businesses, regardless of size, are required and expected to abide by such environmental legislation. The Agency is a firm but fair regulator. Where any requirement of these all-encompassing laws is not met, then the Agency is obliged to act, but will take into account all the circumstances surrounding the event. However, in responding to a pollution incident, the Agency can find itself in a position whereby it is required to take legal action on the first contact with a smaller company.

1.4 The requirement on smaller business to comply with environmental legislation is no longer limited to "avoiding being caught by the regulator". Many larger companies now require their suppliers to comply with environmental legislation and include this as a contract condition.

1.5 In 1998 the insurance sector developed a document, with Agency support, on the underwriting of pollution risk[2]. The recommendations in this document are likely to impact on business insurance with premiums reflecting environmental risk.

1.6 The Agency is committed to addressing the needs of SMEs. The Agency believes that companies should be aware of their environmental obligations, and provides guidance on how to implement systems to meet these in a cost-effective manner. However, where companies do not comply with the law, the Agency will use its enforcement powers in a proportional manner to maximum effect.

2. EXAMPLES OF AGENCY INITIATIVES TO DATE

Links to the European Union

2.1 During the UK's presidency of the European Union, the Agency organised a seminar, on behalf of IMPEL, to debate the practicalities of enforcing environmental legislation in SMEs, and if alternative approaches could be adopted instead. IMPEL is an informal network of the environmental regulators of the Member States of the European Union. The Agency plays a key role in the network, which promotes the exchange of information and experience, and the development of a greater consistency of approach in the implementation, application and enforcement of European environmental legislation.

2.2 The seminar brought together a wide range of representatives from Member States, including local authorities, Government Departments and Agencies, and experts in the field of environmental management in the SME business sector. Some of the key recommendations from this seminar were that a sector-specific approach to helping SMEs is important; that better and simpler interpretation of guidance and legislation is needed and that a better co-ordination of initiatives by environmental support organisations is required.

UK Partnerships

2.3 At a national level, the Agency enjoys a strong relationship with both DETR and DTI on issues relating to SMEs. Firm links have also been established between the Cabinet Office Better Regulation Unit and the Agency STAR group which looks at the application of "simple and transparent Agency regulation".

2.4 The Agency actively supports and provides guidance to the Environmental Technology Best Practice Programme (ETBPP). In addition, the Agency welcomes the development of DTI's new Small Business Service Unit and looks forward to working closely with the unit when it is established.

2.5 The Agency was represented on the UK Round Table sub-group on SMEs and contributed to the recent UK Sustainable Development report on SMEs. The report recommended that the Agency and SEPA should "co-ordinate and promote the development of guidance for small firms on environmental legislation". The Agency welcomes this recommendation and is actively working on this area (see Present and Future Initiatives below).

2.6 In 1998 the Agency contributed to the Groundwork report *Small firms and the environment*.

Local initiatives

2.7 The Agency places a priority on working with industry at a local level. The day to day interaction with businesses by Agency area and regional staff is critical to getting the right information and messages across. Information ranging from awareness raising materials to good practical guidance is produced on a national level (often in conjunction with other UK environmental regulatory bodies). For example, the Agency has produced Pollution Prevention Guidance Notes (PPGs) which cover 22 key issues, including the storage of waste oil, construction and operation of fuelling stations and working at construction and demolition sites.

2.8 Under section 4(3) of the Environment Act the Agency has a duty to encourage waste minimisation. The recently published Agency policy on waste minimisation[3] states that "the Agency will work directly, with government, and in partnership with others, to inform, educate and facilitate measurable reductions in the

---

[2] *Recommendations for the Underwriting of Pollution Risks,* Association of British Insurers, Joint Pollution Working Group (web site: http://www.abi.org.uk).

[3] For more information and a copy of the policy contact Jon Foreman on 0117-914 2779.

generation of all types of waste". Although primarily focused at directly regulated industry, the benefits of promoting the sustainable use of natural resources will also impact on smaller businesses.

2.9 The Agency is currently involved in over 100 regional waste minimisation projects in England and Wales. These projects typically involve "clubs" working together and sharing information. SMEs often take part in these initiatives and feedback allows a constant refinement of how best to communicate with and assist SMEs.

2.10 The Agency has produced a "waste minimisation good practice guide" and a video entitled "money for nothing: your waste tips for free[4]. Both of these products have been designed with smaller businesses in mind and have been well received by industry.

2.11 Working in partnership with the ETBPP and the BOC Foundation, the Agency helped produce the Waste Minimisation Interactive Tools (WMIT). WMIT is a software tool geared toward SMEs and introduces the concept of waste minimisation. The Agency is also involved in presenting a number of joint training programmes to industry which aim to minimise the generation of packaging waste.

2.12 The Agency has co-ordinated the production of several sectoral based Codes of Practice (CoPs) in conjunction with the industrial groups, for example with the timber industry and the printed circuit board industry. This has been a successful initiative as the CoPs are effectively written by the industrial sector, and are, therefore, more acceptable to the target audience.

2.13 The Agency also believes there is much to be gained from an environmental management systems approach. We have supported the Jaguar/Rover initiative, which promotes this approach through the supply chain. We also expect to demonstrate the value of environmental management systems by implementing programmes at our own sites to a standard, which will be capable of certification to ISO14001 by the end of this year.

3. WHAT WE HAVE FOUND TO DATE

3.1 Recent surveys of business attitudes to the environment reveal the extent to which many SMEs remain unaware of environmental legislation. In general, the smaller the business, the less resource and time is available to deal effectively with environmental compliance issues. This, and other evidence, suggests that many SMEs are unaware of their environmental responsibilities, but are apprehensive about contacting regulators for advice in case they are found to be in breach of environmental legislation.

3.2 There has been rapid development of technologies, such as the Internet, which may assist in communicating more effectively with SMEs. Evidence suggests that uptake of the Internet for business usage by SMEs is steadily growing.

3.3 It is clear that business would prefer guidance that is specific to their sector rather than just generic. In addition, uncoordinated or conflicting guidance can result in rejection of all forms of advice. Guidance that is from, or backed by, a credible source such as Government or Government Agencies is preferred.

4. PRESENT AND FUTURE INITIATIVES

4.1 The Agency is currently devising a national strategy which will outline how the Agency will assist SMEs, understand their environmental responsibilities, prevent pollution and contribute to sustainable development.

4.2 As part of a pilot project, SMEs in the printing sector were invited in April 1999 to test out a new Internet tool called NetRegs[5]. The tool is designed to give practical, sector-specific tips on water, waste and air issues and to clarify the environmental responsibilities of smaller businesses. There are plans to develop the Netregs concept over the next few months.

4.3 SMEs make up over 99 per cent of the businesses in the UK and many are generally lacking in awareness about their environmental responsibilities. The Agency recognises that on many occasions, first contact with an SME may be as a result of a problem. We will continue to make special provision for the needs of SMEs through the provision of appropriate guidance.

4.4 Some SMEs will fall within the scope of the Integrated Pollution Prevention and Control Directive, which will be implemented over the next few years. Within this regime the Agency proposes to regulate industry in proportion to the risks involved, and will therefore take account of the smaller business.

4.5 Government Departments and Agencies with responsibilities for environmental protection need to communicate more effectively with SMEs in order to raise their awareness and to prevent pollution incidents. The Agency will play an active role in this, and will collaborate with others to achieve consistency and efficiency. In particular, the Agency will make best use of its local networks to disseminate materials and raise awareness on environmental responsibility and we will continue to look at how we communicate with those we come into contact with on an infrequent basis.

July 1999

---

[4] Both the good practice guide and video are available free by telephoning 0345-337700.
[5] For more information visit: http://www.environment-agency.gov.uk/epns/netregs.html.

Memorandum by HM Customs and Excise about VAT

Customs and Excise has long recognised the importance of Small and Medium Enterprises (SMEs) to the overall health of the UK economy. Over the years our approach has been to try to support these businesses by keeping to a minimum any regulatory compliance costs and by providing advice and assistance which recognises their special needs. This submission sets out what in the VAT area Customs and Excise already does to assist SMEs, what further work is planned, and the opportunities and difficulties associated with a range of current EC VAT issues.

1. Differences in EU VAT Systems and Rates

1.1 *General*

Although VAT is governed by EU law, the Sixth VAT Directive (77/388/ECC) provides only a broad framework for the coverage and machinery of the tax: the details are filled in by national law. The Directive allows (through permissive provisions and derogations) much scope for national variations to suit the revenue requirements and business needs of individual countries. This works to the UK's advantage, allowing us for example to retain our zero rates despite the "normal" minimum 5 per cent reduced rate; offer special accounting schemes under UK-specific derogations; and operate the EU's simplest periodic VAT declaration (only nine data elements have to be completed).

The Commission have long pressed for greater harmonisation of the VAT rules and rates, and get some support for their vision of a Common VAT System from large businesses trading multi-nationally. But the UK (along with most other countries) is opposed to forced harmonisation, and prefers to look at the merits issue by issue. We support efforts to simplify and modernise EC VAT law and procedures that will genuinely benefit business, but are wary of proposals that would increase bureaucracy for businesses, or would reduce our ability to offer flexible, simplified systems nationally. This last point is particularly important for SMEs, given that only a small proportion (approximately 120,000–130,000) of the 1.67 million UK VAT-registered businesses trade internationally.

1.2 *Rate Harmonisation*

At the 25 May 1999 ECOFIN Meeting, Member States agreed to retain a 15 per cent minimum standard VAT rate but not to introduce a maximum standard rate of 25 per cent. Although the Commission would prefer to have a narrower range of VAT rates, when they put forward the proposals they acknowledged that a range of 10 percentage points does not appear to create any significant competitive distortions within the Single Market (Luxembourg has a rate of 15 per cent and Sweden and Denmark 25 per cent). During discussions the Government was content to continue with the current minimum standard rate which has been in force since 1992, as it establishes a floor across the Community and prevents the competitive down bidding of rates and the distortions of cross-border trade which might result.

1.3 *Reduced VAT rates for labour intensive services*

The Commission recently brought forward a proposal (COM (1999) 62: Explanatory Memorandum submitted on 30 March 1999) to allow Member States to apply a reduced rate of VAT (not lower then 5 per cent) on an optional, experimental basis, to certain local, labour-intensive services. The intention behind the proposal is to boost employment for small businesses, but it could also encourage businesses out of the shadow economy. While a reduced rate would address the financial burden of VAT where it is at its greatest (ie small service providers), and could be targeted on particular sectors (eg builders), the rates would apply regardless of the size of the business. The proposal is currently under discussion in a Council working group, where officials are drawing up a list of services to which the experiment might apply.

The Government does not object in principle to the introduction of an optional, experimental scheme in other Member States. However, the UK does not at present intend to participate in any experiments.

2. The Single Market and the "Transitional" VAT System

2.1 *Abolition of "Import" and "Export" declarations*

The present VAT system (the so-called "transitional" system which will operate until a definitive origin based system is eventually adopted) was agreed in order to abolish fiscal controls at internal European Community borders and so complete the Single Market. It is a destination based system which means that VAT revenue accrue to the Member State where consumption takes place. The introduction of the Single Market arrangements on 1 January 1993 led to the abolition of the requirement for customs "import" and "export" declarations for goods moving between EC Member States.

Businesses trading with other Member States now send periodic EC Sales Lists to the fiscal authorities showing the value of their supplies to VAT registered businesses in the other Member States. This information can then be used under mutual assistance arrangements—the VAT Information and Exchange System (VIES)—to verify that VAT has been properly accounted for on intra-EC trade. The removal of the requirement for import/export declarations has significantly reduced paperwork for the majority of businesses and so helped to stimulate trade within the Single Market.

These changes have benefited SMEs to a greater extent than large businesses who often had their own import/export departments, or for whom the cost of employing specialist shipping agents to complete all the necessary cross-border documentation was less significant.

2.2 *Intrastat Declarations*

With the completion of the Single Market a monthly Intrastat return replaced individual frontier declarations as a source of trade statistics for the intra-EC movement of goods. However, only larger VAT registered businesses (approximately 28,000 at present), whose value of either receipts from, or dispatches to, other Member States exceed the Intrastat threshold (currently £240,000), have to submit these forms. Consequently the Intrastat requirements do not generally represent an administrative burden for SMEs. It should also be noted that as a result of the Simpler Legislation in the Internal Market (SLIM) initiative, the amount of information to be provided by declarants will be reduced with effect from 1 January 2001.

3. SLIM II

The SLIM initiative was launched in May 1996 and covers both Community legislation and harmonised national legislation. VAT was part of SLIM II announced by the Commission in March 1997. The SLIM VAT Task force comprised five experts from national administrations and five representatives of users of the legislation. Its remit was to focus on measures which would ease burdens on business. It reported in October 1997 and recommended:

— simplifying the rules on tax representatives (see paragraph 6)

— reforming the 8th Directive refund mechanism (see paragraph 7)

— updating the arrangements governing mutual assistance on debt recovery (draft Directive COM (1998) 364—EMs submitted 24 July 1998 and 18 June 1999—proposes enhancing existing procedures and extending the scope of the current arrangements to include direct taxes)

— introducing common standards for electronic invoicing (currently awaiting a proposal from Commission)

— simplifying and increasing the efficiency of the VIES system used for verification of international trade (currently under consideration in Brussels by the Standing Committee on Administrative Co-operation)

The SLIM team favoured the UK's simplified procedures with regard to VAT returns and registration.

4. VAT REGISTRATION THRESHOLD

4.1 *Current threshold*

Recognising that compliance costs tend to be proportionately greater at lower levels of turnover, EC VAT law permits special schemes for small undertakings, including a small business exemption. The UK utilises these provisions to the full by having a high VAT registration threshold (currently £51,000) and in recent years has increased the threshold by at least the rate of inflation. By contrast most other Member States have lower registration thresholds, although interestingly earlier this year France significantly increased its threshold from 100,000Ffr to 500,000Ffr, bringing it up to a level very similar to that in the UK. The main reasons the French gave for their change of approach were to encourage business start-ups and increase employment opportunities.

4.2 *Current study of the registration threshold*

Although a high registration threshold is welcomed by SMEs, in recent years representations from business have suggested that it can cause competitive distortions between registered and unregistered businesses and can create a financial "cliff-edge" for growing businesses. Following an initial consultation exercise last year and an announcement in this year's Budget, Customs are currently working with business representatives to identify ways in which the impact of crossing the threshold could be cushioned. It is too soon to predict the outcome and any potential arrangements will need to be discussed with our EU partners.

5. Special Accounting Schemes

Under various provisions of the Sixth VAT Directive the UK has put in place a number of special accounting arrangements which are designed to enable traders to use their existing accounting systems and records and as a consequence to minimise the administrative burdens of the VAT system.

5.1 *Annual Accounting*

The UK operates an Annual Accounting Scheme for businesses with an annual turnover of £300,000 or less. It allows businesses to submit just one VAT return per annum with estimated instalments being paid throughout the year. Despite changes in 1996 to enhance the scheme and make it more attractive, take-up is only approximately 9,000 out of a possible 800,000 businesses. In consultation with business representatives, we are therefore exploring ways in which the scheme could be made more attractive to a larger number of eligible traders.

5.2 *Cash Accounting*

Under a special derogation obtained under the provisions of Article 27 of the Sixth VAT Directive the UK operates a Cash Accounting Scheme which allows businesses with a turnover below £350,000 to account for VAT on the basis of cash received and paid, rather than on the basis of the normal "time of supply" rule or invoice date. This simplifies bookkeeping and helps to alleviate the burden of bad debts or delayed payment. When last measured in 1996 take-up was over 40 per cent of the eligible trader population. But again we are exploring ways in which the Scheme could be improved whilst ensuring that any changes do not provide increased opportunities for tax evasion or avoidance in what is a high revenue risk sector.

5.3 *Retail Schemes*

Under another Article 27 derogation the UK operates a range of special schemes to give retailers an alternative (and often simpler) method of accounting for VAT. Their main purpose is to help retailers who cannot identify the liability and value of every sale. For larger businesses this is less of a problem as information technology now allows them to make greater use of "normal" accounting or the point of sale arrangements. But this is not always an option for smaller retailers, some of which do not even have a till. Changes were made to the schemes in 1997, mainly because of tax avoidance by large traders, but the benefits were retained for smaller businesses.

6. Person Liable for Payment of VAT (Fiscal Representative)

The EC Sixth VAT Directive provides Member States with a number of options for dealing with businesses which have no place of establishment in the Member State where they are liable to be registered. The UK has chosen to allow non-established taxable persons (NETPs) the option to take responsibility for their own VAT affairs *or* to appoint a fiscal representative or agent to act on their behalf. Such a flexible approach allows overseas businesses to minimise their administrative costs, whilst providing overall benefits to the UK by encouraging investment and trade. Generally speaking, we would only require appointment of a fiscal representative where we consider there is potential revenue risk.

However, some Member States insist on the appointment of a tax representative in all circumstances, and take financial guarantees that can be bureaucratic and burdensome, for SMEs in particular. There is inconsistent practice across the EC, with the UK at the liberal end of the range.

The European Commission's recent proposals to modify the present rules (draft Directive COM (98) 660: Explanatory Memorandum submitted on 13 January 1999) aim to simplify the obligations for such persons. The principles contained in the Directive are broadly in line with the UK's already flexible approach, and would have little effect on the treatment or obligations of NETPs operating in the UK. The proposals offer the prospect of simplification, more consistency of treatment and, in particular, a lighter administrative burden for UK businesses trading on a non-established basis in other Member States.

7. Rules on Deduction of VAT/8th VAT Directive Refund Scheme

The 8th VAT Directive (79/1072/EEC) provides a mechanism whereby businesses can recover VAT which they incur in other Member States where they are not VAT registered. Claims must be made to the tax authority in the Member State where the tax has been incurred and, in practice, businesses often encounter difficulties and delays in obtaining a refund. Small businesses are the most disadvantaged as, in terms of cash-flow, they are generally less able to cope with the delays and the additional administrative burden.

The Commission has put forward a proposal (draft Directive COM (98) 377: Explanatory Memorandum submitted on 21 July 1998) to simplify the refund system by allowing businesses to recover (as input tax), in the Member State in which they are registered, VAT incurred in other Member States. The Commission also proposes to standardise rules on business expenditure on which VAT cannot be recovered (input tax blocking rules). These proposals are still under discussion at EC Working Group level and the shape of any final measure is far from clear. While the UK recognises the potential benefits of simplifying/harmonising the current procedures, we are concerned about some aspects of the proposals (eg potential administrative burdens of the Commission's proposed refund arrangements; complexity and high revenue cost of the proposed harmonised rules for treatment of input tax on cars). The results of our recent consultation exercise show that there is strong support among businesses for reform of the 8th Directive, although there is hostility to any complex blocking rule proposals.

8. PLACE OF SUPPLY

8.1 *Current rules*

The VAT "place of supply" rules determine where a supply of goods or services is made and the tax jurisdiction in which any VAT has to be accounted. The primary purpose of the rules is to give certainty and thereby to try to avoid situations where there is either no or double taxation. However, the rules are complex, and in certain areas they can cause difficulties, particularly for SMEs. For example, the rules for passenger transport in Article 9(2)(b) of the 6th VAT Directive define the place of supply of transport services as being "the place where the transport takes place". This is a problem for SMEs such as coach tour operators who may as a consequence have to register for VAT in several Member States. The UK has alerted the Commission to such difficulties and will continue to press for reform of the rules deciding place of supply.

8.2 *Electronic commerce*

The need for a fundamental revision of the place of supply rules has in any case been highlighted by the rapid growth of e-commerce. E-commerce makes it much easier for any business to trade internationally, but as most large businesses already trade on a global scale the real impact/opportunities will be for SMEs. But differences in place of supply rules can lead to double or non-taxation. Fiscal authorities, including Customs & Excise, have been working with business representatives in OECD and EU fora to develop common rules under which e-commerce will be taxed. It has been agreed that for e-commerce, indirect taxes will be levied at the place of consumption and we are now working on the detailed rules—and ways of applying them—to ensure that the arrangements minimise the administrative costs to business whilst protecting tax revenues. The UK is at the forefront of a two-year programme instituted by the OECD after a Ministerial Conference in Ottawa in October 1998. Work is also going on at an EC level and will probably lead to proposals within the next year to modify and simplify the rules for deciding the place of supply.

9. ELECTRONIC VAT RETURNS AND REGISTRATION

Legislation was introduced as part of this year's Budget to allow tax information, such as VAT and Income Tax returns, to be submitted via the Internet as an alternative to paper communication. A live pilot of electronic VAT returns will take place during 1999–2000 and, if this is successful, the service will be expanded during 2000–01. Sending returns electronically will be conditional upon businesses also making the associated payments electronically. In the Budget, the Chancellor also announced that, in order to encourage small businesses to join the electronic age, discounts would be offered to those filing tax returns electronically. We are currently working up proposals in this area with colleagues from IR, DTI and the Treasury.

We are also developing a system to allow businesses to submit and amend VAT registration details via the Internet. We plan to pilot an interactive system early in 2000.

10. TRADER ADVICE AND EDUCATION

To help SMEs comply with their UK and EC tax obligations, in recent years we have implemented a number of business advice and education programmes:

— *Learn About VAT Menu.* A number of options are given to newly registered VAT traders to facilitate their understanding of the tax, including seminars and a video which has recently been re-packaged to be more user-friendly. These options are provided by our business education teams.

— *New Business Starter Pack.* This is a joint development with the Inland Revenue to provide those thinking of starting their own business with information concerning their legal tax obligations.

— *Business Support Programme.* A developing education programme to provide new importers and exporters with guidance about the Department's various import and export regimes, and generally to increase trade awareness of the facilities available.

— *Business Advice Open Days.* Following a successful pilot we are organising a number of further events over the next 18 months at which businesses, especially SMEs, can come and meet the revenue departments, local authorities and representatives of other regulatory authorities to get comprehensive advice and answers to problems.

— *Business with Government.* A cross-Departmental project to provide online information to citizens thinking of starting their own business. The Department is represented on both the project board and steering group.

— *Call Centres.* We are currently piloting call centres, with the aim of replacing over 40 business advice centres by 2002. The new call centres will be accessed through a national one-number enquiry line.

July 1999

Memorandum by the Inland Revenue, Business Tax Division

DIRECT TAX SUPPORT FOR SMEs

1. The Inland Revenue has been invited to submit evidence to the Committee on what, within EU policies, the European Commission, national governments and their agencies are doing to promote small and medium sized enterprises (SMEs).

2. The Commission policy on SMEs is described in a 1994 document *The Improvement of the Fiscal Environment of SMEs*, which was the subject of an Explanatory Memorandum (7663/94 dated 25 July 1994). Given the importance of direct taxation for European Member States' sovereignty and the principle of subsidiarity, Community action on direct taxation is limited to the minimum necessary to ensure that the internal market functions smoothly. There are, therefore, no current Community proposals specifically on the direct taxation of SMEs, but Member States are encouraged to tackle the problems that SMEs face in obtaining finance, incorporation of businesses and administrative complexity of taxation systems.

3. Fiscal measures aimed at SMEs fall within the scope of Community state aid law, and there are special guidelines which apply to SMEs. Tax measures directed towards SMEs are also potentially within the scope of the Code of Conduct on business taxation. The Government is confident that none of the UK SME measures being assessed under the Code is harmful and is robustly making that case in the Code Group.

4. This paper concentrates on direct tax initiatives in the UK. The paper is in two parts. Part A (paragraphs 2 to 20) describe the UK's direct tax measures to help small and medium sized enterprises and comments on SMEs and cross-border trading. Part B (paragraphs 21 to 35) gives a brief description of how the UK taxes small businesses.

PART A: UK DIRECT TAX MEASURES

5. The present government has cut the corporation tax rate for small companies from 23 per cent to 20 per cent, and has given a commitment that the rate will remain at or below 20 per cent for the rest of this Parliament. This will encourage investment by small companies and increase the post-tax return on that investment.

6. From April 2000 a new 10 per cent starting rate of corporation tax will focus help on the smallest companies. The new rate will benefit 270,000 companies, of which 85 per cent employ fewer than 10 people. The 10 per cent rate is the lowest ever rate of corporation tax in the UK and the lowest rate for small companies among the major industrialised countries and the major EU economies.

7. The abolition of ACT in April 1999 gave small companies a cashflow boost of £1 billion.

8. Enhanced first year capital allowances of 50 per cent (double the normal rate) were introduced in the July 1997 Budget for assets bought between 2 July 1997 and 1 July 1998. This was extended in 1998 for a further year at 40 per cent and was extended again this year to assets bought up to 1 July 2000.

9. A new research and development tax credit is proposed for introduction next year. Businesses already benefit from the 100 per cent first year allowance for R&D (under the Scientific Research Allowance), but the new credit will increase the allowance for SMEs to 150 per cent for current R&D spending. It will also allow SME companies to sell unused R&D losses to the Exchequer at a discount from their tax value. This will directly address the cashflow constraints faced by high tech firms who have long lead times between R&D and marketing.

10. Capital gains tax (CGT) has been reformed to promote long-term investment and encourage entrepreneurs. The new CGT taper relief is of particular benefit to individuals who hold "business asset" investments in trading companies (or holding companies of trading groups). A shareholding qualifies as a business asset if, in the case of a full-time working officer or employee, it provides at least 5 per cent of the voting rights, and, in the case of other investors, it provides 25 per cent of the voting rights. These thresholds are more likely to be exceeded in SMEs, so there will be a greater number of business asset shareholdings in these. Gains arising on the disposal of such holdings after 10 years or more will be taxed at an effective rate of 10 per cent or less.

11. The Enterprise Investment Scheme (EIS) and Venture Capital Trusts provide a range of tax incentives for individuals to invest in small higher risk unquoted trading companies. The schemes target investment in companies whose gross assets are no more than £15 million immediately before the investment, and no more than £16 million immediately afterwards. The EIS caters for direct investment in such companies, and VCTs

for indirect investment in them through the medium of a quoted investment fund. Following changes made last year to the EIS, entrepreneurs are able to defer CGT charges on gains by reinvesting the gains in new shares in EIS companies they control. Changes made this year provide for serial investors in EIS companies to benefit from CGT taper relief on a cumulative basis when they reinvest a chargeable gain arising from one EIS investment in shares in another EIS company. The holding period for taper relief purposes for the gain will be the aggregate of the holding periods for the two investments.

12. Investment companies and individuals are able to set capital losses on investments in new shares in small higher risk unquoted trading companies against income if they cannot offset them against chargeable gains.

13. The Inland Revenue has recently consulted on a proposal to introduce a corporate venturing relief to encourage companies to make minority equity investments in small higher risk unquoted trading companies. The intention is to improve the supply of venture capital and to encourage the development of mutually beneficial relationships (which may include sharing of skills, product or market knowledge or facilities). Draft Clauses are to be published later this year for consultation with a view to including legislation in next year's Finance Bill.

14. In the last Budget the Chancellor announced his intention to introduce a new targeted tax break on equity remuneration in 2000. This will be available to a few key individuals who are prepared to share in the risks and rewards of running small higher risk trading companies. It will offer them considerably more tax-advantaged equity remuneration than is available under existing tax-advantaged schemes. The measure will broadly be targeted on the same companies as the EIS/VCT schemes. By enabling these businesses to recruit and retain high calibre people, it will help them to succeed and grow and so create wealth and jobs.

15. The last Budget also increased the limit for quarterly payments of PAYE. This will help small employers' cashflow and will benefit over 60 per cent of employers (some 700,000 businesses).

16. The Government has been putting considerable efforts into helping SMEs meet their obligations. A new Small Business Service will give support to the whole range of small businesses from the self employed and micro businesses through to businesses with up to 250 employees. The Inland Revenue already provides a wide range of assistance. It has recently introduced a new business guide, business starter pack and guidance for new employers which focuses on helping them through their first pay day. There is also a national helpline facility and a nationwide network of Business Support teams offering face to face help.

SMEs AND CROSS-BORDER TRADING

17. We have been asked to comment on the disadvantages faced by SMEs vis-à-vis large firms because they have fewer options for managing their tax liability when cross-border trading. Our views are in paragraphs 18 to 20.

18. Where the UK enterprise is engaged in trading across an international border, the same rules apply to the taxation of the profits of the trade whatever the size of the enterprise.

19. The transfer pricing rules in Schedule 28AA to the Income and Corporation Taxes Act 1988 are particularly relevant in the context of trading across international borders. These apply where a UK enterprise is involved in transactions with another enterprise with which it is associated, and that other enterprise is not within the charge to UK tax in respect of the activities in question. The law says that the UK enterprise cannot enjoy a more advantageous position in relation to UK tax than the position it would have been in if the transactions had been at arm's length between independent enterprises.

20. The 1999 Finance Bill contains provisions for advance pricing agreements for transfer pricing issues. These enable an enterprise to reach an agreement with the Inland Revenue about an appropriate method to use in calculating an arm's length price in the circumstances of the particular business of the enterprise. The advantage for the enterprise is that it has the certainty that, if it applies the method as specified in the agreement, the resulting prices will be accepted by the Inland Revenue. The purpose of these agreements is to establish an appropriate way of addressing complex transfer pricing issues on a prospective basis. The Inland Revenue is willing to enter into discussions about an agreement whenever the issues are sufficiently complex. It acknowledges that complex transfer pricing issues can be encountered by small and medium sized enterprises and it is willing to enter into discussions with such enterprises wherever the general conditions are met.

PART B: HOW THE UK TAXES SMALL AND MEDIUM SIZED ENTERPRISES

Introduction

21. There is no definition of a small or medium sized enterprise for tax purposes. Instead there are different definitions for the 1985 Companies Act, the Small Firms Loan Guarantee Scheme and Department of Trade and Industry statistical purposes. Broadly speaking, a small firm may be said to be one with 50 or fewer employees and a turnover of £1.5 million or less. A medium sized business might have 50 to 250 employees and a turnover between £1.5 and £3 million.

22. Small businesses come in a variety of different forms from the sole proprietor who is self employed, through normal companies limited by shares (or on rare occasions guarantee) to specialist professional operations such as lawyers, accountants etc, who tend to form partnerships. Partnership taxation is a specialist area and therefore this note will deal in broad terms with the UK's tax and National Insurance systems as they affect the self employed and companies.

The self employed

23. The trading income of the self employed is taxed along with their personal income under the UK's normal personal tax regime. They are allowed to deduct from their income the normal personal allowances and their income is then taxed at the following rates.

The tax bands and rates are (after deducting expenses and personal allowances):

	1998–99	*1999–2000*
Lower 20 per cent	£0–4,300	£0–1,500
Basic 23 per cent	£4,301–27,100	£1,501–28,000
Higher 40 per cent	over £27,100	over £28,000

24. Class 4 National Insurance Contributions are collected by the Inland Revenue at the same time as tax. Class 2 contributions are paid direct to the DSS. There are various classes and structures for this, but the self employed pay the following which is calculated solely on their trading income.

Self employed NICs for 1998–99 comprise:

Class 2. A flat rate charge of £6.35 a week due from all self-employed with earnings above £69 a week.

Class 4. A 6 per cent charge on taxable profits, between £140 a week (the Lower Profits Limit) and £485 a week (Upper Profits Limit).

Companies

25. Companies pay corporation tax on their trading and other income and on their capital gains. They are allowed to deduct from their taxable income any revenue (ie day-to-day) expenditure that they incur in generating that income and get capital allowances in place of depreciation against their capital expenditure.

26. The small companies' rate of corporation tax, for companies with profits up to £300,000, is currently 20 per cent. There is marginal relief for companies with profits between £300,000 and £1,500,000, to ease the transition to the main rate of 30 per cent.

27. The new 10 per cent starting rate will apply to companies with profits up to £10,000. There will be marginal relief for companies with profits between £10,000 and £50,000.

28. The profits limits for the lower rates are reduced proportionately where companies are grouped or have associated companies.

Capital allowances for SMEs

29. In the UK tax system capital allowances take the place of commercial depreciation of capital assets, which is not allowed for tax purposes. Capital allowances are normally given on machinery or plant at 25 per cent of the cost remaining each year after deducting allowances given in previous periods. But there is special treatment for SMEs.

30. For the period from 2 July 1997 to 1 July 1998 an increased first year allowance of 50 per cent is available for expenditure by SMEs on machinery or plant.

31. For the period from 2 July 1998 to 1 July 2000, the rate of first year allowance for SMEs is 40 per cent. SMEs purchasing machinery or plant for use in Northern Ireland between 12 May 1998 and 11 May 2002 may qualify for a first year allowance of 100 per cent.

32. The allowances are available to both companies and unincorporated businesses (ie self employed).

Payment of tax

33. The self-employed pay their income tax and NICs under a self assessment system in which half of the tax is paid within the year with the balance payable three months after the end of the tax year.

34. Companies pay under a new corporate self assessment system. Those with profits below £1.5 million pay their corporation tax nine months after the end of their accounting period. The overwhelming majority of companies pay on this basis.

35. Companies with profits over £1.5 million have started to pay some of their corporation tax in-year (with the balance due nine months after the end of their accounting period). This is a new system which is

being phased in over four years, at the end of which such companies will pay all of their corporation tax in four quarterly instalments (two of which will be in-year), based on their current year liability.

July 1999

Memorandum by KPMG

1. Further to your letter of 7 July I am writing to provide KPMG's views on "what, within EU policies, the European Commission, national governments and their agencies are doing to support and promote SMEs, and what they should or should not be doing for such enterprises . . . in particular:

— the special characteristics of management training for SMEs;

— any significant differences between SMEs and large firms in the management skills needed in European markets; and

— whether current EC policies cater for the particular requirements of SMEs with respect to management training."

2. We have restricted our response to three key areas. They are:

— access to finance;

— training; and

— support services.

3. For each we consider the fundamental questions:

— what is being done well;

— what is being done less well; and

— what are the areas for concern.

4. *Access to finance*

Small firms face unique issues with regard to accessing finance. They include:

— the business's securities are not publicly traded, so that valuation of a small business is much more subjective than that of a large quoted business;

— the owner's investment in the business constitutes a major portion of their personal wealth, so that as a business increases in stature, the owner-manager may become more risk adverse and less prepared to pledge his assets as security for finance;

— limited liability is often absent or ineffective, particularly in respect of bank finance which is frequently secured by guarantees against personal assets;

— the business is likely, especially at an early stage, to have an incomplete management team, lacking breadth of management skills in, among other areas, finance;

— financiers among other factors consider the track record of the borrowing entity to date. New start ups and fast growing businesses often find it difficult to demonstrate record that is credible; and

— the business is potentially subject to various constraints, both internal and external, on borrowing, equity participation by outsiders and on the scale and growth of the business. These constraints arise due, among other factors, to the smallness of the business relative to other market participants (banks, big firms), the psychology of the management team, the information the business makes available to the market and the information the business is able to acquire itself.

5. KPMG undertook an evaluation of the Small Firms Loan Guarantee Scheme (SFLGS) for the Department of Trade and Industry, published in March 1999. The SFLGS was introduced to address a gap in the market for small firms' access to finance by providing a guarantee to encourage banks and other financial institutions to lend where small firms are unable to raise conventional finance. We concluded that the SFLGS has provided much needed financial support to a large number of small firms. The majority of the support was found to be additional to that which would have been available from other sources.

6. However, gaps still exist in the provision of finance to small firms, notably at the very low end of the employment size band and the higher risk ventures such as seed capital and higher technology firms.

7. Furthermore, it is our experience that entrepreneurial firms that are growing often have the need for investment equity of between £100,000 and £500,000 which is both difficult to access and costly to finance. Traditional venture capital firms are often unwilling to back this level of investment preferring to complete larger transactions. It is these medium sized businesses which are the engines of employment growth.

8. *Training*

It is our experience that managers in SMEs have different training and development needs from those in larger firms. These include:

— business planning;

— investment appraisal;

— personnel development; and

— IT skills

9. SMEs do not have access to the range of skills and internal support structures found in larger firms.

10. It is our experience that SMEs currently turn to their peer group (Small Business Federations, friends, business colleagues) and local support systems (Chambers of Commerce, Training and Enterprise Councils and local authorities) for help and support in this area. The majority are not well served by current publicly provided courses. This is due to a lack of flexibility, effective marketing and the provision of timely and appropriate support and information.

11. *Support services*

SME support services, in the UK at least, have historically been fragmented, poorly signposted and poorly delivered. The creation of the Business Link Service in the UK partly addressed this issue. However, the provision of public support remains fragmented and overlaps between different agencies, with Business Links often existing alongside Enterprise Agencies, Regional Supply Offices (part of the Regional Supply Network working to develop supplier relationships between SMEs and local customers) and Innovation programmes. Furthermore, there are wide variations in the quality of service provided. Public sector and private sector can often find themselves competing for the same customers.

12. The UK government is attempting to streamline this situation through the development of a small business service and the inclusion of business representation on the planned National Learning and Skills Council, but provision is likely to remain disjointed and fragmented. The creation of the Regional Development Agencies in England is a positive move especially with regard to the strategic overview they will take in areas such as venture capital and inward investment.

12 August 1999

Memorandum by Mr David Milborrow

1. I am a freelance energy consultant and carry out work for clients in both public and private sectors in Britain, Europe and North America. My specialist areas are the economics of electricity generation and the renewable energy sources. I have acted as an expert adviser to the European Commission and am currently working on two contracts with EU funding. I am registered for VAT (this is essential for EU contracts) but am not a limited company. I collaborate with other consultants and academic and industrial partners, but, as a "sole proprietor", might possibly be regarded as the ultimate in small businesses.

2. My overall impression of the attitude of the European Commission towards small businesses is that "its heart is in the right place" but that efforts to assist them are diffused—the net is spread too wide. Small businesses are also frustrated by increasingly bureaucratic procedures and ever more complicated rules for contracts.

3. These concerns about bureaucracy are not mine alone. A few years back, I participated in a survey (organised by the Commission) which went to small businesses. One of the clear-cut conclusions from the survey was "EC procedures are too bureaucratic". More recently, there has been a steady increase in the volume and complexity of proposal forms for submissions to the research programmes. Several organisations with whom I have spoken recently indicated that they would not be making submissions as a result.

4. The attitude of the Commission's contracts services towards one-man enterprises is particularly frustrating. About four years ago, I participated in an EU-funded research project and, at the Commission's insistence, devised the business name "DM energy" as they were not prepared to deal with a real person. About a year ago, with another contract, the position was reversed; and, after much hassle, I became a real person again, but it was necessary to become a sub-contractor to one of the project partners. I understand this attitude stems from problems with some consultants who have declared bankruptcy at an early stage in a contract. Nevertheless, it should be possible to distinguish between consultants with a good track record (my connections with the Commission go back to 1986) and newcomers or defaulters.

5. I have not sought assistance from any of the programmes targeted specifically at SMEs. The impression I have is that application to one of these programmes simply involves an additional layer of bureaucracy. I do, however, receive the journal *Cordis Focus* which is a valuable source of information on Commission activities, publications and calls for proposals.

6. In conclusion, I suggest that much more needs to be done if the Commission really wants to promote and assist small businesses. As the upper size limit for SMEs is 250 employees, it is unrealistic to expect that small businesses of, say, 50 employees and below have the same needs as the much larger ones. If the bureaucratic and contractual procedures were simplified, for a start, it would aid all SMEs. The support measures cover a very wide range of business sizes and might be targeted more specifically at the smaller end of the spectrum.

4 August 1999

Memorandum by the National Centre for Business & Ecology (NCBE), the Co-operative Bank

INTRODUCTION

The NCBE is a sustainable solutions organisation offering environmental protection and social responsibility advice to businesses and other organisations. The Centre recently completed a large demonstration project using European Regional Development Funds to help over 40 SMEs to achieve environmental improvements. The introduction of practices including greater use of the Internet and the use of sustainable product design were key components of the project. The NCBE is currently making use of ADAPT funds to offer 40 more SMEs the chance to develop and remote learning packages to enhance environmental performance, and more ERDF funds to link 20 SME suppliers to Manchester Airport to comply with environmental requirements through innovative telecommunication techniques.

During the course of this work the NCBE has identified faults in the current SME environmental support strategies. Solutions are proposed to this House of Lords Committee Enquiry that would enable European and other funds directed at SMEs to be more effective and efficient.

THE NORTH WEST OF ENGLAND AS AN EXAMPLE OF THE CURRENT SYSTEM

Large-scale "Demonstration Projects" for the environmental improvement of small companies have become an established point of delivery in the UK. Inspired by the success of the Aire and Calder Project in Yorkshire over a decade ago, the North West has hosted Project Catalyst, the Merseyside Waste Minimisation Project, Environet 2000 and the Business and Ecology Demonstration Project (BEDP) all in the space of six years. Excluding many other smaller schemes, this represents over £15,000,000 of investment (most of it from European Structure Funds) solely devoted to the environmental improvement of small companies in the region.

Each of the projects followed a successful formula. A number of small companies (less than 250 employees) aggregated under the banner of the small to medium sized enterprise (SME) were recruited to participate in subsidised environmental improvement programmes. The projects generally offered waste minimisation and/or the means to build an environmental management system into businesses that did not previously have the means or opportunity to take on such initiatives. Most of the projects were directed at particular industrial sectors and were limited to specific geographical areas within the region.

The outputs of the projects varied depending on the source of funding, but all of the end-of-project reports highlighted the monetary benefits accruing to participating companies. Over 2,500 companies have benefited from these projects, which must therefore be considered worthwhile based on the sheer number of individuals that they have touched. However, the mark of success for a Demonstration Project should also be the effect it has on the non-participating businesses in the region and further afield. The aim of a Demonstration Project should be to demonstrate that the methods and techniques designed to improve environmental performance for the few will benefit the many.

It is notoriously difficult to gauge the post-project effects of demonstration projects, partly because the funding rarely allows research outside the immediate beneficiaries, and partly because the decision by businesses to implement environmental programmes can seldom be attributed to information from a single programme. Accepting that there is poor data on this subject, it is possible to use a number of surveys into the environmental needs of SMEs to conclude that there is rarely life in a demonstration project after the funds run out.

Polls and surveys carried out in the North West by (among others) the National Centre for Business & Ecology (NCBE), Manchester Chamber of Commerce and Industry, MORI, and Manchester Metropolitan University show that SMEs still rank environmental issues relatively low on the list of business priorities. Many are still unsure about where to look for advice, and most have never heard of the demonstration projects that have taken place in their region.

RESOURCES AND EFFICIENCY

There are over 180 organisations in the North West purporting to offer small companies advice on environmental matters. These organisations make use of many different sources of funding offered by a wide range of bodies. The following bodies have funded just a few of the recent initiatives in the North West:

— European Commission (Regional Structure Funds, Millennium/Lottery Sources, LIFE, ADAPT and others);

— UK national sources (DTI, DETR, Single Regeneration Budget preceded by various Challenge initiatives);

— UK regional sources (Welsh Development Agency, The Welsh Office, English Partnerships and County Councils); and

— local sources (Landfill Tax Credit Schemes, ad hoc support from the Business Links and Training Enterprise Councils and match funding from private sector and local government).

The rules that govern the way bidding organisations can obtain these funds vary widely and combine a diverse mix of qualifying criteria. Each fund also has different outcomes or output requirements. This diversity could be seen as an advantage as it offers a number of ways to obtain funds, but the reality is that the current situation is confusing and many of the resources on offer are inefficiently spent, and some even fail to be claimed. Rationalisation of both the qualifying criteria and the outcomes would help bidders to put together integrated proposals. It would also help auditors to produce coherence, region-wide reports against unified performance targets.

Recent change in the administration and management of European Structure funds make it even more difficult to gauge how much value is being added to the region through environmental programmes. Devolving management duties from Government Offices to thematic partnerships cuts down on central costs, but seriously harms the ability to co-ordinate programmes across a whole region. While most funding bodies have some form of ex-post audit system, these are mainly designed to identify misappropriation of funds, and rarely raise issues of substance on a more holistic scale.

There are three elements that need to be addressed before the radical improvements to the UK SME environmental assistance programme can begin to make significant inroads into current levels of performance. These are:

— the need for consistent, high quality advice;

— the need for co-ordination of effort; and

— the need for a unifying vision of achievement.

The Quality of Advice

There are over 180 bodies offering environmental advice to SMEs in the North West of England. Many of these service providers make use of European match funding to carry out their work. With so many providers it is hardly surprising that conflicting advice of variable quality is encountered from time to time. Most service providers use experienced professionals or trained graduates to advise participating companies. For the majority of the time, participants benefit from a good standard of support.

However, there is some evidence that small company schemes and environmental consultants in general are being discredited by the poor work of a handful of advisors. A Business in the Environment conference on green business clubs last year featured the Managing Director of a small company arising some of his grievances:

— Poor quantified business advice—advisers often suggest that businesses invest in solutions with open-ended payback periods, or seek to extend the investigation without stating the likely outcome.

— Poor environmental advice—advisers can fail to bring sufficient expertise to the client, often because they have an alternative speciality (such as health and safety). The lack of experience shows in suggestions that companies should do their checks to determine whether they are breaking the law without providing the necessary skills to carry this out.

— Unfocused or formulaic advice—recommendations to produce an environmental policy or implement an environmental management system may be less appropriate than more direct and immediate measures.

It seems reasonable that a minimum standard of qualification and experience should be set for any organisation offering advice under a small company scheme. Although there is no such requirement for those offering advice on the open market, individuals operating under a subsidised scheme are rarely under the same scrutiny.

Co-ordinating Effort

One outcome of the many European funded small company programmes in the North West is a wealth of innovative and inspiring approaches to solving environmental problems. This produces an impressive number of satisfied participants, particularly where considerable sums of money have been saved through waste minimisation or energy conservation measures.

The disappointing aspect of these success stories is that so few companies benefit from this enterprising work. The ripples of innovation that should travel through the region and beyond rarely make it further than the participant's site boundary. This is sometimes due to a unique solution that is sector-specific or can only be applied to certain process technologies. Most of the time, however, it is simply due to a lack of dissemination funds at the end of the programme, or unimaginative communication methods. Linked to this is the evidence that many companies would like to participate in certain programmes, but are excluded because of their location or sector.

There needs to be some mechanism to maximise efficiency, and to manage and maintain the momentum of small company schemes. The best way to achieve this is to appoint an overseeing or co-ordinating body responsible for identifying gaps in funding, and the dissemination of best practice. Ideally, this body should not just concentrate on environmental issues, but should have the remit to consider the larger task of building industrial competitiveness. It should have sufficient financial and political weight and require service providers to take note of its views.

Funding for a co-ordinating body could come from a percentage of the funds directed to each small company programme. Whatever the administrative arrangements, small company environmental schemes will continue to scatter both light and shadow across potential beneficiaries until a single body illuminates the whole of the region.

The obvious candidate to perform this function is the newly created Regional Development Agencies (RDAs). The RDAs have a number of responsibilities that would sit well with the role of co-ordinating body including:

— Promotion of inward investment;

— Promotion of commercial competitiveness;

— A mandate to adopt an integrated policy approach linking economic, social, and environmental objectives;

— An advisory role for TECs and Business Links.

The regional focus of the RDA fits with the geographical delineation of regional Structure Funds from Europe and regional assistance from central government. Whitehall could direct all regional fund managers (not just those in Government Offices allocating European regional funds) to work with the RDA in an attempt to co-ordinate the diversity of programmes.

A UNIFYING VISION

Many schemes that are designed to improve the environmental performance of small companies cite job protection as a main output of, and justification for, the project. Whilst important, this is hardly a progressive aspiration. Similarly, while accepting that it should be a societal goal to increase the level of social and environmental responsibility in the business world, this is unlikely to be the prime motivation that engages small business to invest time and resources in sustainability initiatives.

Without diminishing the diversity of small business schemes, there should be a better vision that links all initiatives in the future. This vision should seek to reduce environmental impacts and promote social responsibility within the context of increased regional prosperity. These three elements, taken together, form the basis for a vision of a sustainable future. This is not an aspirational view. Instructions to Member States wishing to bid for the latest round of Objective 2 (ERDF/ESF) regeneration funds explain that sustainable development should be at the heart of their strategy.

The vision should be embedded in guidance for fund managers and providers. Even the prescriptive conditions attached to Structure Funds allow additional local criteria to be added to the programme. A common objection raised when the Environment Agency was proposing environmental screening criteria for Structure Fund Programmes in the North West was that it hindered the ability of fund managers to allocate the money to needy beneficiaries. This is a shortsighted view if the waste of resources caused by poor co-ordination and an unfocused approach is included in the calculation on value for money.

Better and more imaginative indicators of sustainable progress should be developed and built into the early stages of new projects. This strategic approach will allow service providers to promote bottom-line benefits to potential beneficiaries, while being aware of their more far-reaching duties to the prosperity of the region.

CONCLUSION

A wide range of approaches designed to help SMEs to improve their environmental performance has been tried in the UK over the past decade. These vary from the ad hoc assistance offered by government sponsored assistance bodies to multimillion pound demonstration projects making use of large amounts of European funding initiatives. The main lessons that have been learned during this period are that the majority of the SMEs have yet to fully appreciate the reasoning behind environmental improvement initiatives.

This is borne out by service providers that report difficulty in recruiting participants, even when programmes are running at 100 per cent subsidy rates. This is partly due to the limited relevance of environmental protection legislation for small companies, but is also due to the supply-led nature of funding for SME assistance. Much of the available funding for these projects is awarded to bodies that have learned how to submit a winning bid. A demand-led system would ensure a much higher take-up rate from companies that have taken the trouble to explain their needs to fund managers.

A combination of consistency, co-ordination, and vision will radically transform small business environmental improvement programmes in the UK. A regional body that has joint responsibility for sustainable development and economic growth would be ideally placed to co-ordinate such a programme, proving that it adopted a progressive style of management. While this would require widespread co-operation amongst the diverse range of fund providers (particularly the Government Offices) all parties would ultimately gain from the pooling of experience and knowledge. This would allow all projects to cause ripples far beyond the businesses that directly benefited from the original advice.

21 July 1999

Memorandum by Professor Hannah M Scobie, Director, European Economics and Financial Centre

1. The evidence is submitted in two parts:

— The disadvantages for SMEs outside the Euro-zone

— Measures adopted to assist SMEs in other countries

THE DISADVANTAGES FOR SMES OUTSIDE THE EURO-ZONE

2. With respect to the role of a single currency, it is useful to draw attention to the practical experiences of British SMEs that have been involved in exporting goods and services. Undoubtedly these SMEs have suffered from the considerable appreciation of the pound sterling over the period 1995–98. This is demonstrated in Figure 1 when the value of the pound sterling rose by some 40 per cent going from 2.2 DMarks to the pound in the second quarter of 1995 to 3.1 DMarks in the third quarter of 1998.

3. Such a sizeable appreciation of the pound against the Deutschmark and some of the other European currencies has had adverse consequences on the business of these SMEs and has eroded their competitiveness.

4. The strong sterling made it very difficult to sell their products in Europe. Under these circumstances they were forced either to:

— Absorb the sterling appreciation themselves and cut their prices, or

— Lose the business altogether, as it no longer was cost effective for them to absorb all the currency appreciation themselves.

5. A great many firms have reported the loss of some sizeable business over the time period 1995–98 through no fault of their own. Figure 1 clearly depicts the continual erosion of competitiveness of UK goods and services within the EU.

Fig.1. UK Pound Sterling Exchange Rate against German Mark

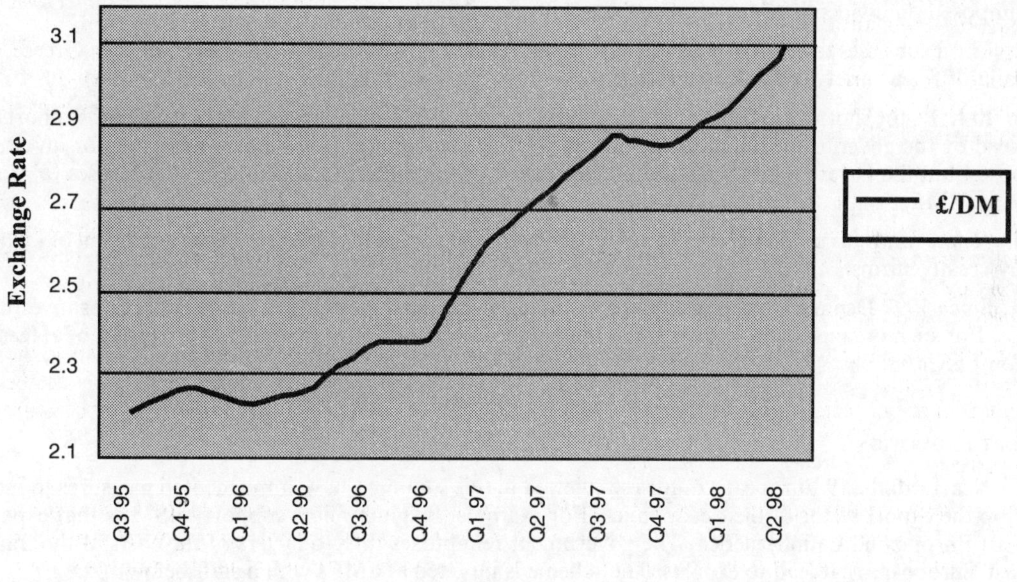

ASSISTANCE PROVIDED BY THE EUROPEAN COMMISSION, NATIONAL GOVERNMENTS AND THEIR AGENCIES TO SUPPORT AND PROMOTE SMALL AND MEDIUM-SIZED ENTERPRISES (SMES) IN EUROPE

6. The presented analysis covers 19 European countries and examines the support offered for SMEs in these regions.

Financial Assistance

— Provision of finance and other support for start-ups.

— Loans subsidised by governments both for start-ups and specific investments of SMEs.

— Loan guarantees of 75 per cent on average.

— Tax allowances for innovative projects.

— Financial assistance for staff involved in research and development.

— Venture capital guarantees for innovative projects and firms.

— Stimulation of networks and co-operation between research centres and firms.

Export Promotion

7. Measures implemented for the provision of better conditions for the generation of international business include:

— Financial assistance for staff involved in exports.

— Financial support for exports.

FINANCIAL ASSISTANCE FOR NEW BUSINESSES

8. Belgium has aided business start-ups in two principal ways: (a) through loan guarantees, and (b) through reduction in social security payments. The French government has allocated new finance for business start-ups. From 1996 Austria has introduced a scheme whereby the founder's initial saving for the start of a business would be uplifted by 14 per cent by the government with a ceiling of 55,000 ECUs. This scheme has been operated through a savings account which also entitled the business initiator a line of credit worth 110,000 ECUs. The Netherlands has established new financial assistance and capital for SMEs in the technology sector. Finland has offered the SMEs a similar scheme to Austria.

ADDITIONAL FORMS OF FINANCIAL HELP

9. Portugal introduced a financial package for SMEs in 1996 to help those enterprises without an adequate security for their loans. From 1997 entrepreneurs under the age of 35 were assisted further by additional guarantees provided by the Portuguese government. The objective of such actions was to reduce the lending risk by protecting 25–50 per cent of the loan risk left uncovered by the entrepreneur's collateral.

10. Measures to increase the level of investment undertaken by SMEs have been taken in Austria, where support is targeted on companies with a staff of less than 250.

11. Belgium has been concentrating on diverting risk capital from the private sector towards small firms with a staff below 100. Further support for SMEs has taken the form of a lowering to 15 per cent of the tax rate imposed on dividends of the shares of small firms.

12. Extra subsidies towards interest on investment by SMEs is offered by the government in Greece. This is available for a variety of SMEs for start-ups.

13. In Italy, the short-term debts of SMEs can be converted into medium-term debt via a new support fund financed by the government. In addition, not only is finance from the government available for investment purposes, but the government has also chanelled funds to commercial banks and finance houses to provide loans for SMEs.

14. A new fund was put in place in Spain in 1997 with the particular objective of the provision of loans for highly creative firms.

15. Since 1997 Denmark has put in place a system of financial guarantees for organisations investing in SMEs. For such organisations to qualify for these guarantees they must possess SME equities of at least 2.7 million ECUs.

EXPORT PROMOTION

16. Nearly all the 19 European countries reviewed in this summary have implemented measures to further develop the export sector of their economies. For example, Belgium offers support to SMEs that export to Eastern Europe and Latin America. The government reimburses three-quarters of the costs of the training of East Europeans that lead to exports. The scheme is targeted at SMEs with a staff below 100.

17. Similarly, the government of Denmark offers financial assistance towards the training of export staff. Unlike Belgium, however, this is not specifically targeted to any particular region, and has taken the form of wage subsidies. The French stance has been to induce all SMEs to take steps towards exporting goods and services by offering loans.

SUPPORT TOWARDS RESEARCH AND DEVELOPMENT

18. The provision of financial support for Research and Development by the SMEs is quite common in the European Union. The Spanish government, for example, has taken noticeable initiative in this area by offering tax allowances, wage subsidies and funding to provide incentive for innovation during the 1997 to 1999 period. Similarly, in the Netherlands financial support for SMEs in the area of R&D has been provided, as well as granting tax allowances for employees carrying out R&D. This is subject to a cap of 7.5 million ECUs per individual enterprise.

19. France's financial support to SMEs includes subsidies for the purpose of employing graduates. This is in aid of increasing innovativeness. In Norway the government has designated specific funds providing 2.25 million ECUs per year for SMEs employing new graduates in order to improve innovation.

20. The approach adopted by Austria has been to encourage closer links among research centres and universities in order to increase the penetration of modern technologies. To this end finance has been provided for the Austrian Research Promotion Fund.

21. In Denmark between five and 10 regional "innovative" projects have been supported by the Danish Ministry of Business and Industry. Finance in the form of venture capital has been provided by the Finnish government to benefit Research and Development. Luxembourg, Switzerland, France, Germany, Greece and Italy have also been supportive of the transfer of technology by earmarking finance, interest-free loans, tax allowances, or subsidised loans to this end.

22. Table 1 is a summary of measures introduced by European governments in order to improve the performance of SMEs in the EU.

Table 1

SUMMARY OF MEASURES DESIGNED TO ASSIST SMEs IN DIFFERENT

EUROPEAN COUNTRIES

● Indicates implemented or planned action.

Country	Finance	Innovation	Late Payments	Labour	Internationalisation	Information	Administrative Burdens
Austria	●	●		●	●		●
Belgium	●			●	●		●
Germany	●	●			●	●	●
Denmark	●	●		●	●	●	●
Finland	●	●		●	●	●	●
France	●	●	●	●	●		●
Greece	●	●		●	●	●	
Iceland	●						
Ireland	●	●	●	●	●	●	●
Italy	●	●	●	●	●	●	●
Liechtenstein	Only general economic policies; no direct support measures for SMEs						
Luxembourg	●	●		●	●		●
Netherlands	●	●			●	●	●
Norway	●	●		●		●	●
Portugal	●	●		●	●	●	●
Spain	●	●		●	●	●	●
Sweden		●		●	●	●	●
Switzerland	●	●		●	●		●
United Kingdom		●	●	●		●	●

Source: European Networks for SME Research, 1997.

EXPERIENCE OF UK SMEs

23. As far as help by the UK government is concerned, sadly the experiences of SMEs have not been very favourable in this country. The attitude of the UK government towards the SMEs has been one of "sink or swim". The assistance that is frequently offered is in the form of consultancy or advice which often SMEs do not find useful. Small firms are offered subsidised consultancy services on how to run their businesses where the government covers the lion share of the consultancy fee. Indeed, this does not fulfil the SMEs' immediate needs and these firms often feel rather disappointed whenever they explore the possibility of any form of assistance from the government in the UK. In our opinion the offer of consultancy is a waste of government resources. More appropriate forms of assistance which are offered in other parts of the European Union (as outlined above) could be more beneficial to UK SMEs.

July 1999

Memorandum by the Trades Union Congress (TUC)

INTRODUCTION

1. This submission examines the importance of the SME sector to the UK economy as a whole and the economic performance of the SME sector. It concludes that there is an important role for national and EU level policies to fulfil in terms of promoting best practice and improving the management of small firms.

THE ECONOMIC IMPORTANCE OF SMALL BUSINESSES

2. In 1997 2.5 million or 68 per cent of all businesses in the UK had no employees and a further 1 million or 27 per cent had between one and nine employees. Together these accounted for 95 per cent of the 3.7 million firms identified by the DTI Small Firms Statistics Unit using the Inter-Departmental Business Register.

3. The remaining portion of the 3.7 million firms is made up of:

— 157,000 or 4 per cent were small firms with 10–49 employees;

— 25,000 or 0.7 per cent were medium sized firms with 50–249 employees;

— 6,600 or 0.2 per cent were large firms with over 250 employees.

4. Whilst the number of micro and small firms can be seen to make up an overwhelming proportion of all UK firms their contribution to employment is far less significant. Only 16 per cent of workers worked in a small firm and an additional 14 per cent were self-employed or worked in a micro firm.

5. Approximately 21 million people were employed in the 3.7 million UK firms identified by the DTI Small Firms Statistics Unit in 1997 (this total excludes public sector workers). When this total is broken down by firm size it can be seen that:

— 2.8 million or 14 per cent worked in 0 employee firms;

— 3.5 million or 16 per cent worked in firms with 1–9 employees;

— 3.0 million or 15 per cent worked in firms with 10–49 employees;

— 2.5 million or 12 per cent worked in firms with 50–249 employees;

— 9.1 million or 43 per cent worked in firms with over 250 employees.

6. It can therefore be seen that whilst 6.3 million or 30 per cent of market sector employment was accounted for by small and micro firms, large firms employing over 250 people, whilst accounting for only 0.2 per cent of the overall number of businesses, made the greatest contribution to overall employment of any individual sizeband.

CONTRIBUTION TO UK TURNOVER

7. Overall turnover (the value of sales, work done and services rendered) in the UK was concentrated in large businesses in 1997. The DTI estimates that the total turnover (excluding VAT) was £1,797 billion. In 1997, 23 per cent of total turnover came from micro firms, 16.4 per cent from small firms, 14.3 per cent from medium sized firms and 46.3 per cent from large firms. In total therefore large and medium sized enterprises accounted for 60.6 per cent of turnover with small firms accounting for only 39.4 per cent.

8. Whilst micro firms accounted for 95 per cent of all businesses in 1997, their 30 per cent share of total employment and 23 per cent of total turnover were much less significant. Only 0.2 per cent of firms were classified as large, however, these firms accounted for 43 per cent of overall employment and 46.3 per cent of total turnover.

ECONOMIC PERFORMANCE

9. The performance of UK SMEs has been analysed by the DTI's UK Benchmarking Index (UKBI) since 1996. A report published in 1998 examined the data that had been collected and reported that: "significant gaps . . . exist between the best and worst performing companies and sectors".

10. Specifically it found that the top 25 per cent of UKBI user companies had profit margins five times greater than companies in the lower quartile. Well over 50 per cent of companies had significantly more cash than necessary to cover current liabilities indicating that the companies were not as well run as they could be. There were significant differences between the best and worst companies in terms of their supplier performance. The best companies, those in the upper quartile, achieved 98 per cent supplier accuracy and 99 per cent delivery reliability, whilst those in the bottom quartile achieved only 60 per cent accuracy and 85 per cent reliability.

11. There was also a clear difference in the way that staff are treated. The highest quartile companies were spending £294 on training per person per year and the lowest quartile only £30 per year. Absenteeism was also four times higher in the lower quartile companies than in the higher quartile.

12. It is clear that within the SME sector performance varies greatly. Some SMEs are able to compete at a world class level. They are competitive and perform efficiently whilst other SMEs are poorly managed and therefore achieve poor results.

ARE SMALL FIRMS MORE INNOVATIVE?

13. Recent Government policies aimed at helping SMEs have been skewed towards assisting high tech and innovative firms. A recent study[6] has shown that whilst small firms, especially in manufacturing have been found to be of responsible for a greater proportion of innovations than employment, these innovations tend to be of a relatively low value.

14. Tether (1999)[7] examined recent studies on innovative and technology based firms and drew the following conclusions:

— Innovative new and small firms are more likely to create employment than other similarly sized firms.

— The average rate of employment creation within these firms tends to be small—less than 10 jobs per firm per year, but job creation is in fact concentrated amongst only a few firms.

— Even in these fast growing firms the job creation levels are modest. Tether and Massini[8] found that the fastest growing innovative or technology based new or small firms created hundreds rather than thousands of new jobs throughout the 1980s.

15. Policies that are aimed at improving innovation should therefore be aimed at business as a whole rather than simply at the SME sector.

MANAGEMENT PERFORMANCE

16. A key issue for promoting the performance of the SME sector is the issue of management. Many entrepreneurs face problems as their business expands. They lack the experience and management skills to capitalise on their company's potential growth. The SBS must address this key area and encourage and support the management of small businesses in a number of different areas.

17. A recent study[9] examined the barriers to growth experienced by a sample of SMEs and by monitoring the performance of two groups of firms: a "sustained growth" group and a "stalled growth" group. The study found that the sustained growers were able to plan strategically and were able to recognise the importance of developing management expertise as a tool for growth. This group also cited the availability of qualified management with good project skills as their main constraint on growth.

18. The "stalled growth" group were more likely to have ill defined strategic objectives, poorly specified managerial responsibilities and little devolution of managerial tasks. These problems were then exacerbated by poor management training and information systems. The "sustained growth" group valued their internal resources and were able to make good use of them:

"internal operations of sustained growth business were directed expanding the capabilities and ambitions of, and opportunities for, their people, through training, HRD programmes and sometimes by recruitment of the skills which cannot be grown in house."

19. In other words they valued their employees and invested in improving and making the most of their skills and abilities. Good management is vital for the growth of a small business. Strategic planning is needed as well as the ability to overcome hurdles such as constraints on finance or people.

20. This highlights the differences between the small business that is run by a good manager and those where the manager lacks sufficient skills. The poor manager will need support to enable them to understand the regulations that apply to them and how to fulfil their legal obligations. They will also need support in terms of assisting them with long term planning and employment issues such as health and safety and training.

DOES SIZE AFFECT HEALTH AND SAFETY?

21. Working in a small firm can be bad for your health. The rates of fatal injury and of amputation injury in small manufacturing workplaces (fewer than 50 employees) are double those in large workplaces (more than 200 employees). The rate of major injuries which require immediate medical treatment is also 25 per cent higher in small manufacturing workplaces than large ones.[10]

22. A report in Labour Market Trends concludes that after differences in cultures, mix of occupations and processes are controlled for there is still a greater risk of serious injury in small workplaces. There must therefore be inadequacies in the management of small workplaces that enable the conditions for the occurence of these serious injuries to persist.

23. A TUC report *Safety in numbers?*[11] revealed the details of a survey carried out by health and safety reps in small firms. The results showed that small firms, unionised and non unionised, did not have the formal

---

[6] *Small and Large Firms, sources of unequal innovations?,* B S Tether, Research Policy, 27, 1998.

[7] *A Question of expectations. . . ,* B S Tether, CRIC, University of Manchester, March 1999.

[8] *Employment creation in small technological and design innovators in the UK during the 1980s,* B S Tether and S Massini, Small Business Economics, 7(2),1998.

[9] *Growth constraints on small and medium sized firms,* Hughes, 1998, ESRC Centre for Business Research, University of Cambridge.

[10] *Workplace injuries in small and large manufacturing workplaces 1994–95 to 1995–96,* Graham Stevens, HSE published in Labour Market Trends January 1999.

[11] *Safety in Numbers?* TUC, August 1998.

structures in place needed for a traditionally strong health and safety culture. The report therefore urged the HSE, unions and small firms organisations to develop health and safety structures that would bolster the genuine but informal commitment to safety which exists in the best small firms and to push the worst towards better practice.

REGULATION AND SUPPORT

24. It is important that a coherent strategy is put in place to provide support and information for small businesses to ensure that they are able to grow into larger, more productive businesses and contribute fully to a dynamic, growing economy. The sections above show that there is a large gap between the best and worst performing small businesses. There is also a clear gap between the productivity and relative profitability of small and large firms.

25. Small business managers should be encouraged to think strategically about the long-term future of their company and made aware of the training opportunities that exist for them and their employees. Combining all sources of information into a one-stop shop may help to make small employers aware of initiatives such as Investors in People, Modern Apprenticeships, National Traineeships and Export Services and their importance. Small business leaders need to be able to embrace such initiatives and to work to apply them to their company. Investing in skills and training is invaluable if the small business is to be able to grow into an efficient larger business.

26. Helping small businesses to know and understand the regulations that apply to them is an important part of supporting SMEs. This includes both national and European level regulations. It is important that the ultimate aim of the regulation is not compromised by allowing exceptions for small firms. Allowing too many exceptions and exemptions adds to the complications involved in applying regulations causing difficulty and confusion. Keeping regulations simple will help small businesses to know what applies to them, why the regulation is in place and how to apply it.

CONCLUSION

27. Improving the performance of small firms across a variety of indicators is essential for the long-run competitiveness of the economy as a whole. Support policies have an important role in helping to reduce the gap between the best and worst performing small firms and in helping the small firm sector as a whole to boost its productivity and profitability.

28. In examining ways of creating an environment that will encourage the growth of small firms it is worth noting that trade unions have played an important role in the formation of Framework Agreements. Where matters can be put into more flexible language than would be the case in detailed prescriptive legislation with scope to apply to different sectors and sizes of firm to different extents. The thought that SMEs should be excluded from regulation collapses when put under detailed scrutiny.

· If the trade unions, as is often the case for these industry sectors, agree the nature of derogations and flexibility then this may be to the advantage of industry, the workers and the consumer.

An experiment could be carried out, and the TUC has written to the Secretary of State for Trade and Industry, suggesting that the Fixed Term Contract Directive should be implemented in the UK through specific consultation with the TUC and the CBI as the national centres for employers and employees.

This would avoid criticism made separately by Social Partners in the UK that the Working Time Directive and aspects of the Part Time Work Directive, amongst others, did not have enough regard to some specific concerns from the TUC and the CBI.

Therefore the Committee is asked to give particular attention to the way that these transpositions are carried out. It is well known that the Committee's conclusions on these matters are given high regard and the TUC would be very happy to come and explore these matters further with the Committee.

July 1999

Printed in the United Kingdom by The Stationery Office Limited
11/99   446293   19585